**WITHDRAWN
UTSA Libraries**

EGYPT AND THE SUDAN

By the same author
The Sudan under Wingate
Islam, Nationalism and Communism in a Traditional Society:
The Case of Sudan

(*co-editor with Uri M. Kupferschmidt*)
Islam Nationalism and Radicalism in Egypt and Sudan
in the 20th Century

EGYPT AND THE SUDAN

Studies in History and Politics

GABRIEL R. WARBURG
Institute of Middle Eastern Studies
University of Haifa

FRANK CASS

First published 1985 in Great Britain by
FRANK CASS & CO. LTD.
Gainsborough House, Gainsborough Road,
London, E11 1RS, England

and in the United States of America by
FRANK CASS & CO. LTD.
c/o Biblio Distribution Centre
81 Adams Drive, P.O. Box 327, Totowa, N.J. 07511

Copyright © 1985 Gabriel R. Warburg

British Library Cataloguing in Publication Data

Warburg, Gabriel R.
   Egypt and the Sudan.
   1. Egypt—History—1798–   2. Sudan—History
   I. Title
   962'.04   DT100

ISBN 0-7146-3247-3

All rights reserved. No part of this publication may be reproduced in any form or by any means, electronic, mechanical, photocopying, recording or otherwise, without the prior permission of Frank Cass & Co. Ltd. in writing

Printed and bound in Great Britain by
A. Wheaton & Co. Ltd., Exeter

*To my mother Ilse,
and to Rachel
with love*

Contents

Acknowledgements ix
Abbreviations x
Introduction 1

PART ONE
BRITAIN'S MOMENT IN THE NILE VALLEY

1. From Conquest to Independence: 1882–1956   11
2. The Sudan in Anglo-Egyptian Relations: 1899–1924   48
3. The Sinai Peninsula in Anglo-Egyptian Relations: 1906–1947   89
4. 'The Three-Legged Stool': Lampson, Faruq and Nahhas 1936–1944   116

PART TWO
REGIONAL AND POLITICAL CONSIDERATIONS

5. Egypt's Regional Policy in the Nineteenth and Twentieth Centuries   161
6. Islam and Politics in Egypt and the Sudan under the Military   188

Index   243

Acknowledgments

Most of the studies which make up this book were originally published in the following journals or collections: *Asian and African Studies, Journal of Contemporary History, Middle Eastern Studies, The Jerusalem Quarterly; The Contemporary Mediterranean World*, eds. C. F. Pinkele and A. Pollis, New York, Praeger 1983; *The Great Powers in the Middle East 1919–1939*, ed. U. Dann, New York & London, Holmes & Meier (forthcoming). I am grateful to the editors and publishers of the above for kindly enabling me to use these studies for republication. I would also like to thank the staff of the Public Record Office, London, for their kind help. Crown Copyright records appear by permission of the Controller, Her Majesty's Stationery Office.

All the studies in this volume have been rewritten and in some cases considerably enlarged, to take account of new material which has become available since they were first published.

Gabriel R. Warburg
Haifa

Abbreviations

AAS	*Asian and African Studies*, The Israel Oriental Society, The Institute of Middle Eastern Studies, Haifa University
F.I.B.S.-M.E.A.	*Foreign Broadcasting Information Service – Middle Eastern Affairs*
FO	Foreign Office Archive, Public Record Office London
IJMES	*International Journal of Middle East Studies*, The Middle East Studies Association of North America, Cambridge University Press
M.E.C.S.	*Middle East Contemporary Survey*, (eds.) Colin Legum and Haim Shaked, New York & London, Holmes & Meier Publishers Inc.
MEJ	*Middle East Journal*, Washington D.C., The Middle East Institute
MES	*Middle Eastern Studies*, London, Frank Cass & Co.
SAD	Sudan Archive Durham, the Wingate Papers and other private archives relating to the Sudan; deposited at the School of Oriental Studies, Durham University
SIR	Sudan Intelligence Report
SSIR	Secret Sudan Intelligence Report

NOTE ON TRANSLITERATION

Due to technical reasons no diacritical marks have been used in Arabic terms or names, except for the *ayn* (') and the *hamza* (').

Introduction

The studies included in this volume attempt to examine certain aspects of the history of Egypt and the Sudan in the nineteenth and twentieth centuries. Most of these studies are concerned with the triangular relationship between England, Egypt and the Sudan which evolved during the period of Britain's rule in the Nile Valley between 1882 and 1956.

The Nile is indeed of central importance in the study of Egypt and the Sudan and justifies a comparative study of these two separate political entities. The search for the sources of the Nile in the second half of the nineteenth century brought the Egyptians to the Equatorial regions of the Sudan and ultimately led to their conquest and incorporation into the Turco-Egyptian Sudan. Thus, even in a study limited to the political rather than the economic aspects of the Nile Valley, the Nile predominates as the single most important factor in the relations between these two regions. The fear of a hostile regime in Khartoum became a crucial consideration for whoever ruled in Cairo. For the free use of Nile waters for irrigation in the Sudan, or, even worse, their diversion to some hitherto uncultivated lands, became a constant threat to Egypt's very existence. Egypt's rulers were therefore opposed to their forced evacuation from the Sudan in 1883–1885 and regarded the Mahdist state, throughout its existence, as a possible threat to Egypt. This threat became even more acute when Britain ruled the Sudan under the guise of the Anglo-Egyptian Condominium. The 'Unity of the Nile Valley', which had been propagated by the Egyptian Nationalist party under Mustafa Kamil since the 1890s, remained the cornerstone of Egyptian nationalism throughout the period of British occupation.

In a study comparing British rule in Egypt to its rule in the Sudan an attempt is made to determine if, and to what extent, British ability to dominate these regions was influenced by the availability and exploitation of indigenous collaborating elites. Furthermore, while it is recognised that various Eurocentric components determined imperial expansion, the conquest of Egypt and the Sudan and their eventual emergence as independent nation-states are also examined against the background of the breakdown of collaboration between rulers and ruled. This study, which embraces the whole period of British rule in the Nile Valley, is an attempt to examine if and to what extent the workings of British imperialism were determined by indigenous collaborative systems connecting its European and African components.

Several findings emerge. First, it is quite clear that an examination such as this enables us to understand better the various methods by which imperial powers ruled the vast areas of their colonies with negligible use of military power. Second, the fact that there were two imperial powers, England and Egypt, simultaneously seeking to control the Sudan meant that the local elites tended to split into anti-Egyptian and anti-British factions, thereby facilitating each power's quest for collaborators. In Egypt the situation was more complex since all the components of the indigenous elite sought an early end to British occupation and the reunification of Egypt and the Sudan. Nonetheless, the internal power struggle between the King and his allies, on the one hand, and the Wafd on the other, enabled Britain to retain its paramountcy through collaboration with one or the other of the two power blocs. A third finding which emerges is that collaboration was not a one-sided affair − the indigenous elites had their own reasons for collaborating with the imperial power. Thus the Wafd in Egypt and the Ansar in the Sudan sought to exploit their alliance with Britain in order to further their own political and economic ambitions. This of course proved to be a two-edged sword, for while they benefited from British support in the short run, they found themselves at least partly discredited later on. Finally, while taking into account the complex reasons for Britain's departure from Egypt and the Sudan in 1955−1956, the fact that she had run out of effective collaborators in both these territories should be borne in mind.

A study of the Sudan as a factor in Anglo-Egyptian relations examines this problem in one of its most acute periods, namely from the beginning of the Condominium in 1889 to Lord Allenby's ultimatum in 1924. For while the terms of the ultimatum were generally humiliating, there can be no doubt that the major threat, as far as Egypt was concerned, was Allenby's announcement that the Sudan would thereafter be allowed to use the Nile waters freely for its own irrigation projects, without consideration for Egypt's requirements.

Introduction

Although this part of Allenby's ultimatum was neither endorsed nor enforced by the British cabinet, it continued to cloud Anglo-Egyptian relations as long as England maintained its paramountcy in the Nile Valley. A close examination of Anglo-Egyptian treaty negotiations between the two world wars clearly indicates that while a compromise over the gradual withdrawal of British troops from Egypt could have been attained even before 1936, the Sudan question remained a constant stumbling block. No Egyptian king or political party was willing to compromise over the future of the Sudan, and England's insistence on the Sudanese right of self-determination was dismissed as a blatant imperialist plot, aimed at undermining Egypt's legitimate rights in the Sudan. This study, dealing with the most crucial years of the Condominium, which ended with the evacuation of the Egyptian army from the Sudan, is also a case study of the workings of collaboration between the co-domini and sections of the young Sudanese elite. The encouragement of the Ansar, under the able leadership of Sayyid 'Abd al-Rahman, became an important factor in Anglo-Sudanese policy, since this movement as well as the Khatmiyya *sufi* order gave full support to the explusion of the Egyptians. But Egypt also managed to find allies within the Sudanese elite, and especially in the army where Egyptian influence was far greater than in the civilian administration. Early Sudanese nationalists were therefore split right from the beginning between the two centres of power, with England emerging as the winner of this first round, which ended in 1924.

Whereas the Sudan represented Egypt's lifeline and its vast arable lands were regarded as a natural outlet for Egypt's ever-growing population, the Sinai peninsula was regarded as an area of potential danger both during the heyday of the Ottoman Empire and in later years when Israel emerged as a political threat. The problem of Egypt's north-eastern borders was therefore of crucial importance ever since the Taba Incident of 1906. The agreement signed following that incident, whereby a 'Separating Administrative Line' was drawn from Rafah to the Gulf of 'Aqaba, left the Sinai under Anglo-Egyptian administration but did not grant Egypt sovereignty over the peninsula. Just as in the Sudan, the British authorities were tempted to use the peculiar status of the Sinai whenever their relations with Egypt reached a low ebb. Some suggested claiming British sovereignty in that region and turning it into a permanent British military base. These suggestions were studied seriously in 1946–1947, when it became clear that Britain was running out of time in Egypt and alternative ways to protect the Suez Canal were being ardently sought. But by then it was too late. British experts on international law argued that England could have claimed the Sinai after World War I and probably until the Anglo-Egyptian agreement of 1936. However, once that agreement was signed and Egypt had been accorded full membership in the League of Nations a year later, her borders were recognized by the international community, thereby granting her *de facto* sovereignty over the Sinai Peninsula. Furthermore, the British foreign office believed that a negotiated settlement with Egypt, protecting imperial interests, was still possible and hence rejected the 'Sinai solution' as undesirable. It is of special interest to note that even at this late stage the British Chiefs of Staff rejected the proposal to consider the Sinai as an alternative military base, because it lacked adequate facilities, such as airports, railways and roads.

A special study is devoted to the period between 1936 and 1944 in Anglo-Egyptian relations and their impact on internal Egyptian politics. The choice of these years is not accidental. It was influenced by the fact that three personalities – Lampson (Killearn), Faruq and Nahhas – dominated the political scene and hence presented the 'three legs' on which the Egyptian 'stool' was precariously balanced. But even more important, Killearn was the first British ambassador in Egypt to advocate and enforce collaboration with the Wafd, Britain's foremost enemy since its appearance in 1918. As a result of this collaboration, and especially of the Wafd's desire to rule at all costs, even with the aid of British military force, the party had been discredited to such an extent that the whole constitutional pattern was undermined. The centre of power therefore shifted to the King, the ex-parliamentary forces and especially to the Muslim Brothers. In other words it seems that these crucial years were in a way detrimental, in that they paved the way for the Free Officers who, in July 1952, gave the *coup de grâce* to the Egyptian constitutional monarchy.

The unique importance of the Sudan in Egypt's regional politics was, however, not limited to the period of British rule in the Nile valley. In a study dealing with the multifaceted aspects of Egypt's regional ambitions and interests, this problem is examined over a longer period starting with Muhammad 'Ali and ending with Anwar al-Sadat. What emerges as far as the Sudan is concerned, is that its unique position in Egypt's regional interests has remained a constant factor throughout the whole period, while Egyptian policies in other

Introduction

regions, both in the Middle East and Africa, have fluctuated according to circumstances. Thus, for example Egypt's conquest of Syria in the 1830s or its active involvement in the Fertile Crescent under Nasser, were, in comparison with its interest in the Nile valley, of lesser importance or duration. These shifts in emphasis, which characterised Egypt's foreign relations since the beginning of the 19th century, were based to a large extent on Egypt's perception of and reaction to international power politics. Muhammad 'Ali's misinterpretation of British interests in the Ottoman Empire led him to believe that his expansionist policy in Syria would be welcomed by Whitehall. Once he was rebuffed he was left with the Sudan as the only prize for his many conquests.

When over one hundred years later Egypt, under Nasser, once again ventured into the Fertile Crescent under the banner of Arab unity, it did so assuming that the Cold War, which was then at its height, would stop both the United States and the Soviet Union from active interference, thereby enabling Egypt to become the regional leader of a non-aligned Arab world. But, just like Muhammad 'Ali in 1839, Nasser too overplayed his hand and was rebuffed in the June 1967 War into which he was dragged as a result of his regional leadership ambitions. Under Sadat Egypt's main concern was once again centred on Africa. Soviet attempts to seize power in the Sudan, and their success in controlling the regimes of South Yemen, Ethiopia and Libya, were interpreted in Cairo as a Communist plot aimed at encircling Egypt. Sadat's interpretation of the international scene thus led Egypt to mend its bridges with the United States, and sign a peace treaty with Israel, in order to be able to face the Soviet threat and to alleviate Egypt's internal problems. In the turmoil which ensued, in which Egypt was castigated and isolated by most of the Arab states, the Sudan stood firmly by its Egyptian ally.

The final chapter in this volume moves from the period of colonial rule to that dominated by the military elites of the Free Officers, and it attempts to observe and analyse the impact of Islam on Egyptian and Sudanese politics. The political decline of the Wafd and its secular nationalist allies in the wake of World War II brought about the demise of their Western imported ideologies. Egyptian territorial nationalism was replaced by broader loyalties to Arabism and to the Islamic *umma*. And instead of the principles of the French Revolution or of British parliamentarianism, Islam re-emerged as a main source for government. Thus, Sayyid Qutb illustrated how the concepts of social justice were propagated in Islam long before they arrived in Europe. Similarly, the foundations upon which Western democracy rested were derived, it was claimed, from the Qur'anic principle of the *shura*. Another factor which contributed to the re-emergence of Islam as a way towards salvation was the Arab, and especially Nasser's, defeat in the June 1967 War. It is noteworthy that many of the fundamentalist Islamic movements, both in Egypt and elsewhere, mushroomed after 1967. Their rationale, stated in rather simplistic terms, was that God had punished the Muslims because they had abandoned Islam. A return to Islam was therefore a pre-condition for reversing the results of the 1967 catastrophe.

Neither Nasser nor Sadat, though probably aware of the problem, has ever really addressed himself seriously to the challenge of popular Islam. They both harnessed the Muslim hierarchy through financial dependence and political favouritism, and made it a submissive tool of central government. But despite their own religiosity, their attitude to the challenges of Islam to present-day society and politics, especially among the lower classes, can only be defined as superficial.

In the early 1970s Sadat needed the cooperation of the Muslim Brothers in order to overcome the strong Nasserist opposition. He enabled them to renew their propaganda and once again to publish their journals *al-Da'wa* and *al-I'tisam*, in which an Islamic state based on the Shari'a was constantly advocated. Sadat's willingness to compromise through increased Islamic legislation on the one hand failed to satisfy the more militant Islamic movement and, on the other hand, brought about an upsurge of sectarian strife, especially between the militant Muslims and the Copts. Thus Sadat, like Nasser, seems to have underestimated the staying power and popularity of radical Islamic movements such as the Muslim Brethren or the more violent neo-Mahdist fundamentalist groups.

If we move to observe the Sudanese scene many differences come to mind. First, in the Sudan, unlike in Egypt, the 'return of Islam' was not primarily a reaction against Western imported ideologies. Popular Islam led by so-called holy families was dominant in Sudanese tribal society even before the Egyptian conquest in 1821. Despite attempts to undermine its strength through the importation of Egyptian-style Azharite Muslim leadership, popular Islam survived and proved its vitality in the Mahdist uprising. The historical reasons for this phenomenon need not be dealt with here. What is important

Introduction

for an understanding of the present situation is the fact that the Mahdiyya, a radical militant Islamic movement, gave the Sudan its first independent centralized theocratic government. Indeed many regarded the Mahdi as the forerunner and founder of modern Sudanese nationalism and the Ansar, the neo-Mahdist movement of the twentieth century, therefore became a prime contender for power in the new independent Sudan. But the lack of alternative political or social organizations on a municipal or rural basis was also one of the main reasons for the predominance of radical Islamic movements in the independent Sudan. Sectarian divisions helped to bring about the first military coup of General Ibrahim 'Abbud in October 1958, and, following a brief and unsatisfactory parliamentary interlude in 1964–1969, the military under Col. Ja'far al-Numayri once again assumed power. Both military governments attempted to grant greater powers to the provinces, hoping to weaken thereby the sectarian-Muslim leadership.

The two major clashes between the Ansar and Numayri's government occurred in March 1970 and in July 1976. On 27 March 1970, Numayri ordered the bombardment of Aba Island, the stronghold of the Ansar in the White Nile, and between five and twelve thousand of the sect's followers were killed. The spiritual leader of the Ansar, Sayyid al-Hadi al-Mahdi, was killed in later skirmishes, while the Oxford-educated great-grandson of the nineteenth century Mahdi, al-Sadiq al-Mahdi, was exiled to Egypt. If anyone doubted the staying power of the Ansar, these doubts were brought to an abrupt end in July 1976. In that month a considerable number of well-trained and equipped Ansar, who had penetrated into the Sudan from their training camps in Libya, nearly succeeded in capturing the airport of Khartoum where President Numayri was due to arrive. The fact that the President's plane arrived earlier than scheduled caught the rebels unprepared and thus, with the support of the Sudanese army, and Egyptian military backing, Numayri's regime was saved once again. Over seven hundred lives were lost in the ensuing battle and an additional ninety-eight Ansar were later executed.

Unlike Sadat, who in the face of growing Muslim radicalism sought in September 1981 to crush their movement through the arrest of its leaders, Numayri had since 1977 realised that conciliation would probably serve him better. In July 1977, Numayri met secretly with al-Sadiq al-Mahdi in Port Sudan and worked out an agreement for 'national reconciliation'. Since then the leaders of both the Muslim

Brethren and the Ansar have, on the whole, supported the regime. This was for both pragmatic-political and ideological reasons. On the political level the failure of the July 1976 coup brought home to the sectarian leaders that as long as Numayri enjoyed the support of both the Sudanese army and his Egyptian allies, he would be hard to overthrow. Furthermore, while Numayri and his colleagues had started their political careers in the Revolutionary Command Council in 1969–1970 with very little concern for religious issues, this was no longer true towards the end of the 1970s. In March 1970 Numayri had believed that, following the Aba Island massacre, the Ansar had been politically annihilated and relegated to the realm of historical research. Ten years later, in his book: *al-nahj al-Islami limadha?*, Numayri enumerated the stages by which the May 1969 revolution had shifted its orientation towards the Islamic path.

As the 1980s unfold the Sudan, therefore, seems to follow a path towards gradual Islamization: a process in which, for the time being, Numayri's regime leads the way prompted and edged on by the populist Islamic movements. However, as in Egypt, there are those in the Sudan who are less patient and regard violence, rather than collaboration with Numayri, as a faster and safer way towards an Islamic state. The analogy with Egypt is, once again, obvious. The moderation of the older generation of the Muslim Brethren was openly challenged by the young militant neo-Mahdist groups who had no patience with the Brethren's willingness to bide their time and to give up the use of violence.

PART ONE

BRITAIN'S MOMENT IN THE NILE VALLEY

1

FROM CONQUEST TO INDEPENDENCE: 1882–1956

Since the appearance of 'The Imperialism of Free Trade' in 1953 the Robinson and Gallagher controversy has produced a most fruitful and voluminous discussion on nineteenth-century imperialism. Yet while the economic aspects of their approach have been widely debated, and *Africa and the Victorians* has received all the attention it deserves, Robinson's later contribution on the subject of collaboration has not yet been adequately discussed.[1] Robinson's starting point is that no comprehensive historical theory of how European imperialism has worked in the nineteenth and twentieth centuries has as yet been developed. All theories hitherto have focussed solely on Europe and failed to explain 'how a handful of European pro-consuls managed to manipulate the polymorphic societies of Africa and Asia, and how, eventually, comparatively small, nationalist elites persuaded them to leave'.[2] In other words, any new theory will have to recognise that 'imperialism was as much a function of its victims' collaboration or non-collaboration of their indigenous politics, as it was of European expansion'.[3]

The theory Robinson has proposed sees European imperialism as made up of one non-European and two European elements. With respect to the latter, these are the drive to integrate the newly colonised areas into the industrial economy and the strategic need to secure these regions against possible rivals. However, according to Robinson this was 'the stock in trade of the old masters' and did not really explain why a certain region, which for years had been under European tutelage without formal annexation, was suddenly conquered to become part of a European empire. In order to open up the Ottoman Empire to European trade and finance, for instance, the Treaty of Balta Liman (1838) was sufficient, and in fact great power rivalry helped to maintain the integrity of the Ottoman Empire despite its strategic importance until 1914. How then are we to explain the sudden conquest of a new region in Africa or Asia which had hitherto been integrated into the European system of trade and finance without being formally annexed to the empire? The answer, according to Robinson, lies in the non-European component of the new theory of imperialism, 'that of indigenous collaboration and resistance'. The controlling mechanism of imperialism was made up of the relationship between the European agents of expansion and 'their internal "collaborators" in non-European political economies'.[4]

According to Robinson, conquest becomes a possibility only when collaboration breaks down in the 'informal imperialist' stage; without a collaborating elite, Europeans could neither have conquered nor ruled their empires.

Europe's policy normally was that if empire could not be had on the cheap, it was not worth having at all. The financial sinew, the military and administrative muscle of imperialism, was drawn through the mediation of indigenous elites from the invaded countries themselves.[5]

Collaboration, according to Robinson, determined not only if and when a territory was to be conquered, but also the duration of imperial rule. The nationalist movements in the period prior to independence 'had to contrive a situation in which their rulers ran out of collaborators ... Independence became possible, colonial rule impossible, when nationalism had ceased to be merely a tiny elitist movement and succeeded in allying itself to the historic, popular religious forces'.[6]

While this last quotation refers specifically to the Sudan, the author claims that it is applicable to modern colonial rule elsewhere in Asia and Africa. Robinson stresses the point that the term 'collaborators' is not used in a pejorative sense. Furthermore, he rightly states that 'collaborators or not, the social elites of Africa and Asia who made up the great majority of imperialism's involuntary partners, had to mediate with the foreigner on behalf of their traditional institutions and constituents'.[7] Collaboration was not only a natural by-product of imperialism, but an essential part of it as well. We shall see that the collaborators of a certain stage might have been the leaders of resistance during an earlier period and were likely to lead the last stage of the struggle for national independence. Moreover, it is often hard to determine who derived greater benefits from collaboration – the imperial power or the so-called collaborators. Finally, collaboration, as we shall see, is sometimes offered by an elite with which the government is not interested in collaborating. And yet, if this elite is strong

From Conquest to Independence: 1882–1956

enough, like the Ansar of the Sudan after 1924, it can force its collaboration on a reluctant government and benefit from it.

Before examining Robinson's theory in the context of the Nile Valley, the following observations on India seem relevant. Describing the government of the Indian Raj on the eve of the Second World War, Malcolm Muggeridge, then assistant editor of the *Calcutta Statesman*, wrote that 'power only exists in so far as it connects the government and the governed; the gap between them has to be spanned .... In the case of Anglo-India, the gap had widened to the point that it was no longer spannable'.[8] This then was the point at which the British government ran out of effective collaborators, and, according to Robinson, had either to resort to force or pack up and leave. We shall examine this development as it occurred in the Anglo-Egyptian Sudan, Robinson's sole example for his collaboration theory. We shall then move to Egypt, which, as suggested by Robinson and Gallagher, was what brought the British into the Nile Valley and 'trapped them there'.

THE ANGLO-EGYPTIAN SUDAN

The conquest of the Sudan over the period 1896–1898 had nothing to do with either a breakdown in collaboration or a sudden uprising of a proto-nationalist movement in that region. It was British pressure that had forced the Egyptians to abandon the Sudan in 1883, after sixty years of Egyptian rule and following two years of a losing battle against the Mahdist revolt.[9] There had been no substantial British attempts to recruit a Sudanese collaborating elite from the time Khartoum fell into the Mahdi's hands in 1885. It is true that a few Sudanese notables, such as certain leaders of the Khatmiyya *sufi* order, were biding their time in Egypt under British protection and enjoying a British subsidy, praying for the Mahdiyya to come to its end. Similarly, there were Sudanese agents, especially on the Egyptian borders in the Wadi Halfa region and on the Red Sea coast, who collaborated with Sir Reginald Wingate and his Egyptian intelligence department. But as all intelligence reports clearly indicated, there was no force within the Sudan which could or indeed intended to raise the banner of revolt against the Mahdist state and overthrow the Khalifa 'Abdallah. The 'liberation' of the Sudan would have to be undertaken by external forces, and England was of course the most favoured candidate.[10] The decision to invade the Sudan in March

1896 was prompted, as Robinson and Gallagher state, by the defeat of the Italians at Adowa by King Menelik of Ethiopia on 1 March. This in itself did not worry Lord Salisbury, but when on 3 March the German Kaiser urged the British government to save the Triple Alliance, the British were presented with an opportunity to demonstrate the value of their friendship to Berlin. While German pressure provided the necessary occasion for the Anglo-Egyptian invasion, the real motive behind the British move, as stated by Lord Salisbury and Lord Lansdowne in secret memoranda, was to reconquer at least part of the Sudan with maximum international backing, and thus bring the upper Nile under British control.[11] The autocracy of the Ta'aisha (a sector of the Baqqara) under the khalifa 'Abdallah was only advantageous to England as long as it was strong enough to withstand rival European invaders. However, once King Leopold of Belgium could invade the Bahr al-Ghazal from the Congo without serious Mahdist resistance, Britain could no longer rely on the Mahdist state to keep its other antagonists, especially France, at bay. Using Robinson's formula, one could define this relationship as 'collaboration by default': from 1885 to 1896 the Mahdists, or proto-nationalists, as Robinson and Gallagher would have defined them, collaborated or rather served British interests, by keeping the Nile Valley free of its European competitors. Annexation and 'formal empire' became necessary owing to growing Mahdist weakness and to Britain's insistence that the Nile Valley was to become its own sphere of interest.

The principles of collaboration were laid down after the conquest by Lord Kitchener, the first governor-general of the Anglo-Egyptian Sudan, who instructed the British provincial governors and district inspectors 'to make the government of your district as great a contrast as possible to that of the Dervishes'. This was to be achieved through the 'individual action of British officers, working independently, but with a common purpose, on the individual natives whose confidence they have gained'.[12] In other words, Kitchener's main guideline to his subordinates was to avoid any collaboration with ex-Mahdists and to rely on individual collaborators, rather than groups or classes. These collaborators were to be found primarily among the so-called tribal population, especially those tribes which had been suppressed by the khalifa's Ta'ishi autocracy. They included the sedentary riverain tribes and the camel-owning nomads. In the religious sphere collaboration was sought among so-called orthodox Muslim leaders.

From Conquest to Independence: 1882–1956

These included those leaders of the Khatimiyya *sufi* order who, as mentioned above, had escaped from the Sudan to Egypt and hence became the only popular Islamic movement tolerated by the new regime. The government's attitude to other *sufi* orders was clearly enunciated by Kitchener when he ordered Sufism in general to be banished from the Sudan:

> Fikis teaching different tariks [*sic*] ... should not be allowed to resume their former trade. In old days, these Fikis, who lived on the superstitious ignorance of the people, were one of the curses of the Sudan, and were responsible in a great measure for the [Mahdi's] rebellion.[13]

Indeed, the setting up of a British inspired and selected 'Board of Ulema' in June 1901 was probably the best example of an attempt to create a religious collaborating elite. The board was supposed to legitimise Christian rule over a Muslim population by providing the rubber stamp for all government decisions regarding Islam. But the government soon realized that these 'Vicars of Bray' were so weak that when real collaboration became essential it had to look elsewhere.[14] With the outbreak of the war and especially after Turkey joined Germany on 27 October 1914 and declared a holy war (*jihad*) on the entente powers, the British authorities in the Sudan regarded it as imperative to find Muslim collaborators who would be willing and able to resist the sultan's 'command'. In the Arabian peninsula this brought about the famous McMahon-Husayn correspondence and the subsequent Sharifian revolt, probably one of the most controversial of Britain's Middle Eastern activities. In the Sudan it caused a revision of previous anti-Mahdist policies, with far-reaching results for the future of the country. The Mahdi's son, Sayyid 'Abd al-Rahman, who had up to that time lived under the surveillance of the intelligence department, suddenly became the most important potential Muslim collaborator the British administration in the Sudan could hope for. The reasons for this sudden change of heart were as follows: first, the Mahdists, or the Ansar, were by far the strongest politically motivated Muslim group in the Sudan, and their support especially during the war was therefore crucial; second, like the Mahdists of the nineteenth century, the Ansar fiercely hated the Turks (and the Egyptians), and hence had no difficulty in identifying themselves with Britain's anti-Turkish propaganda.

This period of collaboration lasted until the end of 1924. The 1919 nationalist revolt in Egypt had its repercussions in the Sudan, and again Sayyid 'Abd al-Rahman and the Ansar proved themselves loyal supporters of British attempts to eliminate Egyptian presence and influence there. At the height of the troubles in Egypt, when it became clear that nationalist resistance had become a massive, popular uprising, Britain was glad to receive Sudanese support from any quarter. Thus, when the three most popular religious leaders, followed by all the major tribal and *sufi* shaykhs, announced their loyalty to their British benefactors and their disapproval of Egyptian nationalist agitation, this was a most welcome development for the Anglo-Sudanese authorities. Sir Lee Stack, then governor-general of the Sudan, and his compatriots had advocated the complete separation of the Sudan from Egypt for many years. Now the moment seemed opportune, and a delegation of Sudanese notables headed by Sayyid 'Ali al-Mirghani and Sayyid 'Abd al-Rahman al-Mahdi was dispatched forthwith to London to express their loyalty to His Majesty's Government and their desire to end the Egyptian connection.[15] Talk, especially among army officers and the young intelligentsia, that the departure of the 'delegation of loyalty' had been induced by British authorities was dismissed as venomous Egyptian propaganda, which, while unrepresentative, proved the depth and danger of Egyptian penetration and hence the urgency of its removal.[16]

This young and numerically small Sudanese intelligentsia had previously been viewed by the British authorities as a potential ally which would gradually replace the untrustworthy Egyptians. Following the emergence of the first Sudanese nationalist movement over the years 1919–1924, in which the young *effendiyya* class and some young southern Sudanese army officers who had lost their tribal roots played a prominent role, the British authorities had second thoughts and started looking for more 'reliable' allies among the traditional tribal leadership. In doing so, the British alienated this young class of Sudanese, whose sole sin had been the quest for a greater share in the government, leading ultimately to self-determination.[17] According to the 'Ewart Report on Political Agitation' submitted to the Foreign Office in 1925, even 'Ali 'Abd al-Latif, leader of the White Flag League, had not uttered a single word of support for Egypt when he was sentenced in 1919 to a year in prison. It was only while in prison that he became a pro-Egyptian nationalist.[18] But while the White Flag League could be dismissed as a group of disgruntled petty officials of low rank, the uprising of the Sudanese cadets in 1924 was quite a different matter. These had been carefully selected and were the best disciplined, most content, and most loyal military formation

From Conquest to Independence: 1882–1956

in the Sudan. Trained to replace the undesirable Egyptian officers, their rebellion was therefore a real disappointment; it meant in effect that they could not be relied upon in case of tribal uprisings prompted by fanatics, such as the Nyala incident in 1921, which continued to be a definite possibility.[19]

This explains the ambivalent attitude towards Sayyid 'Abd al-Rahman and the Ansar, whose stature had grown immensely over the years 1914–1924 as a result of government policy. Now top government officials were openly suspicious of the Sayyid's great influence, which could easily be turned against them. In November 1924 the assassination of Sir Lee Stack, *sirdar* and governor-general of the Sudan, gave Lord Allenby a convenient excuse for the expulsion of Egyptian troops and personnel from the Sudan, and a new situation arose. First, Britain could theoretically have abolished the condominium, thereby incorporating the Sudan into the British Empire, which was already the case in all but name. Second, with the expulsion of the Egyptians a new Sudanese army had to be established, preferably under British command. Both these possibilities would have required British investments, as the Sudan was under no circumstances paying its way. Further, it was very unlikely that the British taxpayer could be induced to shoulder this additional burden. The way out seemed quite simple: why not retain the de jure status of the condominium despite the de facto de-Egyptianisation of the Sudan? This done, it seemed quite reasonable to force the Egyptian treasury to bear the cost of the new Sudanese Defence Force (SDF). The logic was obvious: Egypt was merely paying for its own security.

It is interesting to note that even during this period of acute crisis the strength of the British garrison in the Sudan was increased from one to only two infantry battalions (some 1,500 men), one detachment of artillery, and one Royal Air Force squadron.[20] Taking into account that by April 1927 the fighting force of the SDF reached some 5,700 men, the ratio of British to Sudanese troops was approximately one to four. Furthermore, in a country of over one million square miles with hardly any adequate communications the security of British rule in the Sudan was by military criteria precarious indeed.[21]

It is in this light that we have to look at Britain's next attempt to find a more suitable and reliable collaborating elite, namely the traditional tribal leaders. Stack's assassination and the consequent expulsion of the Egyptians from the country made the good services of the Ansar redundant, and they were ordered once more to limit themselves to their religious duties and refrain from meddling in politics. The British were basically opposed to religious political movements, the more so as the Ansar's recent history was one of fanaticism.[22]

During the period of so-called indirect rule, an alternative definition for ruling through a collaborating elite, Britain tried to boost tribal leadership and thus encourage a traditional but non-religious elite. The architect of this policy in the Sudan was Sir Harold MacMichael, who had been assistant civil secretary since 1919 and was promoted to civil secretary in 1926. In introducing the principles of Native Administration MacMichael used the experience of Sir Charles Brook, Rajah of Sarawak, and of Lord Lugard's *Dual Mandate* in Nigeria.[23] By relying on local customs and traditional leadership, the pitfalls of colonial administration would, according to MacMichael, be considerably diminished:

There are, of course, two pitfalls which the wary administrator avoids. On the one hand, the chief may abuse his powers: but let it be remembered that a native prefers to submit to a few abuses at the hands of his own chief rather than to be pestered with rules and regulations and viewpoints of alien origin .... On the other hand, if the white man too often interferes, not only will he often make mistakes and unwittingly cause injustice to be done ... but the people will themselves take advantage of this fact both to make a catspaw of the government and to flout their own natural leaders.[24]

But how powerful were these 'natural leaders'? Most of the British governors in the northern Sudan had stated in the early 1920s that tribal leadership had in fact disintegrated. Nonetheless, the government decided that it was worth taking the gamble. Even if tribal organization had all but vanished, it was still possible to recreate it. Legislation was accordingly passed in order to enhance native administration. In 1922 the 'Powers of Nomad Sheikhs Ordinance' was promulgated and put into practice throughout the northern Sudan. Then in 1927, with the full backing of Sir John Maffey, the new governor-general of the Sudan, the 'Powers of Sheikhs Ordinance' was passed to include all tribal leaders of the northern Sudan.[25] This policy continued unhampered until the outbreak of the Second World War. Both Sir John Maffey and Sir Stewart Symes, who succeeded him as governor-general, believed that decentralisation would keep the young Sudanese intelligentsia and the religious leadership from gaining support in the rural districts.[26] While the young and numerically weak and discontented intelligentsia was in fact limited to the major urban centres, this was not true of the Ansar and their spiritual political leader, Sayyid 'Abd al-Rahman al-Mahdi. The Ansar enjoyed the support of large sections of the rural and tribal population, including the tribal chiefs, especially in the western Sudan (e.g., Kordofan and Darfur). They also had the backing of the *fallata* along the Upper Nile and in the Gezira regions. Thus, although the government attempted to persist in its indirect rule, hoping to boost tribal leadership at the expense of that of the neo-Mahdists, the policy failed due to its incorrect interpretation of the nature of the Ansar and the strength of sectarian politics.[27] Indeed, many of the so-called tribal leaders were first and foremost supporters of Sayyid 'Abd al-Rahman al-Mahdi. While it was easy enough to boycott the immediate relatives of the Mahdi and the khalifa 'Abdallah and denounce them as politically undesirable, it was practically impossible to banish the whole Mahdist elite. In fact, when Sayyid 'Abd al-Rahman was ordered to curtail his activities, all he had to do was recruit the so-called tribal leaders and appoint them as his agents in the rural Sudan.[28] Another misconception was the very use of the term 'tribe' for such diverse groups as the riverain sedentaries and the Baqqara or Beja nomads, which made nonsense of the whole concept of tribal leadership. Among the Danaqla and the Ja'aliyyin there was no sense of ethnic cohesion or indeed of political leadership. At most one could speak of a common cultural identity, but this did not provide the basis for a collaborating political elite. In the rural areas of the central Sudan one could talk of ruling families or ruling clans, such as the Nurab of the Kababish, who in periods of strength attracted a large variety of people of different backgrounds under a so-called tribal label. But this mechanism was not strong enough to provide the kind of leadership sought by the British administrators, as in periods of weakness or tough competition it tended to disintegrate.

Considering that it took some 20 years before the Anglo-Sudanese authorities finally realized that indirect rule was a myth which could no longer bring dividends, one is bound to conclude that, despite the quality of British officials in the Sudan, their ability to analyse the situation realistically and elaborate fresh policies accordingly was rather limited. When Neville Henderson was sent in April 1925 to report on the Sudan, he commended devolution as the principal manner in which the Egyptians would be made superfluous and replaced by the Sudanese. Furthermore, he emphasised the importance of limiting education to technical subjects such as agriculture and of not encouraging any higher education 'among a people so profoundly backward as the Sudanese'.[29] But to Henderson's much more serious charge that the young Sudanese graduates felt much closer to the Egyptians than to the British through religion and culture, there was no convincing reply. Sir Geoffrey Archer, then governor-general, admitted that this had been true in the past owing to the massive presence in the Sudan of Egyptians, who had caused the young Sudanese 'to become absorbed into the "effendi" class'. Now these young Sudanese were being convinced by British 'welfare officers' to 'cast off their shoddy European clothes and tarbush and revert to *national dress*'.[30] This rather naive and unrealistic policy could hardly have been expected to succeed. Throughout the 1920s and 1930s, the Foreign Office archives on the Sudan are littered with complaints regarding the disaffected Sudanese intelligentsia on the one hand and the inadequacies of the tribal leaders on the other. The young intelligentsia regarded government policy as both reactionary and inefficient. Not only was higher education halted but even primary schools were regarded as superfluous. Thus, Sir John Maffey and Sir Stewart Symes, the governors-general of the Sudan in the 1930s, proudly reported that they had managed to reduce the numbers of Gordon College graduates and to convince the parents 'that expensive secondary education in Khartoum is not necessarily a gilt-edged investment'.[31] But they admitted that the young Sudanese were alienated as a result of this policy and thus became gradually more hostile to British aims as time went on.[32]

It is this context that Sir Miles Lampson's first impressions of the Sudan seem rather illuminating in their honesty. Having arrived in Egypt in 1934 as the new British high commissioner, he wrote the following less than a year later:

It was a mistake to try and run the Sudan without Egyptian administrative cooperation .... However, we have adopted this policy and it must be allowed to run its course .... With regard to indirect rule and the fostering of the tribal system, I believe with Sir J. Currie that we are working against the stream of natural forces at play in Colonial and Eastern lands today .... Unfortunately, a Sudanese intelligentsia already exists and it regards this system as directed against its own future development which is bound up with the progress of the Sudan on modern state lines. Again, we have adopted this policy and it must be allowed to run its course. Its effects on education must of course be retardatory − not altogether a bad thing in the circumstances.[33]

One is left with the impression that Lampson was hardly convinced that either indirect rule or a de-Egyptianised Sudan would produce

From Conquest to Independence: 1882–1956

the expected results. For some reason, he recommended that both these policies be allowed to 'run their course' despite their obvious shortcomings. Lampson was of course not in a strong enough position to intervene in the Sudan where over the years the Sudan Political Service had gained nearly complete control over the country's fate. Moreover, Egypt was his first priority, and an Anglo-Egyptian treaty seemed a more important goal than the reversal of antiquated policies in the Sudan. It is therefore hardly a wonder that in the Sudan even the more forward looking among the Anglo-Sudanese, like Douglas Newbold who served as governor of Kordofan in the years 1932–1935, did not question these policies.

'Indirect rule', 'devolution', and 'native administration' were still the unquestioned principles of colonial policy, and District Commissioners were patiently working to amalgamate the small units of local government left by thirty years of direct rule into federations large enough to handle their own finances.[34]

Even in 1942, when the Graduates' Congress was already in full swing, the principles of indirect rule and native administration were still propagated by Newbold, now civil secretary, as the only sensible path for the Sudanese government.[35] Yet it was Newbold himself who encouraged collaboration in yet another direction and brought the authorities into direct cooperation with the founders of the Graduates' Congress in 1938. In supporting the founding of this congress Newbold had hoped that a closer association with the educated classes would keep the sectarian schisms out of the graduates' ranks, and thus he took another step in developing the future secular leadership of the Sudan. Newbold's ideas, which by 1941 expressed government policy, were stated in a minute he wrote in September 1941: 'Whatever means we use of associating the Sudanese with a province Headquarters and with the Central Government we cannot confine this association to Sayeds, Nazirs, loyal ex-Kaimakams or Chief Merchants. The maturer educated Sudanese *must* be brought in.'[36] But neither Newbold nor other senior British officials regarded the graduates as a political body or believed that they were ready to assume political responsibilities. In fact, when the Graduates' Congress was founded in 1938, partly to offset the concessions made to Egypt in the 1936 treaty, Sir Angus Gillan, then civil secretary, wrote:

It is possible that the Graduates' Congress may emerge at some future date as a nationalist organization with a political programme .... Today ... it neither seeks formal recognition, nor does it claim to represent the views of any but its own members.[37]

British policymakers in the Sudan were soon to be proved wrong on their two major assumptions with regard to the Congress. First, in the sectarian realities of the Sudan it was impossible to keep the religious schisms out of the graduates' ranks. Indeed, as early as June 1940 the Congress was divided between Mahdists and Khatmi supporters.[38] Second, to hope for a non-political intelligentsia which would limit its activities voluntarily to education and welfare was very much out of tune with the ambitions which had been nurtured by the Second World War. Thus, it is not surprising that by 1942 the Graduates' Congress was deeply involved in politics and regarded itself as the embryonic parliament of the future independent Sudan. It was this involvement which caused the split in the graduates' ranks along sectarian lines. When the first political parties, the Ashiqqa' and Umma appeared in 1943/44, they needed the broad backs of the sectarian leaders as shields. The graduates and others who joined the Umma party did not necessarily do so as supporters of the Mahdist creed. But to fight for Sudanese independence, especially in the face of growing pressure from Egypt for the unity of the Nile valley, in effect meant joining Sayyid 'Abd al-Rahman's camp. During the 1946 Anglo-Egyptian negotiations the sayyid and his Ansar had once again played a crucial role in supporting British claims against the Egyptians. The Ansar demonstrations against the 'Sudan protocol', as well as Sayyid 'Abd al-Rahman's subsequent talks with Prime Minister Clement Attlee, had proven that there was no viable alternative to the Umma party as a collaborating elite. Indeed, the so-called pro-Egyptian parties, led by Isma'il al-Azhari, a one-time protégé of the sayyid, provided the same services for their Egyptian patrons. Many of them regarded their pro-Egyptian stance as a provisional ploy towards expelling British imperialism from the Nile valley.

The boycott by al-Azhari's party of the Legislative Assembly, founded in 1948, created a situation in which the British authorities were forced once again into an even closer coalition with Sayyid 'Abd al-Rahman and the Umma party. Thus, it was not surprising that members of the new body were reviled by all those who boycotted it, as being in the government's pocket. Furthermore, despite the declared policy of self-government and Sudanisation, leading eventually, to self-determination, progress was not fast enough even for the so-called collaborators. Attempts by Muhammad Ahmad Mahjub in 1949 and by the Umma reprentatives in 1950 to force the British to commit themselves to a definite timetable leading to independence met with little success. Nevertheless, the government was well aware that by dragging its feet it might postpone the decision but not overcome the repeated demands, leading ultimately to a more serious crisis. In February 1950 Sir James Robertson, the civil secretary, remarked:

> I am convinced that to wait too long is fatal .... When concessions refused to the moderates, have to be made to extremists after disturbance and civil disorder, there is an immediate loss of sympathy and good feeling between ruler and ruled.[39]

Friction between the Sudan political service and the Umma developed for yet additional reasons. The rural representatives in the Legislative Assembly were the kind of men with whom the British district commissioners had been collaborating for many years under the guise of indirect rule, so there was reason to hope that this collaboration would continue within the assembly and help overcome Umma-type sectarianism. But the Umma leaders, aiming to strengthen their own position both in the assembly and in the rural areas, made an all-out effort to win the support of the newcomers. Thus, the British found themselves in the position of attempting to encourage the rural leadership without alienating their Umma supporters – a near-impossible feat. This was made even more difficult by the abortive attempt to lure the Khatmiyya leaders into the assembly, thereby threatening the *tariqa*'s support for al-Azhari's camp as well as undermining Umma predominance.

Matters came to a head in December 1950, when the Umma tabled a motion in the assembly requesting the governor-general to approach the co-domini with a view to obtaining a joint declaration granting the Sudanese self-government. The British were placed in a predicament: if the Umma motion were carried, it would alienate non-Umma rural leaders and encourage the Khatmiyya and those seeking union with Egypt. Should the motion be defeated, however, the Umma would blame the political service, which would thus lose its only reliable collaborators without assurance of a viable alternative. Furthermore, such a motion would tend to undermine any future prospect of Anglo-Egyptian accommodation regarding the Sudan, as it would be interpreted in Cairo as British inspired. Despite the concerted efforts of the British Foreign Office and the Sudan political service, the Umma refused to withdraw the motion, and it was carried by 39 votes to 38. It was hoped that the narrowness of this victory would encourage the Khatmiyya to join the assembly. It also proved that both the northern and southern rural representatives were a force to be reckoned with.

The appearance of the Socialist Republican party in 1951 was therefore regarded by many in the political service as a step in the right direction. Here was a new political force, willing to collaborate in leading the country toward self-determination but without the sectarian characteristics of the Umma. Furthermore, appearing as it did shortly after Nahhas Pasha had unilaterally abrogated the condominium agreement, the new party was heralded by the political service as a clear indication of Sudanese popular will in the face of Egyptian imperial designs. But the Socialist Republicans, who were in effect a party of rural conservative leaders and included in their ranks many of those who had collaborated with Britain in the days of indirect rule, represented an abortive attempt of the political service to overcome the sectarian predominance.[40] The result was the final alienation of Sayyid 'Abd al-Rahman and the Umma party, leading eventually to a complete breakdown in Anglo-Sudanese collaboration and hence to a reconciliation between the sayyid and the Egyptian government.[41] The new Egyptian prime minister, Hilali Pasha, realized that the Anglo-Egyptian deadlock on the one hand and the alienation of the Umma on the other gave him a real chance to reach an agreement with Britain's most consistent anti-Egyptian ally, namely Sayyid 'Abd al-Rahman al-Mahdi. In order to reach an accommodation Hilali accepted for the first time in Egyptian history the Sudan's right to self-determination, provided the Sudanese agreed to accept King Faruq's sovereignty in the intervening period until they decided about their future. To this the sayyid could not agree; and with the fall of Hilali's government and the consequent deadlock in Egyptian politics there seemed even less sense in making such far-reaching concessions.[42]

The next important move came in September 1952, following the abolition of the Egyptian monarchy and the emergence of the Free Officers regime headed, at least nominally, by General Muhammad Najib. This in itself was a major contribution to the success of the Egyptian-Sudanese negotiations. Najib had been born and educated in the Sudan and hence was aware of Sudanese sensitivities. Moreover, the Egyptian crown, a major obstacle in all previous negotiations, had vanished from the scene following the July revolution. Najib could afford to be much more magnanimous than his predecessors and offered the Sudanese both self-government and self-determination in an atmosphere of complete freedom. Thus, at a single stroke

From Conquest to Independence: 1882–1956

Najib reached an agreement with Sudanese politicians and political parties of all shades, including Britain's latest collaborator, the Socialist Republicans. On 10 January 1953 an agreement was signed in Cairo with the representatives of all Sudanese political parties, and Sir James Robertson noted despairingly in his diary: 'What then do we do? There seems little point of struggling if all political parties are with Egypt.'[43] On 12 February 1953 the Anglo-Egyptian agreement regarding the Sudan was finally signed, very much on the lines agreed between Egypt and the Sudanese party leaders.

As mentioned above, the breakdown of the collaboration between the Sudan political service and the Umma party was largely due to continued British reluctance to regard a party dominated by a religious sect as a legitimate partner in its quest for an independent Sudan under British influence. The abortive attempts to revive the tribal leadership, this time under the attractive though misleading title of Socialist Republicans, was the last straw for Sayyid 'Abd al-Rahman. Moreover, he felt further disenchanted with his erstwhile allies when during his visit in London in September 1952, he was told by Foreign Office officials that the Sudan's salvation was now up to him and to his willingness to negotiate and compromise with the new Egyptian leaders. In other words, the British government, under constant pressure from the United States, was willing to opt out of the Sudan and thus reach the elusive agreement with Egypt, while the Anglo-Sudanese political service was still attempting to hang on to the Sudan. The Anglo-Egyptian Sudan therefore terminated its existence on 31 December 1955, and independent Sudan emerged as a new state.

For more than 50 years of what was British rule in all but name, the Sudan served as an excellent example for the 'theory of collaboration'. True, Robinson's description of the workings of this collaboration suffers from certain inaccuracies and generalisations. Nonetheless, one can state with certainty that 'the country of the Blacks ruled by the Blues', as the Sudan had often been called, could not have been ruled by the handful of British officials backed by a symbolic British military presence, without the voluntary collaboration of large segments of the Sudanese populace and its elite. It seems clear that the Ansar, under the able leadership of Sayyid 'Abd al-Rahman, provided this support despite British rebuffs. Indeed, one could almost claim that they chose to collaborate with Britain, despite the latter's reluctance, in order to overcome what they regarded as the major danger, namely the Sudan's annexation to Egypt. Once this danger had vanished following the removal of King Faruq in July 1952, it was relatively easy to reach an accommodation with Egypt; hence the British presence in the Sudan had lost its raison d'être.

Viewing developments from a British point of view, one observes repetitive futile attempts to create a Sudanese 'secular' elite in Britain's own image. In the absence of such an elite Britain had to rely on the only adequate alternative, though sectarianism was anathema to its beliefs. When the Ansar were finally able to achieve their aims in agreement with Egypt's new military rulers, Britain was already on its way out. India had become independent in 1947 and Palestine had been handed over to the United Nations in the same year. Egypt's Free Officers made it quite clear that they would not tolerate British troops on Egyptian soil, and the United States was using its economic muscle to drive Britain out of the Nile valley. If one adds to this Britain's bankruptcy following the war and the realization that it could no longer adequately police the empire, it becomes clear that there was no real alternative but to relinquish its hold on the Sudan.

BRITAIN AND EGYPT, 1882–1952

Egypt is the 'central exhibit' in Robinson and Gallagher's theory for the partition of Africa. The Egyptian crisis of 1879–1882, according to them, led to 'the breakdown of the Khedivate', and the British government's 'misdealings with this new proto-nationalism brought the British stumbling on to the Nile and trapped them there'.[44] Whether in fact this crisis was a genuine one, as described by Robinson and Gallagher, bringing anarchy in its wake, or whether 'it was engineered by Sir Aukland [sic] Colvin and others who regarded the Egyptian government which came into office in February 1882 as a threat to Anglo-French control over Egypt's finances',[45] as claimed by Roger Owen, is not the issue with which this paper is concerned. The question is if Whitehall viewed it as a genuine Egyptian crisis requiring military intervention.

'The Official Mind of Imperialism' under Gladstone, with which Robinson and Gallagher are concerned, first viewed 'Urabi and his comrades as Egyptian nationalists deserving British sympathy and tried to reach a workable solution which would bring about a compromise between the khedive, the legitimate ruler of Egypt, and the new nationalists.[46] Indeed, even Sir Auckland Colvin, reporting his interview with 'Urabi and his two colleagues on 1 November 1881,

From Conquest to Independence: 1882–1956

noted the respect of the Urabists for the khedive Tawfiq, who, 'to them, represented the Sultan: the Sultan, the Prophet; the Prophet, God'. Furthermore, it was quite clear that 'Urabi understood British interests in Egypt and was fully aware of Britain's ability to destroy him and his movement if it chose to intervene.[47] Prior to the naval demonstration and the British bombardment of Alexandria in May 1882, the Urabist movement had limited itself to a fight against the Turco-Circassian control of power and for a certain reduction of European economic and financial control. The rather exaggerated and hence misleading description of this movement as xenophobic tending to anarchist was first adopted by Colvin, the British controller of the debt, and later also by Malet, the British consul-general in Egypt and helped convince the British government that intervention was imperative unless Britain was willing to face complete chaos in Egypt, the Suez Canal, and even the Far East. The fact, so ably proven, that 'Gladstone had little idea of what had produced the violence that had made the occupation of Egypt inevitable' is immaterial as far as Robinson's theory is concerned. What matters is that decisions reached by the so-called 'cabal', including Hartington, Northbrook Childers, and Granville, who acted as a self-appointed group, led first to the bombardment of Alexandria and later to the unplanned military intervention and occupation of Egypt.[48]

The British conquest of Egypt created a number of problems for the conquerors. Even after the invasion they had no intention of staying in Egypt indefinitely. They were eager to restore law and order and to come to terms with the local Turco-Egyptian elite. Moreover, they sought, in agreement with the Ottoman sultan, a formula for the evacuation of British troops from Egypt, thereby enabling a return to the status quo ante of informal empire. It was only after French and Russian intervention with the sultan caused the Drummond-Wolff negotiations to end in a fiasco in 1887 that Britain's 'brief' sojourn in Egypt became an indefinite occupation. In fact, despite the British declaration of Egyptian independence in February 1922 and the Anglo-Egyptian agreement of 1936, Egypt remained a British dependency in all but name until President Nasser signed the 1954 agreement for the evacuation of all British troops from Egypt.

What were the alternatives open to Britain in its search for local allies or collaborators who, according to Robinson, were essential for its 72 years of supremacy in Egypt? There was, of course, the khedive, who, despite Robinson and Gallagher's claim regarding the 'breakdown of the Khedivate', was still the legitimate and supreme ruler of the country. During the British sojourn in Egypt there were five such rulers, three of whom were strong enough to lead their country and would have been ideal collaborators had the British authorities opted in that direction. 'Abbas Hilmi II (1892–1914), Ahmad Fu'ad (1917–1936), and Faruq (1936–1952) possessed both the necessary leadership qualities and the desire to rule. However, all three were alienated soon after they came to power by their treatment at the hands of their British overlords, who decided that Egypt should have a constitutional but not a ruling monarch. Examining the attitudes of the chief British officials in Egypt to the legitimate Egyptian rulers from the consul-generalship of Lord Cromer in 1883–1907 to that of Lord Killearn in 1934–1946, we find a striking similarity despite the changed circumstances. The Egyptian Kings were by and large viewed as a necessary evil. They were 'to reign but not to rule', as the new Egypt had no place for despotic kings. It was at least partly British interference which saddled Egypt with a constitution full of inconsistencies, for which the country was politically, socially, and economically unprepared in 1923. Indeed, Sir David Kelly, a senior British diplomat in Cairo during the last years of King Fu'ad's life, recounts how the latter told him

he was especially bitter against the British for having 'imposed a constitution on the Belgian model' on the Egyptians, who were completely unsuited for parliamentary government on those lines .... Why had we [the British] not been content to leave him to run the country, as he well knew how to do.[49]

There are many examples one could pick at random to describe the humiliation suffered by the legitimate rulers of Egypt at the hands of the British consuls-general or high commissioners. Lord Cromer in his book, *Abbas II*, describes the Egyptian khedive as 'a master of petty intrigue ... so wedded to tortuous courses that he was incapable of steadfastly pursuing for long any really loyal and straightforward course of action'.[50] Indeed, Cromer asked himself, when young 'Abbas came to power, 'Was it conceivable that an inexperienced youth of eighteen, fresh from the scholastically sound but rather narrow training of an Austrian college, would possess the intelligence, patience, judgement and self-restraint necessary to conform himself to the exigencies of a system of this sort?'[51] The system was that the khedive had in fact to bow to British 'advice' as formulated by the consul-general. Cromer's attitude becomes even clearer in the following passage:

It had to be borne in mind that a mischievous child of ten years old, armed with some straw and a box of matches, can cause a conflagration as well as a man of forty who is bent on committing arson. It was not easy to draw the line between the indulgence due to youth, and the severity necessary to prevent youthfulness from incurring the consequences of its own unreflecting and headstrong folly.[52]

Cromer rightly assumed that he and his fellow-British officials were disliked by the khedive and the Turco-Egyptian elite, who regarded British occupation as unlawful. From the point of view of the Egyptians, 'British civil and military administrators prevented the Khedive from doing what he liked, whereas he thought his will, however whimsical and capricious, should invariably be law.[53] There were clearly two alternatives open to Cromer: first, to withdraw into the background and let the khedive and his Turco-Egyptian elite rule the country as best they could. This was indeed the line followed, at least partly, by Cromer's successor, Sir Eldon Gorst, in the years 1907–1911.[54] But Cromer chose the second alternative, namely to teach the khedive a lesson. The occasion chosen was the khedive's dismissal of the Egyptian prime minister and the appointment of a new one in January 1893. 'If the Khedive had consulted me previously, I should not ... have made any strong objections ... But the whole affair had been planned and executed without my being taken into council.'[55] Cromer of course received the full backing of the British government, despite the fact that the Liberals under Gladstone were from 1892 until 1897 again in office. Cromer received the following message from the cabinet at his request: '*Her Majesty's Government expect to be consulted in such important matters as a change of Ministers. No change appears to be at present either necessary or peremptory.*'[56] This 'ultimatum' was submitted to the young khedive, and 'Abbas was forced to make the following declaration, dictated to him by Cromer: 'He was to say that he "was *most anxious to cultivate the most friendly relations with England, and that he would always most willingly adopt the advice of Her Majesty's Government on all questions of importance in the future*".'[57]

With regard to Cromer, then, one can conclude that collaboration, at least at the highest level of government, was not granted voluntarily and that the Egyptian elite, from the khedive downwards, were treated as subordinates of British officials. In concluding his study of British colonial rule in Egypt until 1914, Robert Tignor wrote:

Between 1892 and 1914 there was a steady growth of British influence over the Egyptian administrative system. Inspectors and subinspectors were appointed in virtually all branches of the government .... These British officials, although technically the subordinates of the Egyptian officials, became the real executive power in the country. No Egyptian official could afford to disregard the advice they proffered.[58]

Having dwelt at some length on the treatment of 'Abbas II by his British superiors, and having quoted Fu'ad's resentment of British policy under Lord Allenby in imposing the 1923 constitution, let us now turn to another strong high commissioner, Lord Lloyd, who served during King Fu'ad's reign and whose views regarding the authority of this ruler are therefore of importance. In weighing the alternatives open to the British government in Egypt in 1925, Lloyd stated the following:

> There were only two alternatives possible in the existing state of Egypt. The first was the government of the Wafd, which could compel the suffrages of an ignorant electorate, but showed no quality of reasonableness or foresight. Such a government had come into existence as a result of the first elections and there had followed the utter destruction of all hopes of a reasonable Anglo-Egyptian settlement .... The other alternative was a government based upon the autocratic power of the King — such a government would derive its strength from causes which still operate strongly in Eastern countries ... From the British point of view it need hardly be pointed out that both our past and our present policy would be rendered utterly fruitless by the appearance, at this stage, of autocratic government in Egypt, when the democratic constitution which was our declared goal had hardly yet come into being .... Neither eventuality could be contemplated and our intervention became inevitable.[59]

Lloyd thus justified British intervention in Egyptian politics during his term of office. In fact his rejection of the only two local political alternatives quoted above as unacceptable to British interests clearly proves that King Fu'ad's autocratic ambitions had no chance to flourish under Lloyd's tutelage. Indeed, as Lloyd stated in his conclusions, whichever side ruled in Egypt 'would owe the maintenance of its power to the presence, however passive, of our army and our influence'.[60] Lloyd's own preference, therefore, was for collaboration with the least significant force, namely the small political parties, most of which had split away from the Wafd and had no chance to gain power without the backing of either the king or the British high commissioner. Lord Allenby had steered a similar course in 1922–1924, when he had hoped to undermine the Wafd through collaboration with the Liberal Constitutionalists. The 1924 elections, however, had proved that the so-called political alternative to the Wafd was a figment of Allenby's imagination.[61] Lloyd followed in Allenby's footsteps with the full knowledge that he was backing a non-existent force, one which would owe whatever power it wielded to the goodwill of the British high commissioner in Egypt and to its cooperation with the palace.

Surveying the first half of the 1930s we see that Britain's new high commissioner, Sir Percy Loraine, adopted a position of greater neutrality in internal Egyptian politics. He refused to be lured by the Wafd or other opposition groups into active intervention and only went so far as to suggest to Sidqi Pasha, the new prime minister, that in the long run he should 'secure the moral cooperation of the country'; in other words, hold elections.[62] When such elections were finally held in May 1931, Loraine felt that despite Sidqi's victory he had not really been morally accepted by the people and therefore Britain should keep aloof from him rather than giving 'moral cover to a possibly fraudulent election'.[63] Attempts to force a reconciliation between King Fu'ad and the prime minister, or between the latter and the Liberal Constitutionalists, thereby creating a viable political base for Anglo-Egyptian negotiations excluding the Wafd, seemed to Loraine an unrealistic dream. Indeed, it was quite clear that as long as the government was composed of minority parties their inability to cooperate gave real power to the king. Britain's choice, therefore, was limited to a pro-palace coalition or a Wafdist-dominated one.[64]

As Marius Deeb rightly concludes, one of the characteristics of these years was British neutrality between the palace and the Wafd, with a certain bias towards King Fu'ad. The British regarded the king as unreliable and defined him as a liability, but thought that it was in his interest to retain British influence in Egypt.[65] The king accumulated greater influence during these years than he had ever had since the British occupation. This was mainly the result of the 1930 constitution which gave so much power to the executive that a Sidqi-Fu'ad combination could survive longer than any previous cabinet in Egypt, namely from June 1930 to September 1933.

The change came after two events – Sidqi's fall and the arrival of Sir Miles Lampson (later Lord Killearn), the new British high commissioner. Unlike his predecessor Lampson did not believe in Britain's continued neutrality in Egyptian politics which, in his view, helped force a minority government onto an unwilling populace. Moreover, he regarded the continuation of the palace regime, which owed its existence to the presence of British forces in Egypt, as counter-productive. As claims of British neutrality in Egypt's internal affairs were not accepted by the majority of the population he proposed to handle the king more firmly and even to rebuke him openly for the anti-foreign movement which was flourishing in Egypt under Fu'ad's patronage.[66] In Lampson's early correspondence there is already a clear preference for cooperating with the Wafd, which, in his view, was the only real political force in the country; or alternatively, and only provisionally, for backing a minority government against the king. Moreover, shortly before King Fu'ad's death Lampson suggested that he be declared incapable of ruling so as to overcome the danger both of his continued hostility and a possible anti-British council of regents ruling the country after his demise.[67]

Turning now to Faruq, the last king of Egypt, we find a striking similarity between his treatment by Lampson and that accorded to 'Abbas Hilmi II by Cromer: when Killearn left Egypt in 1946 after twelve years' service first as high commissioner and then as ambassador, the Egyptian monarchy was irreparably alienated from the British embassy. Like Abbas II, Faruq was a youth of eighteen when he assumed full power in July 1937, and Miles Lampson, who had been appointed high commissioner in Egypt in 1934, treated him like an immature child. Having arranged for a suitable tutor, an English graduate of Eton and Oxford, to 'improve the King's mind' and mold his character, Lampson rebuked 'the boy' for 'taking things too easily'. By the end of 1938 Lampson had lost both his patience with and his hopes for the young king: 'no one ... has the guts to stand up to the boy. Indeed he is becoming a fair pickle and ... even Aly Maher is losing what little influence he had over him'.[68] When Sir Anthony Eden visited Egypt during the war, Lampson quotes him as stating: 'Miles, I can't think how you have the patience to deal with that boy the way you do, it must be very trying.' By then Lampson himself had reached the conclusion that 'as long as the boy remains here we shall never get real cooperation'. He was therefore glad when Eden agreed 'that the only thing to do was to kick the King out'.[69] The opportunity arose according to Lampson, in February 1942 following the resignation of Sirri Pasha, the Egyptian prime minister. With the German African Corps under Rommel approaching Egypt's western border, and with popular anti-British feelings running high, Lampson decided, with His Majesty's Government's approval, to force a pro-British Wafdist government on King Faruq. When Faruq, having failed to persuade the Wafd to head a national coalition government, refused to accept Lampson's 'advice', the latter handed him an ultimatum on 4 February 1942. Backed by the leaders of all the political parties, Faruq persisted in his refusal to comply with British demands. Lampson therefore at last had his chance. Arriving at the palace, which was surrounded by British tanks, he demanded the king's abdication. He wanted Faruq out of office, and when the latter finally submitted and declared his willingness to form a purely Wafdist government, it was with great reluctance that Lampson withdrew the letter of abdication which Faruq had been ordered to sign.[70] In the years to come Lord Killearn, as his diaries indicate, repeatedly expressed his regret at not having insisted on Faruq's abdication on that date.

Others, both Egyptians and Englishmen, regarded Killearn's attitude to the king as a grave mistake. The extremely pro-British Ahmad Hasanayn Pasha, Faruq's chief advisor during the 1942 crisis, clearly blamed Lampson, who, he stated, 'simply bullied the Monarch' and never tried to treat him in a friendly, humane manner.[71] This view was shared by some of Lampson's colleagues in the Foreign Office, who repeatedly blamed the anti-British feelings of King Faruq on the ambassador's highhanded attitude. Even in the Cairo embassy itself there were more sober views, of which the following is but one example:

> We are dealing with a backward oriental country which is not yet ripe for democracy with a big 'D' and in which the Throne is ... a valuable brake on the activities of self-willed political leaders and unfledged political parties.... The present incumbent is far from ideal. But I submit that our doubts as to his fitness for high office ought not to lead us into a course which might gravely impair the ability of the office itself.[72]

Shone, probably fearing a rebuke from Lord Killearn, had tried his very best during the September-October 1944 crisis to keep the Wafd in office, despite his own misgivings. When Faruq finally dismissed Nahhas Pasha's government on 8 October 1944, Shone emphasised in his report on an interview with King Faruq that not only was the king still bitter about the events of 4 February but he resented even more the fact that due to the ambassador's pressure he had been made to suffer a corrupt Wafdist government as long as he had.[73] In his own so-called Swan Song Lord Killearn told a different story. He blamed his difficulties in Egypt on having to deal with an immature king who was influenced by bad advisors, especially 'Ali Mahir. Under these circumstances nothing but a 'stronghand' policy could have preserved British interests in Egypt. After the war, with the Labour party in office, 'non-intervention in Egyptian politics' became the new British policy. Killearn expressed his disapproval:

To sit back and remain splendidly aloof from Egyptian internal politics sounds extremely attractive in theory .... But with Egypt situated as she is, how long will that be possible? Can we allow Egypt to disintegrate and deteriorate at her own sweet will? ... With all deference I gravely doubt it .... With powder in the gun I maintain that in the East it is usually unnecessary to discharge it. The knowledge we mean business is enough.[74]

However, the British Empire was already in the process of being dismantled, and Egypt's strategic position was no longer the major British consideration. As in the early 1930s so-called British neutrality led to palace-dominated minority governments, with Sidqi once again leading the way. But Faruq's success in splitting the Wafd and ousting it from office did not help him to stabilise the throne. The corruption and the social strife of the post-war era, culminating in the humiliating defeat in the war against Israel in 1948–1949, set the stage for the Free Officers coup in July 1952.

As Lloyd had rightly stated as early as the 1920s and 1930s, the Wafd was the only real nationalist elite in Egypt strong enough to rule the country independently and thus provide the British authorities with collaborators of substance. This was true ever since the Wafd first emerged as a political force towards the end of the First World War. And yet, with the notable exception of the years 1936–1937, and again from 1942 to 1944, when, as a result of international pressures culminating in the war, Britain opted for the Wafd, the latter was in constant opposition and hence a nuisance as far as Britain was concerned.

To start at the beginning, Sa'd Zaghlul, as one of Muhammad 'Abduh's most outstanding disciples, was regarded by Lord Cromer in 1906 as a leading member of the 'only group with whom lay any hope of constitutional advancement in Egypt'.[75] In other words, if the khedive 'Abbas Hilmi was to be checkmated and humiliated, an advancement of Zaghlul and of the Umma party seemed the right method. However, the consul-general's honeymoon with Zaghlul, continued by Cromer's successor Sir Eldon Gorst, came to an abrupt end in 1912 during Kitchener's terms of office. By then it had become quite clear that Zaghlul was a prominent figure in Egyptian political circles and thus an important prospective ally for those who sought to dominate Egyptian politics.

By the end of the First World War Zaghlul, the one-time moderate collaborator of Cromer, had become the most outspoken leader of the opposition, which claimed immediate Egyptian independence.

Zaghlul's transformation was partly due to his personality and the realization that he could not achieve his ambitions under British tutelage. But there is no doubt that the consul-general gave him every reason to regard British intentions with utmost suspicion. It was Sir Reginald Wingate who percipiently wrote to Lord Hardinge at the Foreign Office in 1917 that 'I am not at all sure that we would not be wise to secure his [Zaghlul's] support on the side of the government rather than have him in opposition....'[76] But like his predecessors Kitchener and McMahon, Wingate did not follow up these shrewd observations with positive actions. Zaghlul remained in opposition, coordinated his actions with the new sultan, Fu'ad, and on 13 November 1918 visited Wingate and demanded to represent Egypt at the forthcoming peace conference. In fact, by that date Zaghlul and his delegation (*wafd*) had not only coordinated policy with the sultan, but had also gained the full support of the Egyptian government headed by Husayn Rushdi and 'Adli Yakan, who had faithfully supported Britain throughout the war.[77] None of these leaders could afford to oppose Zaghlul, even if their views and interests differed, for fear of being branded traitors or collaborators of the British. Wingate, who knew of the support Zaghlul and his friends commanded, urged the British Foreign Office to act prudently, but to no avail. He was rebuked for having received Zaghlul and his colleagues and was categorically ordered to refuse any further contact with them. Furthermore, with British attention fully absorbed in Europe and elsewhere, Egypt had to wait its turn, and no Egyptian delegation, official or unofficial, was to be invited either to London or to the peace conference. In this way Britain not only alienated the newly formed Wafd but united nearly all other Egyptian politicians around its leadership. Had Rushdi, 'Adli Yakan, or other leaders of official standing been invited to London to discuss Egypt's future, as Wingate had proposed, the united pro-Zaghlul front might have been broken. Instead, Wingate was made the scapegoat, and Zaghlul was inadvertently helped towards becoming the unchallenged leader of Egyptian anti-British nationalism. Once Zaghlul had tasted power it was impossible to remove him. Even some of his colleagues in the Wafd 'came to regard him as a Frankenstein monster they had created but were no longer able to control'.[78]

It was Lord Allenby who as high commissioner had toyed with the idea of a third alternative. From December 1921 onwards he urged the Foreign Office to abandon the protectorate over Egypt in order to boost the anti-Zaghlul leadership of 'Adli Yakan, Tharwat, and others who would provide the necessary support of a collaborating elite and form the 'basis of a lasting settlement in Egypt'. Should his advice not be accepted, Allenby threatened to resign.[79] A little over a month later the British cabinet reluctantly gave in, and Allenby attained the unilateral declaration he had requested. But the hope of a lasting settlement based on so-called Liberal Constitutionalist collaboration was short-lived. Once the new Constitution was promulgated in April 1923 and elections held in January 1924, Tharwat and his Liberal Constitutionalist supporters suffered a crushing defeat, while Zaghlul and the Wafd enjoyed an overwhelming majority in the new parliament. A period of twelve years followed in which Egypt was nominally independent. But with a British army of occupation and British 'advisors' in the army and administration, even the combined opposition of the king and the Wafd could do little to shake British rule. Needless to say, for most of that period Britain could rely on internal rifts between the king and the Wafd, with the smaller parties doing their utmost to undermine Wafdist support, and even opt for the notorious 'Ministry of the Iron Grip' (*al-qabda al-hadidiyya*), which under Liberal Constitutionalist leadership suspended the 1923 constitution.[80] Britain could thus safeguard its interests in the Nile Valley without a real collaborating elite or the unpleasantness involved in the use of force. Indeed, until 1936 the Wafd, the only party with real grass roots support in the country, could not achieve power owing to its uncompromising attitude both to Britain's demands and to King Fu'ad's despotic tendencies.

One aspect of this controversy was of course the economic one, which although not the prime motive for Britain's entry into the Nile valley became more central as time went on. By the 1920s Egypt had become a dependent economy geared almost exclusively to the cultivation and export of cotton. This meant that the principal sectors of the economy were linked to world markets and depended on the latter's fluctuations and crises. This in turn aided the emergence and consolidation of an Egyptian upper class composed almost exclusively of large landowners who together with the king depended on foreign banks and creditors. Investments by this class centred almost exclusively on the accumulation and improvement of agricultural lands. The few attempts at industrialisation failed for the most part owing to the policy of free trade and lack of government protection. The new political elite was therefore one of provincial notables who found a venue for their political ambitions first in the Umma party of 1907 and later in the

From Conquest to Independence: 1882–1956

Liberal Constitutionalists: 'Through their control of the government machinery this new elite was mainly concerned with enhancing the fortunes of their own class of large landowners.'[81]

The founding of Bank Misr in 1920 was an attempt to break out of the complete dependence mentioned above and to facilitate the emergence of an independent Egyptian bourgeoisie. This, it was hoped, would enable Egypt to put an end to its export-dominated economy and to diversify its resources, leading eventually to economic independence. Tal'at Harb, the founder and driving spirit of Bank Misr and its associate companies, could therefore be described as the antithesis of the run-of-the-mill collaborator. He did not belong to Egypt's great landed families but worked his way up through law school to become one of the leading financial experts and estate managers. It is also noteworthy that Tal'at Harb regarded himself as a defender of Islam against its Westernising detractors. He opposed the liberal attitudes toward women's liberation and defended traditional Islamic dictates as to the woman's place in society. Furthermore, he openly denounced the financial exploitation of Egypt as exemplified in the Suez Canal Company and the enslavement of its economy by foreign banks. Herein then was the solution, according to Harb: an Egyptian bank encouraging Egyptian industries leading ultimately towards Egyptian economic independence. Just as Sa'd Zaghlul, the one-time protégé of Cromer, had become the leader of the 1919 revolution for Egypt's liberation. Tal'at Harb, a one-time director of the Kom Ombo land estate company had founded Bank Misr in 1920 as the economic arm of that same revolution. But while the bank and its various ventures had a populist revolutionary tinge, and all its shareholders and directors could only be Egyptians, this did not stop it from benefitting from foreign expertise and capital. Thus the Misr Cotton Exporting Company, founded in 1929, was a joint Egyptian-German venture. Two years later Misr Air came into being as a joint Anglo-Egyptian company, thereby paving the way for future economic collaboration between Bank Misr and British firms in the early 1930s.[82] It was quite clear to the officialdom that as long as Tal'at Harb remained in charge a real Anglo-Egyptian linkage would not be possible. The chance to replace him came in September 1939 when, with the outbreak of war, Bank Misr was besieged by its stockholders and nearly collapsed. Tal'at Harb was forced to resign and was replaced by the pro-British Hafiz 'Afifi and 'Abd al-Maqsud Ahmad, who announced their desire to work in harmony with British capital. In this way the only serious nationalist attempt at economic independence came to an end owing to the dependent nature of Egyptian capitalism during the interwar period.[83] Tal'at Harb's attempts to achieve economic independence were just as untimely as Sa'd Zaghlul's struggle for political independence. Britain was not ready to quit; and there were still enough members of the Egyptian bourgeoisie, even within the Wafd, who were willing to benefit from continued British presence.

Throughout the first half of the 1930s there were half-hearted attempts by some of the Wafd leaders to regain power through British intervention. While Britain maintained its so-called neutrality and refused to be instrumental in reintroducing the 1923 constituion, the Wafd leadership realized increasingly that without British aid it was unable to combat the palace-dominated minority coalitions. Hence the Wafd's ambivalence in presenting itself as the nationalist party hostile to Britain while at the same time exploring ways and means to benefit politically from British interference.[84] This policy began to be questioned soon after Lampson's arrival in Egypt in 1934, as mentioned above. Although Lampson was told explicitly that the British government opposed the reintroduction of the 1923 constitution, as it would automatically bring the Wafd back to power, he did not believe that it was wise to oppose this step once it was supported by other political parties. He also believed that Britain should play a more active role in safeguarding its interests following the death of King Fu'ad in 1935.[85]

The year 1936 was a turning point in Anglo-Wafdist relations. It marked the beginning of an era in Wafd history, lasting until 1944, which may be labelled the 'period of collaboration with Britain'.[86] The change was a result of both internal factors and international pressures. Internally, the Wafd was tired of opposition: it realized that despite its mass support it could not hope to gain power and maintain it without an accommodation either with the British or with the king, preferably both. The death of King Fu'ad in 1935 and the succession of the young Faruq, then still a minor, seemed to bode well for this. On the international scene, with the fascist threat spreading from Europe to Africa following the Italian invasion of Ethiopia, Britain needed a reliable ally in Egypt. And so in August 1936 the Wafd, under the leadership of Nahhas Pasha, accepted the Anglo-Egyptian Treaty of Alliance, defined by Nahhas as 'honour and independence' but whose terms were actually not much better than those previously put forward by Britain and rejected by the Wafd as unsatisfactory.[87]

It took young King Faruq only a little over one year to form an anti-Wafdist coalition, which enabled him to oust the Wafd from office and dissolve parliament. This was achieved through the unification of all opposition parties and the defeat of the Wafd in the rigged elections of 1938.[88] Lampson had warned Eden that Britain 'might be falling out of the frying-pan into the fire by exchanging the Wafd for a Palace Govt.' He warned of Faruq's contacts with Italy and Germany and insisted that Nahhas was the sincerest believer in Anglo-Egyptian cooperation. But while Eden was willing to back the Wafd, as suggested by Lampson, he opposed open intervention in Egyptian politics except in such cases where the palace or the opposition parties adopted an attitude openly hostile to British interests.[89] And so the first period of Lampson's collaboration with Nahhas came to an untimely end.

From the viewpoint of the Wafd, the continued collaboration with England — which was initiated by Nahhas through his intermediary Amin 'Uthman and which reached its climax in February 1942 when the Wafd resumed power with the backing of British tanks — was clearly the beginning of its end as the standard bearer of Egyptian nationalism.[90] This downhill trend was due to a number of occurrences. Foremost among them were the antagonism between King Faruq and the Wafd and internal dissension within the Wafd. These led to the formation of two new parties by ex-Wafdist leaders: the Sa'dist party (*al-hay' a al-Sa'diyya*), named after Sa'd Zaghlul and founded in January 1938, and the Wafdist party (*al-kutla al-Wafdiyya*), founded by Nahhas's deputy leader, Makram 'Ubayd, in July 1943. The Wafd thus lost some of its most outstanding leaders, such as Ahmad Mahir, Mahmud Fahmi al-Nuqrashi, and Makram 'Ubayd. And through its continued collaboration with Britain, coupled with accusations of nepotism and corruption in its leadership, it lost ground to the more extremist and outspoken Muslim Brothers, among its traditional supporters. Still more important, the young Egyptian officers who started attending the military academy in the years 1936–1937 following the 1936 Anglo-Egyptian Treaty, regarded the Wafd's collaboration with Britain during the Second World War as an act of treason for which many of them never forgave Nahhas and his colleagues. As Anwar al-Sadat wrote, 'The result of the British *coup* of 4th February 1942, was to impose upon Egypt two years of dictatorship by the Wafd — two years of nepotism, jobbery and peculation which thoroughly discredited the major nationalist party in Egypt.'[91] Summing up the British side of the bargain immediately after Nahhas's dismissal by King Faruq, Lord Killearn, whose policy contributed to the Wafd's loss of prestige and who six months earlier had recommended the deposal of Faruq in order to save Nahhas, wrote:

I am really relieved about Nahas being sacked during my absence ... [and] cannot be charged either by Nahas or the Wafd with having let them down .... And anyway the crucial time of danger from the war angle is safely past. Nahas did us well then; and we must stand by our friends. That I have done up to the hilt: indeed many people think too much so .... I know Ahmed Maher well. Of course he won't be so much in our pocket as Nahas. But he is heavily indebted to Abboud (who is 100% with us) and also incidentally in our debt too.[92]

This indeed was collaboration at its crudest, assessing the value of Egyptian political and financial leaders according to the extent they were 'in British pockets', and as we have seen these included the landed aristocracy and even the Misr complex. But while many at the Foreign Office disagreed with Killearn's crude policies, he enjoyed the full backing of those who mattered: Churchill and Eden gave him their full support throughout their term of office. When, following the Labour party's victory in the post-war elections, Killearn was finally removed, the damage done was already irreparable. Every major political party, with the exception of the Muslim Brothers, had been discredited through its submission to British interests. The futile attempts of Sidqi Pasha in 1946–47 to reach an agreement with the Labour government, followed by the failure of Nahhas Pasha in 1951, are the final chapters in the dismal history of Egyptian parliamentarism.

According to Sadat, the Wafd's conduct of the anti-British struggle following its unilateral repeal of the Anglo-Egyptian Treaty in October 1951 did provide it with a last chance. Indeed, its 'ardent patriotism and resolution ... raised the Wafd in the esteem of the Free Officers'. So much so, they approached the Wafd's leadership and proposed to back the government in deposing Faruq: 'We had thought we could count on the Wafd, to the point of entrusting it with the government of Egypt after the *coup d'etat*. We were quickly disenchanted. The Wafd was playing a double game.'[93]

It is true that the endless inter-party strife from the end of the war had allowed King Faruq to tighten his control over Egyptian politics. The chain of assassinations of so-called collaborators started with the Sa'dist prime minister Dr. Ahmad Mahir in February 1945, continued with Amin 'Uthman in January 1946, and culminated with yet another Sa'dist prime minister, Mahmud Fahmi al-Nuqrashi, in December 1948. This bloodshed clearly paved the way for the breakdown of public order which the king believed would enable him to assume full control.⁹⁴ The last two years of Wafdist rule, the so-called people's government, from January 1950 to the burning of Cairo by the mobs on 26 January 1952, indicate that Egypt after the Second World War no longer had an elite strong enough to rule the country and reach an agreement with Britain. To return to Robinson's formula, the various political forces in Egypt headed by the king and backed by sections of the army had contrived a situation in which Britain 'ran out of collaborators'.⁹⁵

CONCLUSION

Judging from this brief examination of one imperial power's policies in one region of the Middle East, it would be presumptuous to pass a verdict as to the extent to which 'collaboration' is an essential factor in explaining the force and duration of colonial rule. However, despite this shortcoming it seems that Robinson's contribution to this theory is a useful addition not only in the case of Egypt and the Sudan, but also to our understanding of an important and neglected element in the workings of modern imperialism.

First, let us re-emphasise that, according to Robinson, collaboration is only one of three components essential in explaining European imperialism. The other traditionally recognized and hence favoured components are purely European-oriented and depend on economic and strategic considerations, outside the scope of the present study. Second, in our examination of collaboration in Egypt and the Sudan we have only briefly mentioned an important factor, namely the strength of the British army of occupation in the Nile valley during the period in question. Clearly, with the strategic importance of this region for Britain, so well demonstrated in two world wars, British military forces played an important role in maintaining British supremacy during periods of crisis. Moreover, until 1936 the Egyptian army was so ill-equipped and badly trained that it could not adequately support an anti-British coalition even if it had decided to do so. As one of the British officials observed, even if all Egyptian parties were united and demanded British evacuation from the Nile valley, 'none of the British were worried because they knew that the Egyptian army had been neutralised: "all their ammunition is in the citadel with a perfectly good British battalion sitting on it".'⁹⁶ Yet it was Lord Allenby in 1922 and British military commanders after the Second World War who repeatedly stated that, if Egypt had to be held through sheer military force, its strategic value to Britain would be greatly diminished.

Comparing British rule in Egypt with that in the Sudan, there is an important difference in the starting points. Egypt, when the British occupied it in 1882, was on the eve of independence, with an indigenous proto-nationalist movement ready to assume power. If at that time the Turco-Egyptian elite had been given the choice, they would most probably have opted for Ottoman rather than British occupation as the lesser of the two evils. In the Sudan, after more than a decade of Ta'ishi autocracy under the khalifa 'Abdallah, large sections of the riverain elite were only too pleased to see this autocracy overthrown by Anglo-Egyptian forces. Moreover, many of the riverain shaykhs were also anti-Egyptian as a result of some 60 years of Egyptian rule in the Sudan in the pre-Mahdist period. This, together with at least two other reasons, made it easier to find collaborators in the Sudan. First, the fact that there were two colonial powers — England and Egypt — ruling the Sudan helped to split the emerging Sudanese elite into anti-Egyptian and anti-British factions. Second, the emergence of militant anti-British nationalism in the Sudan took much longer than in Egypt because of the relative backwardness of the Sudan and its comparatively weak educated elite. Consequently, the traditional sectarian leaders played a predominant role in Sudanese politics and provided essential collaboration when required, even though Britain would have preferred to collaborate with a secular elite. In Egypt this kind of effective collaboration could not emerge for a simple reason. Prospective Egyptian collaborators of any hue were united in their demand for the evacuation of British military forces from Egyptian territories and in their quest for the unity of the Nile valley. There were those who only paid lip service in their pursuit of these aims, but no Egyptian king or politician could ever collaborate fully with the British authorities over a long period without sooner or later coming into an open clash over either evacuation or the Sudan or both. Many Egyptians branded the Anglo-Egyptian Treaty of 1936, which recognized the condominium in the Sudan, as an act of treason by the Wafd. Consequently, the kind of wholehearted support which Britain enjoyed in the Sudan from those who feared Egyptian domination was never available in Egypt.

However, both in Egypt and the Sudan there was a more than adequate supply of prospective collaborators for Britain to choose from. The internal struggle for power in Egypt between king Fu'ad, king Faruq and the Wafd, and the sectarian divisions in the Sudan, made collaboration with Britain an essential part of internal politics. The fact that on the eve of independence the Umma and the Wafd, those most closely associated with the British authorities in the years prior to independence, were at least partly discredited, seems to confirm that collaboration was indeed a two-edged sword. But here again there was a difference between the impact of collaboration on the traditional elites in Egypt and the Sudan. In Egypt of 1951–52 the major components of the elite, including the king and the Wafd, had been discredited to such an extent that new forces had to move in and lead the country to independence. The choice fell on the army as the only alternative to complete chaos and the one element strong enough to force the abdication of King Faruq. In the Sudan Isma'il al-Azhari and others of the educated elite, backed by the traditional sectarian leadership, were in strong enough position to lead the country toward independence in the crucial years 1953–1956. In both cases, however, Robinson rightly suggests that on the eve of Britain's evacuation of the Nile valley she had run out of effective collaborators. True, this was only one of several factors which determined Britain's decolonisation policy in the years 1946–1956, but it was a factor which clearly had to be taken into account. The alternative to evacuation was military force, and Britain lacked both the funds and the will to withstand the prevailing anti-colonial mood in the international arena. If proof of Britain's weakness was needed, it was provided both during and after the abortive Suez War in October 1956.

NOTES

1. R. Robinson, 'Non-European Foundations of European Imperialism: Sketch for a Theory of Collaboration, in R. Owen and B. Sutcliffe (eds.), *Studies in the Theory of Imperialism*, London 1972, pp. 117-140. For the earlier works, see J. Gallagher and R. Robinson, 'The Imperialism of Free Trade', *Economic History Review* (second series), VI/1 (1953): 1-15; R. Robinson and J. Gallagher (with Alice Denny), *Africa and the Victorians: The Official Mind of Imperialism*, London 1961. See also P. Woodward, *Condominium and Sudanese Nationalism*, London 1979 which examines certain aspects of collaboration in the Sudanese context.
2. Robinson, p. 118.
3. Ibid.
4. Ibid., p. 120.
5. Ibid.
6. Ibid., p. 137.
7. Ibid., pp. 120-121.
8. M. Muggeridge, *Chronicles of Wasted Time: The Infernal Grove*, New York 1974, vol. 2, p. 42.

9. Lord Cromer, *Modern Egypt*, London 1908, vol. 1, pp. 371-395.
10. See, for instance, *General Report on the Egyptian Soudan*, March 1895, compiled from statements made by Slatin Pasha.
11. Robinson and Gallagher, *Africa and the Victorians*, pp. 346-354.
12. 'Memorandum to Mudirs', enclosure in Cromer to Salisbury, 17 March 1899, FO 78/5022.
13. Ibid.
14. G. Warburg, *The Sudan under Wingate*, Frank Cass, London 1971, p. 96; for further details, see pp. 95-100, 138-147.
15. Stack to Wingate, 8 May 1919, FO 371/3711; Allenby to Foreign Office, 27 April 1919, FO 371/3725.
16. Report of A.D.I. Khartoum, 28 April 1919, FO 371/3716; see also M. Daly, *British Administration and the Northern Sudan, 1917–1924*, Leiden 1980, pp. 71-74.
17. Memorandum of Sir Lee Stack, 25 May 1924, FO 371/10049; C. A. Willis, 'The Political Situation', 16 June 1924, in Allenby to MacDonald, 13 July 1924, FO 371/10050.
18. Daly, pp. 112-113.
19. Ibid., pp. 119-121.
20. 'Note on Strength of British Garrison in the Sudan', n.d., FO 371/11587; see also Cab/23/60, 23 January 1929, 20 February 1929, where it was decided to retain the above garrison.
21. In June 1933 the force was further decreased following a request by the British War Office; see War Office to Foreign Office, 18 May 1933; Governor-General to High Commissioner, 19 June 1933, FO 141/704. See also minute by J. Murray on British garrison in the Sudan, 29 June 1929, FO 371/13868, in which there was mention that both Chamberlain and Maffey (governor-general of the Sudan) had suggested the removal of one British battalion from Khartoum so as not to spend money on new barracks.
22. See R. Davies, 'Memorandum on the Policy of the Sudan Government towards the Mahdist Cult', *Secret Intelligence Report*, no. 7, 11 December 1927, FO 371/11613 (hereafter *SSIR*); Robinson is wrong in stating that 'the British controlled this dependency up to 1924 through Egyptian and Sudanese subordinate officials in collaboration with anti-Mahdist notables'. See Robinson, p. 135.
23. Sir Harold MacMichael, *The Anglo-Egyptian Sudan*, London 1934, pp. 233-234.
24. Ibid., p. 241.
25. Ibid., pp. 250-253; see also Daly, pp. 173-175. For the reasons underlying a different policy in the south, see R. O. Collins, *The Southern Sudan in Historical Perspective*, Tel Aviv 1975, especially pp. 35-50.
26. Robinson (p. 136) is mistaken in suggesting a reversal of this policy as early as 1933. See also G. Warburg, 'Popular Islam and Tribal Leadership in the Socio-Political Structure of North Sudan', in M. Milson (ed.), *Society and Political Structure in the Arab World*, New York 1973, especially pp. 248-253.
27. G. Warburg, 'From Ansar to Umma: Sectarian Politics in the Sudan, 1914–1945', *Asian and African Studies* 11/2 (1973): 101-153.
28. Ibid., pp. 118-119, quoting from al-Sadiq al-Mahdi, *Jihad fi sabil al-istiqlal*, Khartoum, n.d., pp. 29-30.
29. Henderson's report on the Sudan, enclosure in Allenby to Chamberlain, 21 April 1925, FO 371/10879.
30. Ibid.; Archer to Allenby, 27 April 1925, FO 371/10880 (italics mine).
31. Maffey to Campbell, 3 April 1933, FO 407/217, vol. 1; Symes to Lampson, 14 April 1934, FO 407/217, vol. 3.
32. See, for instance, Maffey to Loraine, 18 July 1930, FO 371/14565; *SSIR*, no. 8, November 1926.

From Conquest to Independence: 1882–1956

33. Lampson to Campbell, 15 June 1935, FO 371/19095. Sir James Currie, who had served as director of education, had expressed his misgivings regarding tribal leadership following his visit in the Sudan in 1935. Yet, on a previous visit he had suggested supporting some of these chiefs as a counterpoise to the religious leaders; see Currie to Tyrrell, 28 August 1926, FO 371/11613; see also Daly, pp. 184-185.
34. K. D. D. Henderson, *The Making of the Modern Sudan*, London, 1953, p. 41.
35. Ibid., pp. 553-558, quoted from a circular signed by Newbold on 10 September 1942, 'On Further Association of Sudanese with Local and Central Government'.
36. Ibid., p. 539. *Sayyid, nazir*, and *qa'immaqam* were the Arabic terms denoting the Sudan's religious, tribal, and military notables; the rank of the latter approximates that of a lieutenant-colonel.
37. Gillan to Lampson, 5 July 1938, FO 371/21999; cf. Lampson to Oliphant, 30 June 1937, FO 371/20914, in which he expresses similar views; see also Woodward, p. 21.
38. Henderson, p. 537, n. 3.
39. Woodward, p. 89, quoting J. W. R. Robertson, 4 February 1950 (papers formerly in possession of Sir J. Robertson).
40. For details, see G. Warburg, *Islam, Nationalism and Communism in a Traditional Society: The Case of Sudan*, Frank Cass, London 1978, especially pp. 67-89; see also Woodward, pp. 111-116.
41. See Warburg, 'Popular Islam and Tribal Leadership', p. 263.
42. Woodward, pp. 116-119.
43. Quoted in Woodward, p. 124.
44. R. Robinson and J. Gallagher, 'The Partition of Africa', in W. R. Louis (ed.), *Imperialism, the Robinson & Gallagher Controversy*, New York 1976, p. 75.
45. R. Owen, 'Robinson and Gallagher and Middle Eastern Nationalism: the Egyptian Argument', in W. R. Louis, op. cit., p. 214.
46. Robinson and Gallagher, *Africa and the Victorians*, pp. 89-94; see also J. S. Galbraith and A. Lutfi al-Sayyid-Marsot, 'The British Occupation of Egypt: Another View', *IJMES* 9/4 (1978): 472.
47. Memorandum of A. Colvin, 2 November 1881, FO 78/3326, quoted in A. Schölch, *Ägypten Den Ägyptern, Die politische und gesellschaftliche Krise der Jahre 1878–1882 in Ägypten*, Zürich, n.d., pp. 167-168.
48. Galbraith and al-Sayyid-Marsot, pp. 484-487; see also Schölch, pp. 198, 263-269; see also R. Jay, *Joseph Chamberlain: A Political Study*, London 1981, p. 49, who adds that Colvin's selection to this post was done by British bondholders and not by the government. Furthermore, it was the bond-holders' view which Colvin represented both in his reports to the government and in his writings in the *Pall Mall Gazette*, which was the only newspaper which Gladstone read with care.
49. E. Kedourie, 'The Genesis of the Egyptian Constitution of 1923', in *The Chatham House Version and other Middle Eastern Studies*, Frank Cass, London 1974, p. 160.
50. The Earl of Cromer, *Abbas II*, London 1915, p. XIII.
51. Ibid., p. 8.
52. Ibid., p. 10.
53. Ibid., p. 16.
54. See R. L. Tignor, *Modernization and British Colonial Rule in Egypt 1882–1914*, Princeton 1966, especially pp. 291-314. It is difficult to assess the success or failure of Gorst's policy; after his death in 1911 his successor, Lord Kitchener, revived the repressive Cromer policy.
55. Cromer, *Abbas II*, p. 22.
56. Ibid., p. 24 (italics mine).
57. Ibid., p. 27 (italics mine).
58. Tignor, *Modernization and British Colonial Rule*, pp. 392-393.

59. Lord Lloyd, *Egypt Since Cromer* (second edition), New York 1970, vol. II, pp. 115-116. On the reasons for dismissing the Wafdist alternative, see below.
60. Ibid., p. 357.
61. R. Wellesley, Ministry of Interior, Cairo, to J. Murray, 8 June 1922, FO 371/7734. Wellesley complains that Tharwat is a nonentity and that all senior British officials oppose Allenby's compromising attitude towards the Liberals.
62. Loraine to Henderson, 21 February 1931, FO 407/213; Loraine to Henderson, 7 March 1931, FO 407/213; Loraine to Henderson, 17 March 1931, FO 407/213.
63. Loraine to Henderson, 5 June 1931, FO 407/213; Loraine to Simon, 3 December 1931, FO 407/214; Loraine to Simon, 19 December 1931, FO 407/214.
64. Campbell to Simon, 28 July 1933, FO 407/217; Campbell to Simon, 16 September 1933, FO 407/217.
65. Marius Deeb, *Party Politics in Egypt: The Wafd and its Rivals, 1919–1939*, London 1979, pp. 238-239.
66. Lampson to Simon, 1 March 1934, FO 407/217; Lampson to Simon, 6 May 1934, FO 407/217.
67. Lampson to Simon, 3 May 1934, FO 407/217; Lampson to Simon, 8 February 1935, FO 407/218; Lampson to Simon, 24 April 1935, FO 407/218.
68. *The Killearn Diaries 1934–1946, the Diplomatic and Personal Record of Lord Killearn (Sir Miles Lampson) High Commissioner and Ambassador Egypt*, T. E. Evans, ed., London 1972, pp. 78-91, 93-94.
69. Ibid., pp. 129-131.
70. Lampson to Eden (highly secret), 5 February 1942 (Tel. No. 491), FO 371/31567. For further details, see G. Warburg, 'Lampson's Ultimatum to Faruq'. *MES* II (1975); 24-33; Dr. Muhammad Anis, *4 Febrayir 1942 fi Ta'rikh Misr al-Siyyasi*, Beirut 1972. Anis emphasises that British interference in Egyptian politics since 1882 was always anti-nationalist. February 1942 was the sole exception since Britain intervened on behalf of Egypt's major nationalist party.
71. Gerald Delany, letter to the young Lord Wavell on the political situation in Egypt during Wavell's period of command in the Second World War, 27 July 1953; in Private Papers Collection, Middle East Center, St. Antony's College, Oxford.
72. Shone to Foreign Office (no. 1839), 18 September 1944, FO 371/41322. At the time Shone was the chargé d'affaires at the embassy; Killearn was on vacation in South Africa.
73. Shone to Foreign Office, 11 October 1944, FO 371/41334.
74. Bowker to Foreign Office, 11 March 1946, FO 371/53287. Bowker was the chargé d'affaires following Killearn's dismissal; the labelling of the above quotation as 'Lord Killearn's Swan Song' is Bowker's.
75. E. Kedourie, 'Sa'd Zaghlul and the British', in *The Chatham House Version*, pp. 82-159. The following, unless otherwise stated, is largely based on Kedourie's study.
76. Ibid., p. 88, quoting Wingate to Hardinge, 29 November 1917, The Wingate Papers at Durham, box 146/8.
77. A. Lutfi al-Sayyid-Marsot, *Egypt's Liberal Experiment 1922–1936*, Berkeley and Los Angeles 1977, p. 48.
78. Ibid., p. 50.
79. Kedourie, p. 155, quoting Allenby's telegrams to Curzon, 20 January 1922.
80. al-Sayyid-Marsot, *Egypt's Liberal Experiment*, pp. 111-137.
81. Samir Radwan, *Capital Formation in Egyptian Industry and Agriculture 1882–1967*, London 1974, pp. 240-243.
82. For details, see R. L. Tignor, 'Bank Misr and Foreign Capitalism', *IJMES* 8 (1977): 161-181; Marius Deeb, 'Bank Misr and the Emergence of the Local Bourgeoisie in Egypt', *MES* 12 (1976): 69-86. See also M. Deeb, *Party Politics in Egypt*, pp. 227-233, 311.

83. Tignor, 'Bank Misr', pp. 178-181. See also L. Binder, *In a Moment of Enthusiasm*, Chicago 1978, p. 375, who explains how the rural middle class allied itself with the large landowners in order to enhance their position.
84. See, for instance, Loraine to Henderson, 28 February 1931, FO 407/213; Loraine to Simon, 14 December 1931, FO 407/214; Loraine to Simon, 18 November 1931, FO 407/214; Campbell to Simon, 24 June 1933, FO 407/217; Peterson to Simon, 12 October 1934, FO 407/217, reporting his conversation with Nahhas.
85. Simon to Lampson, 20 May 1935, FO 407/218; Lampson to Secretary of State for Foreign Affairs, 9 December 1935, FO 407/218; Lampson to Eden, 2 May 1935, FO 407/219; Eden to Lampson, 2 May 1935, FO 407/219.
86. This in fact is the title of the chapter dealing with this period in Zaheer Masood Quraishi's book, *Liberal Nationalism in Egypt, Rise and Fall of the Wafd Party*, Delhi 1967, pp. 131-151.
87. Ibid., pp. 126-128; al-Sayyid-Marsot, pp. 180-187.
88. Deeb, *Party Politics in Egypt*, pp. 330-334. For 'Ali Mahir's role in these events, see 'Abd al-'Azim Ramadan, *Al-Sira bayn al-Wafd wa'l 'Ursh' 1936-1939*, Beirut 1979, pp. 32-34.
89. Lampson to Eden, 16 February 1937, FO 407/221; Lampson to Eden, 28 July 1937; FO 407/221; Eden to Lampson, 30 November 1937, FO 407/221; Eden to Lampson, 10 February 1938, FO 407/222.
90. Quraishi, pp. 189-195; G. Warburg, 'Lampson's Ultimatum to Faruq', pp. 26-27. See also C. D. Smith, '4 February 1942: Its Causes and its Influence on Egyptian Politics ... 1937-1945', *IJMES* 10 (1979); 453-479.
91. Anwar El-Sadat, *Revolt on the Nile*, London 1957, p. 41.
92. *Killearn Diaries*, pp. 314-315. At the time (9 October 1944) Lord Killearn was on vacation with General Smuts at Muizenberg in South Africa. Ahmad Abbud was one of the richest industrialists and landowners in Egypt, director of the Egyptian sugar company, and chairman of the board of directors of the Khedival Mail Line.
93. Sadat, pp. 101-102.
94. P. J. Vatikiotis, *The Egyptian Army in Politics*, Bloomington 1961, pp. 32-35. For Sadat's description of his role in the Amin 'Uthman assassination, see Anwar El-Sadat, *In Search of Identity*, New York 1978, pp. 59-61.
95. Robinson, p. 137.
96. al-Sayyid-Marsot, p. 69, quoting Murray to Ingram, 26 December 1923, FO 371/8963.

2

THE SUDAN IN ANGLO-EGYPTIAN RELATIONS: 1899–1924

The conquest of the Sudan in 1896–1899 was a logical outcome of the British occupation of Egypt in 1882. The Nile Valley and the Red Sea had become areas of major strategic concern to the British Empire, especially since the opening of the Suez Canal in 1869. The fact that Britain did not occupy the Sudan in the 1880s and even compelled Egypt to relinquish her hold over that country in 1883–1884 had logical reasons and grave repercussions. The reasons were primarily economic and strategic. Economically it would have been a great burden to keep the Sudan under the Egyptian crown which had ruled it since 1820. This burden would have made the economic recovery of the bankrupt Egyptian treasury a much longer and near impossible task. When Lord Cromer was instructed to launch the Dongola campaign in March 1896, he obeyed reluctantly — not because he opposed the reconquest of the Sudan, but because he had earmarked the first surplus in the Egyptian treasury for a project which he regarded as more useful and urgent: namely, the building of a new dam at Aswan. Moreover, the Sudan was important to England strategically only in connection with Egypt. In other words, it would have been fatal to have an anti-British power, such as France, in control of the Sudan and the upper reaches of the Nile. However, as long as the Mahdist state was strong enough to defend the upper Nile valley against prospective invaders, there was no reason for direct British intervention. Only when it became clear that the Mahdist state could no longer hold Britain's foes at bay did a conquest become essential.

Herein then lies the root for Egypt's sensitivity regarding the Sudan. First, since Egypt had ruled the Sudan during most of the nineteenth century and, according to Egyptian politicians and historians, would

The Sudan in Anglo-Egyptian Relations: 1899–1924

have continued to rule it successfully had it not been for British intervention, it stood to reason that the Sudan should once again be part of Egypt. Second, if England regarded the Sudan primarily as a territory through which it could control Egypt during periods of crisis, then the Egyptian ruling elite, needless to say, regarded this as a direct threat. If, as they assumed and hoped, England would be forced to evacuate Egypt sooner or later, her control of the Sudan and the upper reaches of the Nile would enable Whitehall to continue giving 'advice' to whoever was in power in Cairo. Even worse, as far as Egypt was concerned, was the fear that British supremacy in the Sudan encouraged Sudanese separatism, thereby creating a dangerous, possibly irreversible, situation in the so-called Anglo-Egyptian Sudan. The 'Unity of the Nile Valley', which had been the only issue around which all Egyptian nationalists were united, would thus be threatened with extinction.

There was, however, another angle to the triangular relations with which this chapter is concerned. In reality both Egypt and the Sudan were controlled by England: Egypt since 1882, and the Sudan since 1899. One might therefore have expected that Whitehall's control would create harmonious relations and policies in what were, in all but name, British territories. The reality was, however, more complex, since from the outset there was a clash of personalities as well as of interests between the British consuls-general (since 1918 high commissioners) in Cairo and the governors-general of the Sudan. Both Sir Reginald Wingate and Sir Lee Stack, who filled the post of governor-general during the years 1899–1924, tried to diminish not only Egypt's role in Sudanese affairs, but also that of the British consuls-general in Cairo and the so-called Anglo-Egyptian entourage.

The Condominium Agreement of January 19, 1899 provided for a joint administration of the Sudan by the British and Egyptian governments. Yet it was clear from the outset that Egypt's part of this administration was to be purely nominal. The supreme civil and military command of the Sudan was vested in the governor-general, who was nominated by the British government. Thus his appointment by Khedival decree had few practical implications.[1] It is, therefore, no wonder that during the whole period of the Condominium, all the governors-general were British, and owed allegiance to the British government.

Wingate's attitude towards Egyptian rule in the Sudan crystallized during the Mahdiyya. He regarded Egyptian misgovernment of the

Sudan as one of the principal reasons for the Mahdi's revolt.² Consequently he aimed at minimizing Egyptian influence in the new administration. To pursue this policy he had to overcome not only Egyptian opposition, but also the reluctance of the British consuls-general who had to face its consequences in Cairo.³ The main difficulty was finance. Until 1913 the Sudan budget was balanced by an annual subvention granted by the Egyptian government and its development projects were financed by the Egyptian reserve fund. Under these circumstances both Cromer and Gorst had adopted the attitude that 'those who pay the piper ... have a right to call the tune'.⁴ This was challenged by Wingate, who aimed at increasing Egyptian financial aid to the Sudan, while diminishing Egyptian influence in the country. In spite of the obvious difficulties, he managed to successfully pursue this policy throughout his governor-generalship.

The Sudan's financial relations with Egypt were laid down in the 'Regulations for the Financial Administration of the Sudan approved by the Council of Ministers', which were appended to the Condominium Agreement. But whereas the signatories of the Condominium Agreement were Britain and Egypt, the Financial Regulations were set down by the Egyptian council of ministers, without formal British participation, the reason being that Britain did not intend to assume any financial responsibility for the Sudan. The regulations stated that the Sudan's annual budget was to be approved by the council of ministers. Any special or unforeseen expenditure had to be applied for by the governor-general. Even appointments or minor administrative changes, if they affected the budget, had to be passed by the Egyptian ministry of finance. Article 10 of the regulations stipulated that the annual Egyptian grant to the Sudan would remain for the following two years the same as in 1899, after which it would gradually decrease.⁵ In May 1901 a new set of regulations was signed by Wingate and by Gorst, who was then financial adviser to the Egyptian ministry of finance. The Sudan was forbidden to impose any new taxes or to increase existing ones. No new appointments affecting the budget were allowed during the financial year. These regulations were in fact stricter than the ones they superseded. Supervision was removed from the council of ministers and entrusted to the Egyptian ministry of finance. In reality, it was executed by the British financial adviser.⁶

Egypt thus became a supplier without any adequate means of control. The amount of the annual subvention, as well as Egyptian aid to Sudanese development, were determined according to the Sudan's needs as assessed by the British finacial adviser and the consul-general. The moral justification of this procedure was enunciated by Cromer in 1904. He claimed that Britain would never have undertaken the reconquest had Egypt not been prepared to pay. Secondly, he stated that Egypt was morally obliged to help the Sudanese following their long maltreatment by Egyptian administration. Lastly, he regarded investments in the Sudan as being of benefit to the Egyptian economy[7] and consequently, Egypt had to pay. Its loans for the Sudan development for the years 1901–14 amounted to £E5,414,525. Egypt's annual contributions, which, according to the financial regulations, should have gradually decreased, in fact grew from the original grant of £E134,317 in 1899 to a sum of £E335,000 in 1912. In 1913 the grants were finally abolished.

This policy evoked a large measure of criticism in Egypt, voiced mainly by the Egyptian nationalist press, as the government, under British control, was not in a position to interfere.

The main points of criticism were:[8]

(a) Egypt had no control over the way the money it contributed was spent.
(b) Many of the investments undertaken in the Sudan were detrimental to Egyptian interests.
(c) Egypt was financing a British administration in the Sudan.
(d) The Egyptian contribution increased while it was supposed to diminish.
(e) As a result of the annual grant, the Sudan was enabled to pursue a policy of low taxation, and did not need to seek any additional sources of revenue.

Most of the points raised in this critique were, in fact, true, the one exception being that concerning Sudanese investments. Apart from Port Sudan, the customs revenue of which proved detrimental to Egypt's income,[9] practically all major investments in the Sudan until 1913 were connected with communication and irrigation, and were, in the long run, beneficial to Egypt.

The Sudan government claimed that Egyptian grants were much smaller than the official figures suggested, as Egyptian customs gained by Sudanese transit goods. Furthermore, Egypt would have had to spend far more on its defence had the Sudan not been reconquered.[10] The Sudan government was far from satisfied with the extent of Egyptian aid, but even more it was exasperated by the limitations which evolved from these grants. The Sudan was forbidden to grow tobacco north of Khartoum. Agricultural development was limited to crops which did not compete with Egyptian products. Irrigation was strictly limited, and only 10,000 feddans could be irrigated during low Nile.[11] Lastly, the Sudan was forbidden to levy customs on any goods it exported to Egypt. These conditions prevailed until the first world war, and it is hardly surprising that the Sudan government was as anxious to find alternative financial resources as the Egyptians were anxious to stop their aid.

WINGATE'S RELATIONS WITH THE KHEDIVE AND THE EGYPTIAN GOVERNMENT

In his relations with the Khedive and the Egyptian council of ministers, Wingate observed certain rules derived from the Condominium Agreement. As sirdar and governor-general he owed his official appointment to the Khedive, and was supposed to report to him on developments in the Egyptian army and the Sudan administration. In fact, this was not fully observed. Wingate visited the Khedive whenever he passed through Cairo, but reported to him only when the Egyptian army embarked on major campaigns. The one field which was actually controlled by the Khedive was Egyptian decorations, but even in this sphere he only bestowed or refused decorations recommended by Wingate. When the Khedive's control over decorations was restricted by Kitchener in 1913, Wingate wrote: 'I am much amused at the subterfuges to which our "ruler" is reduced owing to stoppage of funds from graves and decorations.'[12] In order not to inflate Egyptian influence, Wingate never recommended Sudanese for Egyptian decorations, as he feared it 'would transfer the patronage from the British governing authorities to the Khedive'.[13] If Wingate observed certain formalities with regard to the Egyptian army, there was certainly no pretence of doing this as far as the Sudan administration was concerned. Wingate did not report to the Khedive regarding administrative measures, and strongly objected when a more cooperative attitude was advocated by Sir Eldon Gorst, Lord Cromer's successor as British consul-general.[14] The Khedive's role was thus purely nominal. The anniversary of his accession was marked by an official exchange of letters and by a levee of officers and senior officials held by Wingate in Khartoum. The day was observed as a general holiday throughout the Sudan, and marked the occasion for a bestowal of decorations granted by the Khedive.

Throughout his reign 'Abbas Hilmi II visited the Sudan only three times. His first visit in 1894 ended in a fiasco when, on criticizing the Egyptian army, he was forced to render an apology to the sirdar, Kitchener.[15] His second visit took place in 1901, and was reported by Cromer to have been a failure. Gorst's period of reconciliation brought 'Abbas once again to the Sudan, for the official opening of Port Sudan. Yet it did little to affect 'Abbas's relations with the country. Thus, when 'Abbas was deposed in December 1914, the reports 'were received with equal apathy by the natives both in Khartoum and in the provinces'.[16] Husayn Kamil, the new Sultan, had no more influence over the Sudan than his predecessor. Wingate was already bent on detaching the Sudan from Egypt, and his relations with the Sultan were cordial but of little consequence.[17]

The control exercised by the Egyptian council of ministers over Sudan affairs was practically non-existent. As sirdar, Wingate had to report to the Egyptian minister of war about all expeditions undertaken by the Egyptian army. But he was not required to consult him beforehand; even the reporting was not always carried out, and in certain cases the Egyptian minister of war only learnt of a military engagement from the Egyptian press. In Wingate's reports to his Egyptian superiors, he was extremely careful not to supply them with any confidential information. A good example of this attitude was Wingate's reports on the most important neo-Mahdist uprising, led by 'Abd al-Qadir Imam Wad Habuba, in April 1908. On this occasion Wingate prepared three separate reports: one detailed and confidential for 'internal use'; a second factual report, for the British government; the third for the Khedive and his Minister of War in which no confidential information was included.[18] His attitude to the minister of war was clearly expressed in a secret letter to Cecil, the financial adviser, where he asked him to raise the salary of Najib 'Azuri, the war minister's private secretary. 'Azuri is no more worth his salary than my boot, but it suits our policy to have a purely nominal War Minister and a still more nominal private secretary to that War Minister.' He ended by hoping that his request will not be refused 'as such an attitude would only emphasize the fact that the War Minister and his Secretaries are practically nobodies'.[19] Wingate's attitude to other Egyptian ministers was even worse, and he did not acknowledge their right to interfere in any matters concerning the Sudan. The financial supervision which was originally vested in the council of ministers was transferred to the British financial adviser in 1901. Sudan ordinances, which, according to the first draft of the Condominium Agreement, had to be submitted to the council of ministers for its approval, were later only submitted as a matter of form and the council of ministers had no right to amend them. Gorst also did not refer conventions signed by the Sudan government to the council of ministers, although previously the council used to be consulted.[20]

Cooperation between the Sudan authorities and the Egyptian government was only limited to those spheres where the Sudan could benefit. According to the Condominium Agreement, the Egyptian mixed courts had no legal power in the Sudan. But the Sudan government, as well as Egypt were, for practical reasons, interested in coming to an arrangement whereby judgements given in one country would have legal power in the other. This was necessary in order to deal with Egyptians residing in the Sudan and vice versa. Consequently, arrangements were made which enabled sentences passed in one country to be executed in the other, as well as mutual extradition rights.[21] A certain amount of cooperation was also necessary in the religious sphere. Although Wingate did not tolerate Egyptian interference in the Sudan's religious affairs, he had no option but to rely on Egyptian *qadis* for the *Shari'a* courts and for the *qadis* training course at Gordon College. However, to minimize the danger of pan-Islamic propaganda, the *qadis* were first vetted by the Sudan's inspector-general, Rudolf von Slatin,[22] and only then were appointed by the Grand *Qadi* of Egypt. While the Egyptian Grand *Qadi* was ostensibly in charge of the *Shari'a* courts in the Sudan as well, the policy of the governor-general was that of 'keeping the Egyptian Religious authorities out of any interference in the Sudan'. A policy of educating young Sudanese *qadis* was followed from the early days of the Condominium, and as soon as these graduated, the Egyptian *qadis* were replaced.

The only other exception Wingate made to his rule of non-interference by Cairo's religious authorities was when he needed £E20,000 for the Khartoum Mosque from the Egyptian *Waqf* administration. The latter were quick to seize this opportunity and asked in return for lands in the Sudan and for the right to supervise all Sudanese mosques. Wingate withdrew his request and wrote to Gorst explaining the reasons for his refusal to let the Egyptian *Waqf* administration into the Sudan:

I know of no subject (except perhaps the slavery question) which is of so thorny a nature as this, owing principally to the racial hatred between

Egyptians and Sudanese. Egyptian maladministration, especially in wakfs matters, had a great deal to do with the original revolt and it has been an essential part in our reorganization of the Sudan to keep out of the country any interference on the part of the Egyptian Wakfs administration.[24]

Apart from these fields there was hardly any interference by Egyptian ministers in Sudan affairs. The Sudan irrigation schemes were run by the Egyptian ministry of public works, but as they were entrusted to a British official, they could hardly be regarded as under Egyptian control.

The Egyptian legislative assembly had little occasion to intervene in Sudan affairs. During Wingate's governor-generalship its members were only invited twice, once in 1906, for the opening of the Nile–Red Sea railway, and again in 1909, at Gorst's insistence, for the opening of Port Sudan. Following their first visit, the legislators made certain suggestions with regard to Sudan administration, which were openly disregarded by Wingate. After the second visit, Wingate reported to Gorst that the visit was a failure, and wrote to the Sudan's British civil secretary: 'God help the country that is governed by such rubbish.'[25] When a new legislative assembly was elected in 1913, its members decided to play a more active role in Sudan affairs, and ventured to discuss the legality of the importation of Egyptian convicts into the Sudan. Kitchener had, for reasons of economy, insisted on the employment of these convicts on the Blue Nile dam, much to Wingate's dismay and against the express wish of the governor-general's council. There was little doubt that the sending of Egyptian convicts to the Sudan was illegal, and could therefore have caused a vote of censure against the Egyptian council of ministers. Kitchener, however, warned Sa'd Zaghlul that the convicts would be brought back to Egypt 'but that of course this would settle the question once and for all of the Sudan being in any way part of Egypt'.[26] Thus everything was settled. The convicts stayed in the Sudan, and the legislative assembly refrained from interfering. Consequently, the Khedive, his ministers, and the legislative assembly did not represent a major obstacle to Wingate's policy of excluding Egyptian interference from the Sudan. Wingate sincerely believed that Sudanese hatred of Egyptian rule was deeply rooted. Furthermore, he did not underestimate the power of Egyptian nationalism, and wanted to secure the Sudan for Britain should Egypt turn restive.

THE IMPACT OF PAN-ISLAMIC IDEAS AND EGYPTIAN NATIONALISM

One may assume, as there is no evidence to the contrary, that the majority of the older generation of Sudanese mistrusted the Egyptians, and even regarded them with contempt. Wingate quoted the following from an interview he had with Sayyid 'Ali al-Mirghani, head of the Khatmiyya order:

> Why should you English people be surprised at the thoroughly disloyal attitude of the Egyptians? – They are a race of slaves and never will be anything better; their character is contemptible and, after all, you are to blame for having given them an education altogether beyond their capacity and put them upon a pedestal, and you now find your idol has feet of clay.

Whereupon Wingate commented:

> This opinion is really representative of the bulk of the better class Sudanese, who are in every respect superior in character to the Egyptians and look down upon them with contempt.[27]

However, it is equally probable that many of the younger generation of Sudanese did not share this view. They had not lived under the Turco-Egyptian regime, and had not been influenced by the anti-Egyptian propaganda of the Mahdi. Hence they found more in common with their fellow Muslim Egyptians than with their British Christian rulers. With this in mind, Wingate employed all the means at his disposal to stem the infiltration of Egyptian nationalist and pan-Islamic ideas into the Sudan. A special system of intelligence was devised in order to deal with this subtle penetration. The intelligence department, whose headquarters were in Cairo, kept a close watch on developments in the Egyptian capital and warned its branch in Khartoum to take any necessary action. Special agents were employed 'to ascertain how and to what extent native feeling in the Sudan was influenced from Cairo'. They were instructed to keep in close contact with those Egyptian officers who were most likely to introduce nationalist ideas in the Sudan. But most of the work was done in Khartoum, where the assistant head of the intelligence department kept in constant touch with local dignitaries and had his agents in Omdurman market and other central places. The assessment of the material collected by the intelligence agents was entrusted to Slatin whose long experience in the Sudan was highly regarded by Wingate.[28] To cut down the hazards of Egyptian influence, the Sudanese were discouraged from travelling to Egypt for any length of time.

When a unit of the Shayqiyya, one of the riverain tribes of the northern Sudan, was stationed in Egypt in 1908, Wingate asked one of his subordinates to replace it by Egyptians as 'they may imbibe all sorts of undesirable ideas'. A suggestion made by Sudanese '*ulama*' to send young Sudanese to study at al-Azhar was rejected by Wingate on similar grounds, 'I have always had a strong feeling against Sudanese coming to Cairo where they undoubtedly imbibe ideas which are prejudicial to our system of government in the Sudan.'[29]

After the murder in 1910 of Butrus Ghali Pasha, Egypt's Coptic Prime Minister, Wingate was concerned about its effects in the Sudan. The intelligence department at Khartoum reported that the majority of the Egyptian army officers sympathized with the assassin. Gilbert Clayton, who was at that time Wingate's private secretary, wrote shortly afterwards: 'there is little doubt that there is widespread feeling of pleasure at the news among the Egyptians both military and civil'. He added, however, that the Sudanese were quite indifferent. Slatin regarded these rumours as grossly exaggerated. He wrote to Wingate: 'It is a mistake to make a Copt Prime Minister over a Mohammed. population ... this will only strengthen the so-called Nationalist Party.'[30]

Wingate was convinced that in order to decrease the dangers of Egyptian nationalism in the Sudan, he had to bar the Egyptian press from the Sudan. The attacks on the Sudan government in the Egyptian nationalist press encompassed a large area of subjects. First and foremost they attacked the Condominium Agreement, and the fact that the British flag flew in the Sudan. Then came Egypt's financial liability, which had been enforced against her will. Heavy attacks were launched against the sirdar himself, whose rule in the Sudan was described as similar to that of the Russian Czar. He was accused of not promoting Egyptian officers whose honour was degraded by having to kiss the sirdar's hand. A popular and frequent demand was that the governor-general of the Sudan and the province governors should be Egyptian and not British officers. The most bitter criticism, however, was directed against the government's religious policy, both as regards missionary activities and with regard to Islam in the Sudan.[31] Wingate would have preferred to see all these papers suspended. Like many a military man of his ilk, he regarded the press in general as a nuisance which had to be dealt with firmly. This same attitude prevailed in his comments on sections of the British press. In a letter to Cromer, written during the War, Wingate commented on several articles which had appeared in British newspapers: 'I am only too glad that I have not a large press in the Sudan, but if I had I tell you frankly that I would not allow one of these obnoxious articles to be translated.' Owing to the reluctance of the consuls-general to act as severely as he advocated, Wingate had to devise his own methods for dealing with the press. He was allowed to stop any Egyptian paper from entering the Sudan, and the Sudan agent in Cairo was given full powers to this effect.[32] Wingate also made use of the pro-government papers, *al-Muqattam* in Egypt and the *Sudan Times* in Khartoum, in order to counteract nationalist propaganda. Na'um Shuqayr, one of Wingate's longtime associates in the Egyptian army's intelligence department, was well suited to undertake this task. He used his wide circle of local acquaintances to sponsor pro-government articles in *al-Muqattam*.[33] When Mustafa Kamil, leader of the nationalist party, died in 1908, Wingate expressed his hopes that the nationalist press would die with him. His hopes were, however, not realized. *Al-Liwa, The Standard* and *L'Etendard Egyptien* launched bitter attacks against the Sudan government following the Wad Habuba rebellion in 1908, and accused it of executing seventy of the rebels.[34] The growing vehemence of the nationalist press led to Gorst's decision to revive the 1881 Egyptian press law. Wingate was not satisfied and decided to promulgate a more comprehensive press law for the Sudan. 'I can scarcely conceive anything more undesirable than to introduce into the Sudan the utterly inadequate Press Law existing in Egypt.' However, it was not until after Kitchener's appointment as consul-general in Egypt that Wingate had his way.[35]

Egyptian officials and officers both in the army and Sudan administration were probably Wingate's major difficulty. Apart from his general mistrust of Egyptians, he regarded them as the most likely bearers of nationalist and pan-Islamic ideas. Yet he could not dispense with their services while no alternative source of manpower existed. He therefore followed a line of policy whereby the Egyptians were relegated to positions of minor importance, both in the army and the administration. The mutiny of the Egyptian army in Omdurman in 1900 was a convenient peg upon which to hang his policy. All the accounts of the mutiny indicated that its major cause was to be found in Kitchener's maltreatment of the Egyptian army. Wingate, however, was convinced that the centre of the trouble lay in Cairo and was supported by the Khedive. Hence both he and Cromer concluded that the size of the Egyptian army as well as its composition presented a major threat to the security of the Sudan.[36] The policy pursued was to reduce the Egyptian army by recruiting territorial units in the Nuba mountains and the southern provinces and placing them under British command. Furthermore, Wingate dispersed the Egyptian battalions over the Sudan and entrusted the security of Khartoum to a British detachment. Senior Egyptian officers, both in the army and the civil service, were passed over for promotion or retired prematurely in order to make place for British personnel. Lastly, a military school was opened in Khartoum in 1905, and an ever-increasing number of Sudanese officers replaced the lower-rank Egyptians.[37]

A similar policy was pursued in the Sudan civil service, as stated by Wingate in 1906:

> Our principle is not to allow these young [Egyptian] officers to hold any of the higher Civil appointments, which are reserved exclusively for the young British civilians. Therefore they have no hope of advancement in the Civil Service.[38]

Even in those cases where the government had to employ non-British personnel it preferred Copts and Lebanese who, as Christians, were regarded as more loyal and more intelligent. Finally special courses at Gordon College were devised for training Sudanese for the lower echelons of the administration. In executing this policy Wingate enjoyed the full support of the majority of his British subordinates who wished to purge the Sudan civil service of its Egyptian element. These views were most adequately expressed by the civil secretary when he wrote:

> The wording *'British Influence'* is a mistake, but it of course means the influence of *honest* administration as opposed to Egyptian .... Later on our part of the pink of the African map must be effectively British as well as honest ....[39]

Of the senior British officials only James Currie, the director of education, regarded this policy as unrealistic. He wrote to Wingate: 'To suppose that an English community can *rule* in Khartoum ... is to suppose a vain thing, and for better or worse it is the Anglo-Egyptian Sudan ....'[40]

THE SUDAN AND THE BRITISH GOVERNMENT

There were few direct links between the Sudan and the British government during Wingate's governor-generalship. Control was maintained through the British consuls-general in Cairo, who reported to Whitehall whenever necessary. The prior consent of the British government was only necessary in case of major policy decisions. These included border disputes, large-scale military expeditions, and treaties with neighbouring States. In all other spheres the Sudan government, acting under the guidance of the British consul-general, was free to act and only had to report to London afterwards. The reports sent to London included an annual report on the administration of the Sudan prepared by the consul-general, reports on military expeditions, and Sudan laws and ordinances following their publications in the *Sudan Gazette*. British decorations were only granted to British military and civil personnel. Wingate sent his recommendations to the consul-general who forwarded them to London. Whereas in his capacity as governor-general Wingate had no direct dealings with the British government, as sirdar he communicated directly with the war office. These communications included confidential reports on military expeditions, recommendations for military decorations, the command of British troops in Khartoum, and the service of British officers in the Sudan. Wingate tried to make up for what he regarded as insufficient British influence by increasing the impact of British royalty in the Sudan. This he hoped to achieve by personally cultivating the royal family. Both he and Slatin were regular guests at Balmoral during their summer vacation and attended many of the special functions at Windsor. His major aim was to project the image of British royalty in the Sudan by all the means at his disposal. Coronation day was observed as a holiday throughout the Sudan. A levee and garden party were held at the governor-general's palace, the Royal standard hoisted, and money distributed by the governor-general to the poor of Omdurman and Khartoum. A one-day visit by King George V to Port Sudan in 1912 became the occasion of yet another national holiday. Apart from sporadic visits by the Duke of Connaught, the only other official royal visitor was the Prince of Wales who came to the Sudan in 1916. Wingate, who since the beginning of the first World War had openly sought the complete separation of the Sudan from Egypt, tried to exploit to the utmost the Prince's visit: 'Tell it not in Gath, but I am distributing two or three hundred pounds to the poor ... which they will, I hope, think came from the Imperial Treasury.'[41] Hence it is clear that although official ties between the Sudan and Britain were few and of little significance, Wingate tried to increase their impact to the best of his ability.

Britain had no financial responsibilities in the Sudan. The financial regulations of the Sudan stipulated no British participation in the country's expenses. Hence, despite repeated efforts by Wingate, the British government maintained its policy of regarding the Sudan's finances as a purely Egyptian obligation. The very few occasions on which Whitehall deviated from this line deserve to be mentioned, if only for their pettiness. Britain refused to pay the additional cost for keeping a British detachment in Khartoum. It was only sanctioned after a protracted correspondence, in which Cromer adamantly refused to charge Egypt with this expense.[42] The cost of the British flags in the Sudan was borne by Egypt until May 1900.[43] The British war office refused to pay a gratuity to British soldiers who participated in the reconquest, and it was charged against the Egyptian budget.[44] In 1911 Wingate asked the war office to contribute towards the repair of British graves in the Sudan, and to undertake their upkeep. Out of the £438 Wingate demanded for the repair, he received £300 and the annual upkeep had to be paid by the Sudan as before.[45] On the two occasions on which Wingate demanded a more substantial contribution from Britain, he was rebuffed. In 1910, when the Sudan assumed responsibility for the Lado Enclave, Wingate urged Gorst to demand British aid for the extra expenditure involved. The reasons enumerated by Gorst reiterated many of the Egyptian nationalists' arguments against Egyptian contributions for the Sudan. He argued that payment for the Sudan was generally unpopular in Egypt. Moreover, Egypt was not consulted when the Lado Enclave had originally been leased to King Leopold, and had no direct interest in its return to the Sudan. He further claimed that from an Egyptian viewpoint the East Bank of the Nile, which had been ceded to Uganda, because of British imperial interests, would have enabled Egypt to control the Nile. The necessary money for administering the Lado Enclave was ultimately included in the Egyptian budget without waiting for Whitehall's reply.[46] The second time Wingate requested help was during the world war. In a letter to Sir McMahon, then British high commissioner in Egypt, he described the increasing expenditures incurred in the Sudan as a direct consequence of the British war effort. The British treasury refused Wingate's request and wrote that 'Even if the expenditure cannot be met from Soudan Government balances' Britain would not come to its aid.[47]

Britain's and Egypt's financial liabilities in the Sudan, as described by a correspondent of *The Times* as early as 1900, remained essentially unchanged throughout this period:

> England contributed one third to the cost of the conquest; she contributes nothing to the cost of governing the conquered country. On the other hand, the Governor-General, the Governors of Provinces and their assistants, and all the officers in the Egyptian army in the Sudan are exclusively Englishmen; the lower officials are almost exclusively Egyptians. Two men have jointly bought a horse, A contributing one third, B two thirds of the price. A rides the horse, B grooms it and pays its upkeep. That is approximately the situation in the Sudan.[48]

By 1910 Wingate, who was exasperated by the Sudan's slow rate of progress, devised a plan by which he hoped to achieve a more rapid development. Basically, his plan was to prove that the cotton-growing prospects of the Sudan were second to none. Following which, he would be able, with the help of the Lancashire cotton manufacturers, to force the British government to assume direct responsibility for the country. Wingate, with his senior British officials, embarked on a propaganda campaign amongst British capitalists and politicians. Wingate's aims were as follows:

> It is quite clear that the present attitude of the Nationlists and the Legislative Council is to prevent any Egyptian money being expended in the Sudan; the attitude of the Home Government is also one of 'hands off' in regard to their Sudan responsibilities ... therefore it is a matter of the most vital importance ... to induce British Capital and thus the British Capitalist to have a vested interest in the country .... This is the only sound and practical way of developing the Sudan and keeping the British flag flying, when it is now so seriously threatened by the political attitude of both British and Egyptian Governments ....[49]

It soon became clear that capital would not be forthcoming unless Britain declared its intention to remain in the Sudan. Following a meeting with British capitalists, Clayton reported: 'it is hoped that Milner, Derby and Lovat will be able to bring enough pressure to bear to get a satisfactory assurance as to the permanent character of our occupation of the Sudan'.[50] Wingate himself approached the Prime Minister, while at Balmoral, and gained his full support. In 1912 Kitchener finally decided to ask for a British guaranteed loan for cotton growing in the Gezira. His official request to Grey was forwarded to the treasury with a warm recommendation, in which the following words stand out as proof of Wingate's success: 'We have been strongly pressed from Lancashire to facilitate the development of cotton growing in the Soudan.'[51] On November 19, 1912, the first draft of the Soudan Loan Act 1912 was laid before the Cabinet; and on January 2, 1913, the final draft of the bill was accepted.

It is therefore clear that what little control there was, over the policy which evolved in the Sudan, under the guidance of Sir Reginald Wingate and his close Anglo-Sudanese associates, was exercised by the British consuls-general in Cairo. However, this supervision was never clearly defined until 1910 since, on Kitchener's insistence, it was not mentioned in the Condominium agreement. But there was never any doubt as to the consuls-general's supreme authority. During the seventeen years of Wingate's governor-generalship the control from Cairo gradually decreased. Both Cromer and Gorst exercised their right of control over matters of policy and details of administration. The slackening of supervision during the Kitchener-McMahon era was due to their personalities rather than to a change of policy. Also, Wingate had gained in experience, and with new men at the helm of the British Agency it was only natural that he would assume a greater measure of independence.[52]

Under the terms of the Condominium Agreement the Egyptian government was not in a position to intervene in the administration of the Sudan. Hence, increased control could have only resulted in more direct supervision of Sudanese policies by the British government. Judging by the record of the administration of the Sudan as compared with that of other British colonies during the same period, one can safely conclude that the greater independence of the governor-general of the Sudan improved administrative efficiency.

THE STRUGGLE OVER THE STATUS OF THE SUDAN

Following the declaration of a British protectorate over Egypt in December 1914, Wingate and his colleagues had started to advocate the termination of the Condominium and the establishment of direct British rule in the Sudan. Wingate and the Anglo-Sudanese had no difficulty in finding Sudanese notables to support this anti-Egyptian policy. This was firstly because many of the Sudanese of the older generation were genuinely suspicious of their strong and agressive northern neighbour. And secondly, there was as yet no significant Sudanese elite which was strong enough or independent enough to question the wisdom of their English rulers. It was therefore quite natural that following the termination of the war, when Egyptian nationalism emerged as a mass movement under the leadership of

Sa'd Zaghlul and the Wafd, the bulk of the Sudanese leaders opted, with Anglo-Sudanese blessings, for their own brand of nationalism under the slogan 'the Sudan for the Sudanese'. Wingate, who since 1917 had been Britain's high commissioner in Egypt, emphasized in his correspondence that the interests of the British Empire made it imperative to keep the Sudan totally separate from the 'Egyptian question'. He warned against Egypt's authority extending to the Sudan once Egypt became independent.[53]

This position hardened as Egyptian views and actions became more extreme in late 1918 and early 1919, culminating in the national revolt of March 1919. Wingate, whose career had been brought to a premature and disastrous end through these events, devoted a great deal of time and energy to justifying his policies in Egypt and the Sudan and at the same time attempting to eliminate Egyptian influence from the Sudan. He went so far as to suggest to Lord Curzon, in April 1919, that 'His Majesty's Government may find the present a suitable moment to definitely take over the Sudan, thus eliminating the intensely unpopular Egyptian element.'[54] There is no doubt that both Wingate and his successor, Sir Lee Stack, tried their very best in this crucial period to change the status of the Sudan from that of a Condominium into a British dependency. Failing a change in the legal status they were willing to compromise on a *de facto* de-Egyptianization of the Sudan.

The impact of the Wingate-Stack propaganda can be seen in the views expressed by the Milner Mission which was established in order to investigate the reasons for the Egyptian crisis in 1919 and to propose recommendations as to Egypt's future. While the Sudan was not mentioned in the Commission's terms of reference, Lord Milner delegated Alexander Keown-Boyd, a one-time member of the Sudan Political Service, to report on the Sudan, and the latter produced a most detailed account in which, not surprisingly, he followed the line propagated by Wingate and Stack. In a covering letter, sent to Allenby, Keown-Boyd suggested:

the ideal solution would be an immediate clean cut from Egypt .... Egypt's only legitimate interests in the Soudan are the safeguarding of her water supply and the protection of her frontiers from external aggression. For these His Majesty's Government would assume full responsibility .... As the last Egyptian soldier left the country the Egyptian flag could be hauled down .... Alternatively, if no mention of the Soudan is made by Lord Milner in his report ... the programme of freeing the Soudan from all influences can be gradually followed out until the time is ripe for an understanding with Egypt.

Keown-Boyd enclosed detailed memoranda in which he specified ways and means by which the Egyptian presence, both in the army and the administration, would be eliminated from the Sudan. He even informed Allenby that the annual cost of the new Sudanese army would be about £E800,000.[55] Wingate himself collected all the relevant letters and documents dealing with the status of the Sudan and presented them to Lord Milner's mission in order to convince them and His Majesty's Government that drastic change was essential.[56] Thus, the rather extreme Anglo-Sudanese view had succeeded in becoming part of a semi-official British report. The British government continued to deny that any change in the political status of the Sudan was contemplated. Yet the main reason for maintaining the status quo was the unwillingness of the British government to undertake the expenses involved in expelling the Egyptians from the Sudan. Both Stack and Wingate regarded a yearly British subsidy towards the upkeep of a Sudanese army as a logical price to pay for the final expulsion of the Egyptians. But already in 1920 they were toying with the idea that failing a British subvention Egypt might be 'persuaded' to undertake the cost, as it was in their view a logical price to pay for Egypt's security and the uninterrupted flow of the Nile waters. In order to convince Egypt of the desirability of this solution Wingate suggested that Egypt be promised 'a measure of self-government ... (to be withdrawn if they refused to accept the new arrangement as regards the Sudan)'. In other words, Egypt would pay a £E1,000,000 annual subsidy for the independent Sudanese army, in return for her own security, her water supply and a measure of self-government.[57]

A close look at Stack's and Wingate's letters from March 1919 to 1924 proves that the Anglo-Sudanese lobby had decided that the time had come to force the issue of the Sudan's complete separation from Egypt. They regarded the connection between Egypt and the Sudan as a dangerous pipeline through which Egyptian nationalist anti-British propaganda would continue to flow in order to undermine the peaceful development of the Sudan. Wingate claimed that the British high commissioner (previously the consul-general) for Egypt was the sole means by which either Britain or Egypt had exercised their control over the Sudan. He stated that this had been the case ever since the reconquest and that 'no other control should be officially admitted'.[58]

It is certainly true that both Kitchener and Wingate had attempted since the reconquest to diminish outside interference in the Sudan, and had consequently tried to enhance the semi-independent role of the British governor-general and his Anglo-Sudanese entourage. But neither Cromer nor Gorst had followed that line, and both of them, while opposing Egypt's political claims for unity of the Nile valley, had repeatedly emphasized the official connection between Egypt and the Sudan. Wingate was therefore attempting to formulate a new and more radically anti-Egyptian policy. The attempt was forced through in the years between 1919 and 1924 with Allenby and Stack at the helm in Cairo and Khartoum. Both had been appointed to their respective posts in May 1919, following Wingate's dismissal. From then onwards Stack had consistently regarded the expulsion of the Egyptians from the Sudan as a cornerstone of his policy.[59] Allenby, on the other hand, vacillated between two extremes. Soon after he assumed power and following his first extensive visit to the Sudan, he suggested a redefinition of the status of the Sudan so that it would enjoy a direct link with the British Empire. As a first step he proposed the separation of the office of sirdar from that of the governor-general so that an independent Egypt would not be in a position to issue orders to the commander of the Egyptian army in the Sudan. But, Allenby emphasized, 'Great Britain should have the entire control of the internal affairs of the Sudan.'[60] When later on Allenby's main concern was to reach some form of a settlement with those whom he regarded as moderate Egyptian leaders, he was quite willing to grant them effective participation in the administration of the Sudan, to the dismay of Stack and his colleagues.[61]

In this ongoing battle of words between two British views, one centred on Cairo and the other on Khartoum, the Egyptians had no chance of becoming real partners in the Sudan. The issue at stake was whether they would be kicked out on some pretext or other as Stack would have wanted, or whether their continued presence would be tolerated, provided they remained submissive and junior participants in an Anglo-Sudanese administration, a solution more in line with Allenby's way of thinking.

Throughout these turbulent years the British press was instrumental in carrying the views of the antagonists to the British public and in mobilizing public opinion in England in support of the divergent views. A glimpse at some of these papers during the 'Adli-Curzon negotiations of 1921 indicates that certain papers, such as the *Daily Herald* or the *Manchester Guardian*, generally came out in support of the Egyptian cause, while others, such as the *Daily Telegraph*, the

Morning Post, the *Daily Express* and *The Times* were by and large antagonistic to anything emanating from Egypt and attacked Lord Allenby for his policy of non-interference in Egyptian affairs which some of them viewed as 'an ethically indefensible policy'.[62]

Sa'd Zaghlul was described as 'The Sinister Figure in Egypt' who had only one aim, namely, the expulsion of the British from the Nile valley. The *Daily Express*, which held this view, suggested that Zaghlul be treated with 'a strong hand and the sooner the better'.[63] Meanwhile *The Times* and the *Daily Telegraph*, who were more moderate in their expressions, held similar views, namely that Egypt was not yet fit for self-government and hence had to be guided by Great Britain.[64] When in September 1921 a group of Labour M.P.s were invited by Zaghlul to tour Egypt in order to study the situation on the spot, both Allenby and his close associates were accused of attempting to undermine the visit. The welcome party, prepared by the Wafd, was forbidden by the authorities, while the M.P.s themselves were forbidden by Clayton to travel to various towns 'in the interest only of public security'. Some of the British papers reported that the Egyptians were protesting against the mission which they regarded as an interference in their affairs.[65] The Labour M.P.s returned from Egypt with the solid conviction that the mass of the Egyptians supported Zaghlul and the Wafd, and hence that the negotiations between England and the then Egyptian government headed by 'Adli Pasha were completely futile. Moreover, the M.P.s accused British authorities in Egypt of misleading the public through fabricated reports in the British press. What was required was free elections in Egypt and consequently complete independence leading to a treaty of alliance between Great Britain and Egypt.[66] But when the negotiations finally broke down in November 1921, several dailies, headed by the *Daily Herald*, accused the British government of torpedoing the talks through its obstinacy, while others attacked Curzon for his moderation and for his willingness to withdraw British troops from all Egyptian towns to the Canal zone.[67] It is worth noting that Zaghlul was well aware of the importance of public opinion in England and he admitted quite freely that he and the Wafd had inspired questions in the House of Commons and letters to the British press in order to advocate their case for Egypt throughout the British Isles.[68]

THE SUDAN IN ANGLO-EGYPTIAN NEGOTIATIONS AND THE CONSTITUTION CRISIS

How did the Sudan fare in these early negotiations? The answer in light of subsequent events seems surprising, since the Sudan was not even discussed in the Milner-Zaghlul talks of 1920[69] and was only brought up by Curzon in November 1921 when his discussions with 'Adli had nearly broken down. One may therefore conclude that while Milner, Curzon and other senior members of the British government had already reached a decision not to accept Egyptian participation in running the Sudan, they saw no reason to share their convictions with the Egyptians themselves. Even Lord Allenby, following his visit to the Sudan, had expressed his view that Egyptian propaganda regarding the Sudan presented no real challenge

so long as his Majesty's Government make it quite clear that they intend to continue to govern the Soudan, and that they will not consider any suggestions that the Egyptians should be given a larger share in the control of the Soudanese.[70]

As to how the Sudan question would be settled, the answer seemed quite simple. Following the prolonged and detailed propaganda of Stack and his colleagues, Curzon in 1921 and MacDonald in 1924 suggested that Egyptian interests in the Sudan were in fact limited to security and water. With regard to security Curzon suggested that Egypt continued to assist the Sudan either militarily or financially and that all Egyptian forces in the Sudan should be under the orders of the governor-general. MacDonald was even more outspoken in suggesting that a 'locally recruited defence force' would henceforth be in charge of security and the co-domini would only supply one battalion each. As for Egypt's supply of Nile waters Curzon had suggested entrusting it to a board of three representing Egypt, the Sudan and Uganda. In 1924 MacDonald had proposed that all matters dealing with the Nile waters be determined by the council of the League of Nations.[71] In both cases England would have enjoyed a majority whenever it came to a conflict. But while Uganda and the Sudan were British dependencies and hence could be relied upon to vote 'correctly', the vote in the council of the League contained a certain element of risk. But the most disappointing aspect of this comparison between Lord Curzon and Ramsay MacDonald was that, as far as Egypt was concerned, there was very little to choose between the Tory and Labour governments.

In March 1924, with the Wafd in control of Egypt and the Labour party under MacDonald governing England, it had seemed that prospects for an Anglo-Egyptian settlement were as good as could be hoped for. Both had previously declared their willingness to negotiate. MacDonald, while in opposition, had criticised Allenby's attempted settlement with the moderates whom he had denounced as unrepresentative, and had advocated a policy which would allow Egypt the fullest possible independence. Zaghlul, on assuming control of the Egyptian government following the first general elections, declared his government's willingness to negotiate with Britain, without any restrictions, so as to realise Egypt's and the Sudan's national aspirations.

But once in power neither MacDonald nor Zaghlul seemed willing or able to compromise. For it was quite clear that Zaghlul regarded an acceptance of Curzon's 1921 offer to 'Adli as both humiliating and suicidal, from a political point of view. Having rejected even Lord Milner's formula in 1920, which had been much more conciliatory, it would have been an open admission of defeat to accept the much harsher terms of Lord Curzon now coming from a Labour government. MacDonald, on his side, also showed no inclination to compromise — perhaps as a result of his party's lack of a majority in the House of Commons and his belief that it was up to him to refute Churchill's claim that Labour was not fit to rule. By becoming tough with Egyptian nationalists, whom he had previously supported, MacDonald seemed to indicate that a Labour government was as concerned with the future of the British Empire as a Tory-led government. Or, as *The Times* had written when MacDonald assumed power: 'The great and manifold tasks of Empire must in the end subdue these new forces to their purpose.' What were these tasks? By 1924 England was quite certain about the central role she would continue to play in the Suez Canal and the Nile valley. There could be a gradual withdrawal of British forces from Cairo or Alexandria and a certain reduction in British administrative control, especially in judicial and financial affairs, but no compromise in the Sudan or Suez Canal. Zaghlul felt that what the British authorities were in fact attempting was to discredit him politically. For surely if, once in power, he were to accept what he had rejected in 1920, thereby splitting the Wafd and losing some of its most prominent leaders, he would now lose his prestige as the one and only national leader of Egypt.

The hardening of attitudes developed into a battle of words with the Sudan one of the major topics. Following the anti-British riots in the Sudan, which the authorities blamed on Egyptian propaganda and on Zaghlul's demand of Britain's evacuating the Sudan which was reported in *The Times* on 24 June 1924, Lord Parmoor declared, on behalf of the government on June 25, that Britain did not intend to abandon the Sudan nor change its status, whatever happened. Three days later Zaghlul countered by stating that 'the Egyptian nation will never give up the Sudan'. The negotiations which started in London in September 1924 therefore seemed to have little chance of success. Zaghlul demanded the withdrawal of British troops and advisers from Egypt and the unity of Egypt and the Sudan. Nobody was therefore surprised when the negotiations were suspended soon thereafter.[72]

In between the 'Adli-Curzon negotiations in 1921 and the Zaghlul-MacDonald talks of 1924, the positions of the two parties involved hardened considerably as a result of developments in the Nile valley. In Egypt, following the abolition of the protectorate and the declaration of independence on 28 February 1922, the anti-Zaghlul front tried to marshall support. 'Adli, Tharwat, Rushdi and their colleagues attempted to draw up a constitution which would diminish the autocratic powers of the Khedive, thereby hopefully enhancing their own position both vis-a-vis the Crown and the Wafd. The unity of Egypt and the Sudan thus became a bone of contention. No Egyptian politician in his right mind could afford to concede the sovereignty of Egypt over the Sudan, even had he wanted to do so, for fear of losing support. But there seems to be no evidence that any of the politicians who composed the constitution committee ever had the inclination to relinquish the Sudan. On 9 May 1922 Allenby telegraphed to the foreign office stating that the constitutional subcommittee under Rushdi had inserted a passage on Egypt's sovereignty over the Sudan into the draft constitution. Although Allenby reported that 'Adli and his cabinet fully realised that such a clause could not be included in the final version of the constitution, King George V regarded the matter as serious enough to express his grave concern.[73] In reality Egypt was of course not in a position to effect a change in the status of the Sudan in the face of British opposition. But England was able to act unilaterally and the Egyptians were well aware of it. This was indicated by reports in the Egyptian press at the time as well as in semi-official utterances. In a report of the public security department of the Egyptian government Allenby was quoted as having promised the Sudanese notables that England would never allow a change in the status of the Sudan 'since many millions of British capital are already invested in its development'.[74] But Allenby, who did not want to embarrass the Liberal Constitutionalists who were his main hope for an eventual Anglo-Egyptian treaty, explicitly asked the British government not to make any declaration which would indicate that the Sudan would eventually be severed from Egypt as suggested by Stack and his colleagues. Murray, head of the Egyptian section in the foreign office, and one of those most knowledgeable about Egypt and the Sudan, was however quite certain that the Sudan would ultimately become part of the British Empire and its connection with Egypt would be severed. He predicted that 'the adoption of such a drastic course will have to be justified by some intolerable action on the part of the Egyptians'.[75] But in the meantime the removal of the Sudan from the Egyptian constitution had to be dealt with less drastically. First, the Liberal Constitutionalists insisted that the Sudan was part of Egypt and that the king of Egypt was therefore also the king of the Sudan. They were willing to compromise only with regard to the constitution, which they agreed would not be applied in the Sudan. However, Tharwat and his Cabinet were forced to resign in November 1922. Next, in January 1923, Allenby, eager to produce a settlement, suggested a differently formulated compromise to his superiors in the foreign office, whereby the king of Egypt would be recognised as sovereign of the Sudan while the constitution would be announced as being applicable in all Egyptian territories except the Sudan. This was also rejected by the foreign office.[76] Finally, following an inconclusive academic argument as to whether the title 'Sovereign of the Soudan' had ever been used by the former Khedive, 'Abbas Hilmi, and a search in the foreign office archives for any Ottoman or Egyptian records indicating Egyptian sovereignty over the Sudan, King Fu'ad finally gave in to British pressures on 3 February 1923. This was the result of a series of communications between Allenby and the foreign office in which it was agreed that unless the Sudan issue was removed from the constitution Britain would regard herself free to act in the Sudan as if Egypt had denounced the January 1899 Condominium agreement and the British declaration of 28 February 1922.[77]

Thus, the constitution crisis was finally resolved but at a considerable price. On the Egyptian side the Sudan had assumed a predominant political position, both internally and externally. On the internal front it was now quite clear that any attempt to compromise on the sovereignty issue would be regarded as an act of treason. In the sphere of foreign relations Egyptian politicians, who had previously hardly regarded the Sudan as the most crucial or urgent matter for Egypt, had now realised that England would sooner or later try to force a drastic change in the status of the Sudan and hence were constantly on guard. On the British side there was no unity. On the one hand, there were the Anglo-Sudanese, supported by certain members in the foreign office and by most of the British press, who demanded a clear-cut decision with regard to the status of the Sudan, preferably one which would sever its connection with Egypt. On the other hand there was Lord Allenby's view which still favoured a compromise with moderate Egyptian politicians in order to arrive at an Anglo-Egyptian treaty. This view also enjoyed the support of certain liberal and labour dailies and was regarded as being in line with Labour party policy, at least while in opposition.[78] There is no doubt that the constitution crisis tipped the scales in favour of the Anglo-Sudanese position since it became apparent that there was no hope for a compromise acceptable to England which would be accepted even by moderate Egyptians. Lord Curzon's letter to Allenby, in March 1923, is indicative of this prevailing mood:

If satisfactory settlement of Sudan question cannot be hoped for ... would annexation of Sudan be a feasible alternative: Could it be carried out a) Without further military risk or commitments? b) Without incurring a ruinous financial burden? Would effect of such measure be to inflame or to discredit the agitation which had brought it about? ...[79]

The relatively quiet year which followed the promulgation of the 1923 constitution on 20 April was therefore misleading. The political parties in Egypt were preparing themselves for the first general elections. The British government was eager to promote constitutional government hoping that an Anglo-Egyptian settlement would then be possible. But Stack and his colleagues were forever suspicious and already in October 1923 they warned the foreign office of the consequences of a Wafdist majority in the forthcoming elections. Consequently, Stack did not see any possibility of a compromise with Egypt over the Sudan. Murray, of the foreign office, tended to agree with Stack, and suggested therefore that failing agreement His Majesty's Government should annex the Sudan to the British Empire even at the price of providing £1,000,000 per annum for the Sudanese army.[80]

The Sudan in Anglo-Egyptian Relations: 1899–1924

IN SEARCH OF SUDANESE COLLABORATION

Events in the Sudan and their interpretation by the Anglo-Sudanese lobby in Cairo and London supplied the additional impetus for the drastic action which Wingate, Stack and their colleagues had advocated ever since 1919. The delegation of Sudanese religious and tribal leaders which had visited England in July 1919 in order to express their loyalty to Great Britain, and to dissociate themselves from Zaghlul and from Egyptian nationalism generally, represented the blueprint for future Anglo-Sudanese propaganda. The crux of their message was that the Sudan was a separate entity and did not desire any official links with Egypt.[81] While these anti-Egyptian sentiments were presented as being genuinely Sudanese, the appearance of a secular nationalist opposition which was at least partly pro-Egyptian, was explained in terms of Egyptian propaganda and as being unrepresentative of the vast majority of the Sudanese. Here the Sudan Political Service faced a dilemma which can be noted in their reports throughout these crucial years, namely, how to present Egyptian nationalist propaganda? On the one hand they wanted to prove that the Sudanese hated and feared the Egyptians and hence the latter's propaganda was, by definition, ineffective. On the other hand they sought to expel the Egyptians from the Sudan, but in order to achieve this goal their evil influence had to be exaggerated.[82] One way of dealing with this dilemma was to present those who were affected by Egyptian propaganda as 'ignorant natives' who were disturbed by a feeling of insecurity with regard to the permanence of the present, predominantly British, government. The 'more intelligent natives', on the other hand, despised the Egyptian propaganda and were unaffected by it.[83]

Following the advent of the Wafd to power in March 1924 and the formation of the Labour government in England in January of that year, Stack and his colleagues had reason to fear that an Anglo-Egyptian settlement might be at the Sudan's expense. In April Stack explained at some length, in reply to a foreign office query, why Egyptian personnel should not be introduced into the Sudan. Following the normal pattern, dealing first with their lack of qualifications, Stack went on to state:

No amount of explanation of 'Egyptian rights' would reconcile native opinion to what would be regarded as a betrayal of the trust and confidence they have hitherto given us .... By the younger generation it would be viewed as curtailment of their prospects of an increasing share in their own administration.[84]

This was the beginning of a concerted effort by Stack and his colleagues in London and Cairo to prove that Egypt should under no circumstances gain a real say in Sudanese affairs. In fact he warned that the change of government in England might create fears in the Sudan regarding the permanence of British predominance in that country.[85]

Letters from Sudanese notables from all over the country expressing their desire to remain under British rule until the Sudan was ready for independence were forwarded in bulk to Cairo and London. Some British governors went so far as to state that the inhabitants of their provinces would never submit to Egyptian rule, while a Southern governor warned that 'Egyptians would again reduce the black tribes of the Southern Sudan to a state of slavery.'[86] A suggestion made in England to publish letters of Sudanese leaders expressing loyalty to the British authorities was dismissed by the foreign office on the grounds that 'it would be easy for Egyptian officials in the Sudan to collect signatures to anti-British petitions'.[87] But it is quite clear that the cumulative effect of this Anglo-Sudanese propaganda was felt both in the British press and in government circles. In May 1924 Stack sent a detailed memorandum to the government containing descriptions of all Egyptian misdeeds in the Sudan since March 1919, as well as of Sudanese critical views of their northern neighbour. The message was quite clear: should England give in to Egyptian demands she would be viewed by the Sudanese as a traitor. Moreover, since any compromise suggested to Egypt by the British government would be viewed by the Sudanese as a betrayal, and since the Wafd would reject such a compromise as insufficient, Stack proposed complete British control of the Sudan. He had reached that conclusion since 'the dominating consideration *now* in deciding as to the form of Government for the Sudan must be the interests of the Sudanese themselves'. He was willing to grant the Egyptian government some rights of financial supervision, guaranteed quantities of water and the security of its southern border, but no administrative posts and only a symbolic military presence in the Sudan. So at last Stack had put his cards on the table and it was with this aim in mind that he proceeded to London to represent the Anglo-Sudanese point of view at the Anglo-Egyptian negotiations in August 1924.[88] With him he brought a signed declaration made by Sayyid 'Abd al-Rahman al-Mahdi and several religious and tribal leaders, as well as by Sudanese army officers, to the effect that British rule was superior and preferable to all others hitherto experienced in the Sudan and hence enjoyed their full confidence. On the other side of the negotiating table the Wafd declared in its manifesto to 'our Sudanese brothers ... that the day of their emancipation is near'.[89]

The 1924 disturbances in the Sudan, which included demonstrations and anti-British sermons in several mosques, were therefore heaven-sent as far as Stack and his colleagues were concerned. Some of these were organised by the White Flag League, first founded in 1920, which according to intelligence reports had received substantial political and financial support since February 1924 from both the Wafd and the Egyptian Nationalist party. However, a special intelligence report dealing with the League's connection with Egypt had to admit that there was no absolute proof of Egyptian complicity either in the disturbances in the Sudan or in the White Flag League's activities.[90] This did not stop Stack and his supporters from accusing Zaghlul of complicity in these disturbances.[91] While Zaghlul's continued denials of these accusations did not carry too much weight the following factual report seems rather more conclusive. An official British record of a conversation held at the foreign office on 13 August 1924 stated explicitly that there was no proof whatsoever of Egyptian governmental complicity in the Sudan disturbances, and that the fact that Zaghlul himself was attacked suggested that some outside organisation was involved.[92] Following the demonstration of the Sudanese cadets, who had previously been regarded as the most reliable pro-British element and were earmarked as the future officers of the Sudanese army, it became quite clear that the so-called 'Egyptian propaganda' had much deeper roots among the Sudanese than admitted by Stack and his colleagues. In a candid private letter, Reginald Davies, who was then assistant director of intelligence, wrote that the White Flag League and other such organisations were pro-Sudanese and only secondarily anti-British. Davies warned that it was not Egyptian propaganda which was at the root of the troubles but the fact that 'a generation is now reaching years of discretion which never knew the Mahdia' and hence did not hate or fear the Egyptians as Wingate and Stack had continuously insisted. Also, in contrast to Stack's reports, Davies refuted the claims regarding the spontaneity of the various 'petitions of loyalty', stating that even a loyal tribal chief would never voluntarily sign such a petition.[93]

It is hardly surprising that the Egyptian press during these turbulent months was reporting daily about the intimidation of Sudanese tribal and religious leaders by their British (and sometimes Syrian) superiors. These were accused of forcing the Sudanese to sign their so-called petitions of loyalty to Great Britain. In fact, Shaykhs and *'umdas* were threatened with dismissal unless they agreed to collaborate. Some of the papers suggested that England might learn from the mistakes she had made in Egypt. The British should remember that in Egypt in 1919 'high pressure simply caused explosion ... they are now repeating the same tactics in the Sudan'.[94] But the *Sudan Intelligence Report* drew a completely different conclusion, namely, that the anti-British tone of all Egyptian papers proved that the agitation in the Sudan was in fact undertaken by the Egyptians. The proof was that 'no expressions of a desire for a Sudan for the Sudanese have been found' in the Egyptian press.[95] The following seems to indicate that the Anglo-Egyptian gap regarding the Sudan was growing rapidly and that those in charge of formulating policies, especially in 10 Downing Street, were not inclined to bridge this gap. When asked in the House of Commons whether the people of the Sudan had been or would be consulted with regard to their future, the prime minister replied that while it was impracticable to ask the people directly, the many letters and petitions of loyalty to Britain signed by Sudanese of all classes left no doubt about their desire.[96] Two months later MacDonald stated in a Cabinet meeting that while Zaghlul might be inclined to preserve the *status quo* in the Sudan 'this would not be acceptable as it meant that Great Britain was to remain responsible for the administration while Egypt was to pursue a policy of propaganda and undermining the British position'.[97] Times had indeed changed, since such a *status quo* would have been regarded as heaven-sent by Milner or Curzon in the years 1919–1921. Moreover, had MacDonald really wanted to come to grips with the Sudan question, he would have listened with greater care to Zaghlul, who claimed that the Sudanese were expressing their own feelings rather than Egypt's with regard to their future. For even if there was Egyptian propaganda in the Sudan, the Sudan Political Service, despite its desire, had never succeeded in proving Egyptian complicity in subversive activities. Reports to that effect were readily available for MacDonald throughout these crucial months, leading first to the failure of the Anglo-Egyptian treaty negotiations and later to the mutiny of the black battalion in Khartoum in November 1924.[98]

ENGLAND BREAKS THE *STATUS QUO*

The change in British policy, making a solution which had been desirable in 1921 utterly unacceptable in 1924, was due to several factors. First, Egypt was since February 1922 at least nominally independent and was likely to gain even greater independence in the near future; hence Egypt could no longer be trusted as a 'sleeping partner' in the running of the Anglo-Egyptian Sudan. Second, by 1924, the Sudan had become a far greater economic asset than it had been before the war. The Gezira scheme was regarded as potentially the most important supplier of cotton for the British textile industry. Furthermore, since Britain had guaranteed some £15 million for the Gezira scheme, the Makwar dam and the Sudan railways, the well-being of the Sudan had become a financial concern for England. In other words the financial obligations of the Sudan to England could be met only 'if the minds of the inhabitants are not diverted from agricultural and economic activities to political agitation'. Hence 'the elimination of any connection with Egypt would certainly be an unmixed advantage'.[99] While these were the main arguments used by the Anglo-Sudanese lobby there is no doubt that the Sudan's strategic importance was also enhanced as a result of regional developments. Should Egyptian nationalism get out of hand, what better way was there to restore order than a gentle warning regarding the legitimate extension of irrigation in the Sudan?[100] Zaghlul's docile acceptance of the breakdown of the negotiations, followed by his rather mild rebuke of Stack's communiqué of 14 October 1924, which could have been interpreted as a declaration of a British protectorate in the Sudan, prove that the Wafd did not intend to supply the Anglo-Sudanese authorities with the excuse they were craving for.[101]

Following the general elections of October 1924, the first Labour government was replaced by the Conservatives, and Sir Austen Chamberlain in charge of foreign affairs was less inclined than Mac-Donald to follow Stack's extremist line. He suggested to Allenby that he should follow Zaghlul's mild tone and try to avoid a conflict. He stated explicitly that he intended to keep the Condominium and would try not to make the position of a friendly Egyptian government more difficult than it already was. But, at the same time Chamberlain was well aware that a conflict was possible and he suggested that in such an eventuality Britain would react by removing Egyptian troops from the Sudan and by forming a separate Sudanese army under British command.[102]

In the Sudan, in the meantime, the Anglo-Sudanese officials as well as the British officers in the army were preparing for the next round. They warned Cairo and London against being misled by the present political lull and charged that Egyptian officers were preparing the black and Arab battalions for an anti-British uprising. This was particularly dangerous among the blacks who had just emerged from 'relative savagery'. Also 'the Sudanese are a primitive and fanatical people, whose ignorance makes them particularly susceptible to agitators'. Hence, they advised that, rather than wait for a conflict, all the locally recruited units should be taken over and converted into a Sudan defence force.

> A scheme for this purpose has been worked out in detail ... With the presence of two more British battalions, the Sudan Government are satisfied that the 'Sudanization' of the Egyptian army could be accomplished without serious risk[103]

The replacement of the Egyptian army by a local Sudanese defence force, owing allegiance to British officers only, thus became the most urgent aim of Stack and his colleagues. This plan had been officially proposed by Stack in his memorandum of 25 May 1924. On 18 August Stack wrote in a confidential letter to MacDonald that the details of the establishment of a Sudan Defence Force had been worked out. One month later Stack suggested to MacDonald that he act unilaterally since an army insurrection was likely, and since nearly all the Arab and Sudanese officers were either actively or passively anti-British. Hence, Stack proposed to MacDonald that a communication be sent to Zaghlul informing him of the separation of the offices of sirdar and governor-general and of the formation of a new Sudanese army under the sole control of the governor-general. Stack warned that unless such action was taken immediately 'a mutiny is ultimately inevitable'. Stack, who was at the time in London, had consulted the foreign office prior to making this far-reaching suggestion. It was based on the assumption that the Anglo-Egyptian negotiations, then still in progress, would soon break down and that with Egypt under Zaghlul openly hostile, the continued partnership in the Sudan would become impossible. On 14 September Stack was reassured by

The Sudan in Anglo-Egyptian Relations: 1899–1924

Huddleston from Khartoum that all plans for the evacuation of Egyptian troops and officers from the Sudan were now ready.[104] It seems in fact that all that was needed was the final blessing from the cabinet. There is no indication that anyone either in the foreign office or in the British government was opposed to Stack's plan, but with the general elections in England just ahead and Zaghlul still negotiating in London, no decision was taken until after the assassination of Sir Lee Stack in Cairo on 20 November 1924. When the Wafd claimed in 1927 that it had in its possession the details of a secret British plan to evacuate the Egyptian army from the Sudan, predating Stack's assassination, they were therefore stating the truth. However, 'Scheme E' for the evacuation of the Egyptian army from the Sudan, which had been completed on 10 September 1924, was never dated and hence, according to the governor-general of the Sudan, the Wafd could prove nothing even if the document was in its hands.[105]

Following the assassination of Stack on 20 November 1924 the long-sought-for peg on which to hang the evacuation of the Egyptians from the Sudan had finally been provided. Stack who since 1919 had consistently argued first for the changed status of the Sudan and later at least for the evacuation of the Egyptian army, had achieved his aim only through his death. The British Cabinet, now under Baldwin, sent the following instructions to Allenby to be submitted to the Egyptian government: first, that those responsible for the assassination be punished and an apology be issued; second, payment of indemnity to be left to Egyptian decency; third, that all Egyptian officers and army units be removed from the Sudan and that all black and Arab units of the Egyptian army be converted into a Sudan defence force 'in the pay of and owing allegiance to the Sudan Government alone'; and last, that a special commission be set up, which would include an Egyptian member, 'to examine the possibility of extending without detriment to Egypt, the 300,000 acre area to be irrigated by the Blue Nile dam'.[106] Allenby, however, did not wait for the foreign office instructions to arrive but presented his own ultimatum to Zaghlul at 4:15 p.m. on 22 November 1924. His excuse for not waiting was his fear that Zaghlul might hand in his resignation to the Egyptian parliament which was convening at 5:00 p.m. that afternoon, and that consequently there would be no government to accept his terms. He thus presented his own ultimatum, despite the fact that the foreign office ciphered telegram had arrived just before he left for the prime minister's residence. Allenby's ultimatum was far more extreme and humiliating, both in its tone and in its conditions, especially in so far as it demanded the immediate suppression of all political demonstrations, the payment of a fine of £500,000, and, the gravest demand of all, the unlimited irrigation of land in the Sudan without any reference to Egypt's needs. A conference of cabinet members held at the foreign office in London later that same afternoon was unanimous in condemning Allenby's conduct but decided nonetheless that 'owing to the harm which will result ... in disavowing Lord Allenby's action ... they had no option but to support the authority of Lord Allenby'.[107] Neville Henderson, who was sent out to report on Allenby's action and inadvertently caused his resignation, wrote in his first unofficial communication that he agreed with Allenby's haste in presenting his ultimatum due to his fear of Zaghlul's resignation. Moreover, he praised Allenby's threat regarding the unlimited irrigation in the Sudan 'since it has in it a menace which the Egyptians can understand as well as a basis for a useful concession'.[108]

Realising that Chamberlain would not back their demand to put an end to the Condominium, the Anglo-Sudanese lobby now sought to enforce the lowering of the Egyptian flag, at least from the new army's barracks, and a satisfactory settlement with regard to the financing of this new Sudanese army, without burdening the finances of the Sudan. During December several proposals were made with regard to the introduction of a new Sudan army flag, to be hoisted only over the barracks, instead of the hitherto used Egyptian flag. But this suggestion was rejected as inadequate and dangerous by most of the senior British officials in the Sudan who suggested that the Egyptian flag be replaced by the Union Jack. In the end no drastic action was taken since neither Allenby nor the British government wanted to create further difficulties in the relations with Egypt. Therefore it was decided to fly only a unit flag, whenever feasible, but to continue hoisting both the British and the Egyptian flags on all district and station headquarters. With regard to the Sudan army flag Allenby reiterated the Sudan government's fears of 'dangerous nationalist reactions' and hence rejected it.[109] He also rejected, with Archer's agreement, the elimination of the 4,000 remaining Egyptian officials from the Sudan, since these constituted some fifty percent of all classified staff and their replacement by Englishmen or by Sudanese in the foreseeable future was practically impossible.[110] Next came the problem of financing the Sudan Defence Force, which was founded officially on King's Day (17 January 1925), owing allegiance only to the governor-general of the Sudan. Egypt was expected to carry the financial burden but without having the right to claim that she was paying for the new army. It was feared in the Sudan that such an Egyptian claim might undermine the loyalty of the new force. In the end the Egyptian government agreed to pay £E750,000 per annum 'towards military expenses of the Sudan Government'.[111] Egypt was later even forced to pay the full cost of the evacuation of its own army from the Sudan in the wake of Allenby's ultimatum.[112]

But the Anglo-Sudanese were not really satisfied, as related in the following passages from the diary of Robert Baily, then acting governor of Khartoum. The anger and dismay of the British officials in the Sudan was, according to Baily, based on the fact that Stack had been murdered, a mutiny of Sudanese battalions had been instigated by Egyptian officers, and yet the foreign office insisted on continuing to fly the Egyptian flag in the Sudan. Even the appointment of Archer, the new governor-general of the Sudan, was undertaken by a Royal decree of King Fu'ad of Egypt. To use Baily's words; 'The F.O. are saying in diplomatic language that they want just *one* more murder before allowing us to haul down the flag. How can we explain all this to the Sudanese? ... In the eyes of the Sudanese our action was severence of our connection with Egypt. We mutually congratulate ourselves that henceforth there will be nobody between us and them .... Yet we keep their flag and I suppose are going to salute their King and play his National Anthem.'[113] Baily emphasized the following as the main reasons for his colleagues' frustrations:

1. A conviction that the sirdar was murdered by a concerted conspiracy of Egyptians.
2. A conviction that the mutiny was organized by a concerted conspiracy of Egyptians.
3. A conviction that the Egyptians ... are trying to prove that the murderer was a Sudanese and not an Egyptian.
4. A conviction that the Egyptians have cheated and lied to the Sudanese and now are found out.[114]

The Anglo-Sudanese were therefore anxious to prove Egyptian complicity in all their troubles in the Sudan. Hence a special committee of enquiry was set up to investigate the events leading up to and including the 1924 mutiny. One of the most important conclusions of the committee was that many of the planned acts of violence, scheduled for 1924, never got off the ground. These included the blowing up of the pro-British Hadara printing press; the systematic murder of Anglo-Sudanese officials; armed demonstrations of all black troops; and finally a general mutiny of all Sudanese battalions which was planned for November. The sole outcome of all these gradiose plans was a certain amount of agitation and a mutiny of some sixty Sudanese soldiers and officers all told.[115] But according to the Anglo-Sudanese lobby, Allenby's harsh measures in November 1924 were well deserved while Chamberlain and the Tories were adopting a defeatist policy.

On 26 November 1924 Allenby submitted his resignation to Chamberlain thereby becoming the second high commissioner in Egypt to resign within five years. In a way both Allenby's and Wingate's resignations were brought about by their handling or mishandling of Zaghlul and the Wafd. But while Wingate was made a scapegoat for his own government's lack of a coherent policy, Allenby was blamed for backing the wrong horse in Egypt ever since he had forced his government to issue the February 1922 declaration. But even though the government had appointed Neville Henderson as minister plenipotentiary in Cairo, without consulting Allenby, both Henderson and Chamberlain tried to persuade Allenby to withdraw his resignation. But finally in May 1925 his resignation was accepted and on 14 June 1925 he was replaced by Sir George (later Lord) Lloyd.[116] Thus, the chapter which had started in March 1919 was brought to an end. Egypt had as a result of its violent nationalist revolution gained a semi-independent status. Yet, not unlinked to these same gains, Egypt had lost even the semblance of authority it had in the Anglo-Egyptian Sudan.

NOTES

1. Agreement between Her Britannic Majesty's Government and the Government of his Highness the Khedive of Egypt, relative to the future administration of the Soudan. Enclosure 1 in No. 64, Cromer to Salisbury, 28 Jan. 1899, F.O. 407/150.
2. F. R. Wingate, *Mahdiism and the Egyptian Sudan*, 1891; 2nd Ed., Frank Cass, London 1968, pp. 7-10, 466.
3. G. Warburg, 'The governor-general of the Sudan and his relations with the British consuls-general in Egypt, 1899-1916', *Asian and African Studies*, (hereafter *AAS*) Vol. 5 (1969) pp. 97-132.

The Sudan in Anglo-Egyptian Relations: 1899–1924

4. Cromer to Wingate, 25, Jan. 1904, F.O. 633/8; Gorst to Wingate, 16 Mar. 1910, [see Abbreviations].
5. Inclosure 2 in No. 65, Cromer to Salisbury, 22 Jan. 1899, F.O. 407/150.
6. Financial Regulations to be observed by the Soudan Government, Cairo, 6 May 1901, F.O. 407/157; these regulations were replaced in 1910, following the setting up of the governor-general's council, by a new set of regulations, signed by Wingate and Harvey. Inclosure 4 in No. 33, F.O. 407/175.
7. Reports of His Majesty's Agent and Consul-General on the Finances, Administration and Condition of Egypt and the Soudan, 1904 (CD 2409) pp. 120-21 (hereafter SAR).
8. There are numerous articles in Egyptian newspapers voicing this criticism. One of the most comprehensive articles was written by Ahmad Hilmi in *al-Liwa'*, 21 Oct. 1907.
9. *The Times*, Apr. 11, 1900, put forward a suggestion to build a port in the Red Sea so as to secure British interests in the Sudan. See also R. Hill, *Sudan Transport*, London 1965, pp. 52-3, who suggests that the Sudan railway was never linked to Egypt partly for political reasons.
10. In a special memorandum titled 'The Sudan – Capital expenditure on its restoration and development and its actual cost to Egypt', these arguments were put forward by Bernard, the financial secretary. According to his calculations the Egyptian contribution to the Sudan in the years 1899–1908 amounted to £E655,200, and not to £E4,396,740 as claimed by the official figures. See Bernard's memorandum, 28 Mar. 1909, SAD/286/4.
11. Cromer to Wingate, 25 Jan. 1904, F.O. 633/Vol. 8; Cromer to Wingate, 17 Feb. 1900, F.O. 141/356; see also *Sudan Gazette* No. 60, 1 Mar. 1904; W. E. Garstin, Report on Irrigation Works in the Sudan, 12 Dec. 1900, F.O. 403/312.
12. Wingate to Kitchener, 9 May 1914, SAD/190/2/2.
13. Wingate to Cromer, 30 Oct. 1905 (confidential), F.O. 141/393; see also Wingate to Kitchener (private), 26 Oct. 1911, SAD/301/4.
14. Wingate to Gorst, 4 Apr. 1909, SAD/287/1.
15. P. Magnus, *Kitchener, Portrait of an Imperialist*, London 1961, pp. 89-95.
16. *Sudan Intelligence Report*, 245, Dec. 1914 (short reference, *SIR*); *Sudan Gazette*, 1 May 1909.
17. Wingate's correspondence with Husayn Kamil was more frequent and less formal, as they had known each other over a long period; see for instance Wingate to Husayn Kamil, 14 Aug. 1915, SAD/236/2; Husayn Kamil to Wingate, 27 June 1916, SAD/200/8. Following the declaration of a British protectorate over Egypt on 18 Dec. 1914, the title of the Khedive was changed to Sultan.
18. Wingate to Stack, 12 May 1908, SAD/284/13.
19. Wingate to Cecil ('secret please destroy!'), 13 Jan. 1913, SAD/185/1/1. 'Azuri had been employed in the intelligence department of the Egyptian army at least since 1906. Despite the similarity in names no connection with Najib 'Azuri, founder of the so-called *Ligue de la patrie Arabe*, has been established.
20. Memorandum by Clayton on 'Procedure regarding Ordinances', 1912, SAD/183/3.
21. *Sudan Gazette*, No. 23, 1 May 1901; *Sudan Gazette*, No. 37, 1 July 1902. When in 1910 two contractors, Bencini and Quistas, brought action against the Sudan government in an Egyptian court, the latter decided that it was not competent to pass judgement; see Bencini and Quistas versus the Sudan Government, 11 Apr. 1910, SAD/296/1.
22. Sir Rudolf Karl von Slatin Pasha (1857–1932), joined the Egyptian military administration in the Sudan 1878; submitted to the Mahdists and was kept in captivity in Omdurman 1884–95; following his escape he joined the Egyptian

army intelligence 1895–98; inspector-general of the Sudan 1900–14. For details see R. Hill, *Slatin Pasha*, London 1965.
23. Wingate to Clayton (very private), 27 Mar. 1915, SAD/469/8.
24. Wingate to Gorst (private) 22 Dec. 1908, SAD/284/12/3. In 1912 Wingate learnt to his dismay, that the Tokar mosque had been receiving allocations from the Egyptian *Waqf*. He promptly ordered the subsidy to be stopped; see Wingate to Stack (private) 16 May 1912, SAD/181/2/2; Gorst to Wingate, 12 Dec. 1908, SAD/284/15; Memorandum by Khalil Pasha Hamdi Hamada on the history of the Khartoum Mosque [n.d.] F.O. 141/416.
25. Wingate to Gorst, 4 Apr. 1909, SAD/287/1; Wingate to Phipps, 13 Apr. 1909, SAD/287/1.
26. Clayton to Wingate, 21 Jan. 1914, SAD/469/6/1; Clayton to Wingate, 11 Feb. 1914, ibid.
27. Wingate to Cromer (private) 24 Feb. 1915, SAD/194/2. It is interesting to note that when 'Ali al-Mirghani died on 21 Feb. 1968, the Egyptian press described him as a prominent leader of the Sudanese resistance to British rule since the beginning of the century. See *al-Ahram*, 22 Feb. 1968; *al-Musawwar*, 1 Mar. 1968; *Ruz al-Yusuf*, 25 Mar. 1968.
28. Channer to Wingate, 10 Aug. 1908, SAD/283/8/2. Butler's diary, 13 Oct. 1911; 20 Oct. 1911; 31 Oct. 1911; SAD/400/10.
29. Wingate to Kitchener, 26 Oct. 1911, SAD/301/4; Wingate to Asser (private), 29 Aug. 1908, SAD/283/8/4.
30. Slatin to Wingate, 6 Mar. 1910, SAD/290/3/1; Clayton to Wingate, 1 Mar. 1910, SAD/290/3/1.
31. See for instance *al-Liwa'*, 7 Feb. 1900; 3 May 1900; 30 May 1908.
32. Owen to Wingate, 16 May 1906, SAD/278/5; Wingate to Cromer, 11 Nov. 1915; SAD/236/3.
33. Shoucair to Stack, 24 Jan. 1909, SAD/286/1; see also *al-Muqattam*, 22 Jan. 1909, article on the Sudan written by Ahmad Effendi Yusuf Kandil; and *al-Muqattam*, 21 Oct. 1908 – article signed Ummdurmani, SAD/234/6.
34. *al-Liwa'*, 19 May, 1908; *The Standard*, 1 May 1908. *L'Étandard Égyptien*, 31 May 1908.
35. Wingate to Clayton (private), 15 Dec. 1913, SAD/469/5; Wingate to Bonham Carter, 29 Mar. 1910, SAD/290/3/1.
36. Wingate to Cromer, 19 Feb. 1900, F.O. 141/356; Cromer to Lansdowne, 5 June 1901, F.O. 800/123.
37. Historical notes – Military School Khartoum [n.d.], SAD/106/4.
38. Wingate to Cromer, 9 May, 1906, SAD/278/5.
39. Phipps to Wingate, 7 Sept. 1904, SAD/234/2.
40. Currie to Wingate, 25 June 1908, SAD/282/6.
41. Wingate to Clayton (private), 9 Apr. 1916, SAD/470/1. The money came as usual out of the Sudan civil funds.
42. War Office selected papers, No. 2; British detachment at Khartoum, 1900.
43. Wingate to Cromer, 6 May 1900; Cromer to Salisbury, 7 May 1900; F.O. 78/5087.
44. War Office to Foreign Office, 9 Nov. 1898, F.O. 78/5025. The sum involved was £E29,000.
45. Cheethem to Grey, 10 May 1911, F.O. 371/1113; Slade to Malet, 12 Sept. 1911, ibid.
46. Gorst to Grey, 12 Mar. 1910, F.O. 800/47; Gorst to Grey, 20 Mar. 1910, ibid. The Lado Enclave was created by the Franco-Congolese agreement of 1894, and was administered by the Belgians until King Leopold's death in 1910 when it reverted to the Sudan. For details see R.O. Collins, 'The transfer of the Lado Enclave to the Anglo-Egyptian Sudan, 1910', *Zaïre*, vol. XIV, 2, (1960).

The Sudan in Anglo-Egyptian Relations: 1899–1924

47. Wingate to McMahon, 14 Sep. 1915, F.O. 371/2352; Treasury to F.O., 16 December 1915, ibid.
48. *The Times*, 18 Apr. 1900.
49. Wingate to Clayton, 6 Mar. 1910, SAD/469/2/1.
50. Clayton to Wingate (private), 22 May 1910, SAD/296/2.
51. Kitchener to Grey, 10 May 1912, F.O. 371/1363; Memorandum by E. G. [Grey], 14 May 1912, ibid.
52. For details see my article quoted above (note 3).
53. Wingate to Hardinge (private) 27 Oct. 1918, FO 371/3711.
54. Quoted in M. W. Daly, *British Administration and the Northern Sudan, 1917–1924*, Leiden 1980, pp. 104-105.
55. Keown-Boyd to Allenby, 14 March 1920, FO 371/4981, and enclosures, Alexander (later Sir) Keown-Boyd had served in the Sudan Political Service from 1907 and had been transferred to Egypt in 1917 as Wingate's private secretary. Hence his support of the latter's views is hardly surprising.
56. Wingate's dossier to the Milner Mission consisted of some 87 typed pages. A copy of it can be found in SAD/204/1.
57. Wingate to Hardinge, 1 March 1920, SAD/204/1; see 'Note on the Separation of the Sudan from Egypt', ibid; see also reply of Mr. C. Harmsworth, undersecretary of state for foreign affairs to parliamentary question of Mr. Stewart M.P., 10 Nov. 1920, FO 371/4981; see Cab/23/26 reporting on a Cabinet resolution from 11 July 1921, where it was stated that the Sudan's value for Great Britain lay in the possibilities of growing cotton and in its holding the key to the water supply of Egypt; see also Daly p. 146.
58. Wingate to Curzon, 4 June 1919, SAD/204/1.
59. See for instance, Stack to Wingate, 8 May 1919, ibid; see also memorandum of M. Herbert on the role of the high commissioner in governing the Sudan, in FO 371/10908.
60. Allenby to Curzon, 10 February 1920, SAD/162/5.
61. Daly, pp. 147-148.
62. *Morning Post*, 30 May 1921.
63. *Daily Express*, 24 May 1921.
64. *The Times*, 13 June 1921; *Daily Telegraph*, 24 May 1921.
65. *Manchester Guardian*, 26 September 1921; *Daily Herald*, 20 September 1921, 27 September 1921; *Morning Post*, 3 October 1921, 5 October 1921.
66. *Daily Herald*, 22 October 1921, 28 October 1921.
67. Ibid., 16 November 1921; *Westminster Gazette*, 17 November 1921; *Observer*, 20 November 1921; *The Times*, 29 October 1921; 7 November 1921.
68. *Morning Post*, 26 July 1921, published letter signed by 19 Labour M.P.s warning against the continued negotiations with an unrepresentative government; see also ibid. 10 August 1921 and *Manchester Guardian*, 22 April 1921, where Zaghlul is quoted, as above.
69. Milner to Adly, 18 August 1920, FO 371/4979; minutes by A. W. Cooper on Scott to Curzon, 9 September 1920, FO 371/4987. Murray, of the foreign office, who also commented on above stated that while the Milner Mission did not deal with the Sudan, all its members agreed that it was desirable to reduce the Egyptian share in its administration and in its army as soon as possible.
70. Allenby to Curzon, 18 February 1921, FO 371/6311.
71. G. A. L. Lloyd, *Egypt Since Cromer* Vol. II, New York 1970, p. 397; see also Daly, p. 142.
72. L. C. B. Seaman, *Post-Victorian Britain 1902–1951*, London 1966, pp. 173-175; see also Mahmud Y. Zayid, *Egypt's Struggle for Independence*, Beirut, 1965,

pp. 116-120; for details see debate on Egypt in the House of Lords, 25 June 1924, in FO 371/10050.
73. Allenby to Foreign Office, 9 May 1922, FO 371/7734; Clive Wigram to E. Crowe, 9 May 1922, ibid; Crowe to Wigram, 11 May 1922, ibid; Crowe assured the King that any Egyptian encroachment would be resisted; for details see E. Kedourie, 'The Genesis of the Egyptian Constitution of 1923', in *The Chatham House Version*, London 1969, pp. 169-170.
74. Allenby to Curzon, 13 May 1922, FO 371/7742; Allenby was referring to investments in the Gezira scheme; see also *al-Muqattam*, 18 August 1922, where it was reported that England had decided to transfer the Sudan administration to the Colonial office, and that Egypt's interest in the Sudan was to be limited only to security and irrigation.
75. Allenby to Curzon, 13 May 1922, FO 371/7753; J. Murray, memorandum, FO 371/7734, as quoted by Daly, p. 144; see also *Morning Post*, 22 July 1922; *The Times*, 23 October, 31 October 1922, where it was reported that despite British pressures the Liberal Constitutionalists had adopted the formula of non-separation of the Sudan from Egypt in their party's platform.
76. Foreign Office to Allenby, 25 October 1922, FO 371/7738; Allenby to Foreign Office (very urgent!) 14 January 1923, FO 371/8959; Foreign Office to Allenby, 18 January 1923, ibid; see also *Morning Post*, 30 November 1922, where the reasons for the downfall of Tharwat's government were explained.
77. Allenby to Foreign Office, 25 January 1923, 29 January 1923; Foreign Office to Allenby, 30 January 1923 (two telegrams), FO 371/8959; Allenby to Curzon, 19 February 1923, FO 371/8960; see also Daly, pp. 144-146.
78. For views of the British press see for instance *Daily Telegraph*, 5 February 1923; *The Times*, 6 February 1923; *Daily Mail*, 8 February 1923; *Morning Post*, 9 February 1923; *Manchester Guardian*, 26 February 1923; *Westminster Gazette*, 21 April 1923 (editorial); *Daily Herald*, 13 February 1923.
79. Curzon to Allenby, 13 March 1923, FO 371/8960.
80. Murray's memorandum covering Stack's memorandum, 11 October 1923, FO 371/8991.
81. For details see: G. R. Warburg, 'From Ansar to Umma: Sectarian politics in the Sudan, 1914–1915', *AAS*, 9/3 (1973); see also Daly, pp. 71-79.
82. Ibid., pp. 100-107; see also Stack to Clayton, 21 March 1919, FO 371/3714; Allenby to F.O., 20 April 1919, FO 371/3715; Allenby to Curzon, 4 May 1919; FO 371/3717, enclosing a 'Note on the growth of National Aspirations in the Sudan'.
83. See for instance, Intelligence Department, Annual Report for 1921, FO 371/7746; see also *SIR*, No. 363, October 1924, FO 371/10039, 'Report on Egyptian propaganda'.
84. Stack to Kerr, 6 April 1924, FO 141/777; Kerr was Allenby's counsellor at the Residency in Cairo.
85. Stack to Allenby, 8 May 1924, encl. in Allenby to MacDonald, 23 May 1924, FO 371/10049.
86. *SIR*-358, May 1924, FO 371/10039; see also letters by the Governors of Dongola, Mongalla, Nuba Mountains, Kassala, and Bahr al-Ghazal provinces to the Civil Secretary in May and June 1924, FO 141/777.
87. Minutes by J. Murray, 4 July 1924, FO 371/10050.
88. 'Memoradum on the future status of the Sudan', encl. in Allenby to MacDonald, 1 June 1924, FO 371/10049; it is interesting to note that Mr. Furness, of the Residency in Cairo, commented that Stack's suggestions were fair as far as Egypt was concerned except for his request that Egypt continued to pay £E500,000 per annum for the SDF, see Minutes by Furness, 5 June 1924, FO 141/777.
89. *SIR*-359, June 1924; *Egyptian Gazette*, 27 June 1924, in FO 371/10050; in reply

The Sudan in Anglo-Egyptian Relations: 1899–1924

to an accusation from Zaghlul, Allenby stated that the above-mentioned declaration was the result of a 'spontaneous gathering' and not a British instigated attempt to foster Sudanese separatism; Allenby to Zaghlul, 6 July 1924, encl. in Allenby to MacDonald 6 July 1924, FO 371/10050.

90. *SIR*-359, June 1924, Appendix 'A', 'The League of the White Flag', FO 371/10039; on 29 June the League was accused of attempting to break up the *Hadara* press, for advocating separatist Sudanese nationalism, and of planning to assassinate Samuel Atiyeh of the intelligence department, see also *SIR*-360, July 1924, ibid.
91. Allenby to Zaghlul, 6 July 1924, FO 371/10050; see also Minutes by J. Murray on Allenby to MacDonald, 22 June 1924, ibid., in which he accuses Zaghlul of planning Sudanese disturbances in order to soften British positions prior to his negotiations with MacDonald.
92. Record of Conference held in the room of Secretary of State for Foreign Affairs, 13 August 1924, FO 371/10051. Attending: Prime Minister, Allenby, Stack, Schuster, Murray and Selby. For Zaghlul's denial, see Zaghlul to MacDonald, 29 August 1924, FO 371/10053.
93. Davies to More (private), 20 September 1924, FO 141/669; a similar note can be discerned in Sterry's Memorandum, 21 August 1924, enclosed in Kerr to MacDonald, 30 August 1924, FO 371/10053. Sterry, who based his report on information from the Intelligence department, stated that there was no proof of Egyptian complicity and that the main motto of the demonstrators was 'Sudan for the Sudanese'. See also 'Report on the Mutiny of Cadets School on 9 August 1924' (secret), 1 September 1924, FO 371/10053; Kerr to F.O., 10 August 1924, FO 371/10051 and Appendix in *SIR*-361, August 1924, FO 371/10039, which is devoted to the cadet's demonstration and its aftermath; from these reports it appears that ringleaders were of southern, black origin and that one of their main grievances was 'the unfair distribution of commissions between them and the Cairo Military School'.
94. *al-Mahrusa*, 30 July 1924, *al-Balagh*, 30 July 1924, *al-Akhbar*, 29 July 1924, *al-Ahram*, 31 July 1924, in 'Egyptian Press Resume', FO 371/10052, see also *al-Muqattam*, 28 August 1924, enclosed in Kerr to F.O., 28 August 1924, FO 371/10053; S. Atiyeh was singled out as one of the main culprits.
95. *SIR*-361, August 1924, in FO 371/10039.
96. Parliamentary Question by Lieut.-Commander Kentworthy, 7 July 1924, FO 371/10050.
97. Cabinet meeting 51, (1924) section 2, 29 September 1924, Cab/23/48; see also Supply Committee, House of Commons, 10 July 1924, FO 371/10050, where similar views were expressed by the Prime Minister.
98. 'Record of Conference held at 10 Downing Street on 25 September 1924', present: MacDonald, Zaghlul and four others, FO 371/10054; see also: 'Evidence of semi-official and official Egyptian complicity in subversive propaganda in the Sudan', compiled by J. Murray, 22 November 1924; in the 14 incidents cited there was no conclusive evidence regarding Egyptian complicity. In the three cases where distribution of money and arms was suspected, the source had never been discovered, in ibid.
99. Treasury to F.O. (Confidential), 21 August 1924, FO 371/10052; see also Note on the financial interests of H.M.G. in the Sudan, in Treasury to F.O., 3 July 1924, FO 371/10050.
100. See for instance Murray's memorandum on the financial relations between the Sudan and Egypt, 5 May 1922, FO 371/7753.
101. In his declaration Stack stated that Britain was responsible for the administration of the Sudan 'as trustees of the people of the Sudan'. Egypt was not even mentioned, see Allenby to MacDonald, 2 November 1924, FO 371/10054; for details regarding Zaghlul's response, see file 2426 in FO 141/777.

102. Chamberlain to Allenby, 14 November 1924, 23 November 1924, FO 141/777.
103. Memorandum on the position in the Sudan, 8 November 1924, FO 371/10054.
104. Stack to Allenby, 24 May 1924 (covering letter to his memorandum of 25 May cited above), FO 141/777; Allenby to MacDonald, 29 June 1925, FO 371/10050, (commenting on Stacks' memorandum); Stack to MacDonald (Confidential), 18 August 1924, FO 371/10052; Stack to MacDonald (Confidential), 16 September 1924, and Murray's memorandum based on above, 17 September 1924, FO 371/10053; Hakimam (Khartoum) to Stack (London), 14 September 1924, Stack to Hakimam, 15 September 1924, ibid.; see also Stack to MacDonald, 1 October 1924, FO 141/777, Stack stated that he would remain in London until status of Sudan was clarified.
105. Lloyd to Maffey, (secret), 20 March 1927, Maffey to Lloyd, (secret), 11 April 1927, FO 141/669.
106. Cabinet meeting 61, 20 November 1924, Cab/23/49.
107. Conference of Cabinet Ministers held at foreign office on 22 November 1924, Cab/23/49; see also A. P. Wavell, *Allenby in Egypt*, London 1943, pp. 111-115.
108. Henderson to Selby (private), 6 December 1924, FO 800/264.
109. Minutes by Mr. Wiggin (Cairo Residency) on the two-flag policy after removal of Egyptian army, 14 December 1924, FO 141/777. Chamberlain to Allenby, 23 December 1924, Allenby to Chamberlain, 29 December 1924, FO 371/10055; see also minutes by J. Murray on Schuster to Currie (private), 14 December 1924, FO 371/10883; Col. G. Schuster, then financial secretary of the Sudan and one of the more level-headed among the Anglo-Sudanese, had suggested in his letter that the new Sudan defence force become part of the British army; this was rejected by Allenby.
110. Allenby to Chamberlain, 2 March 1925, FO 371/10879; Archer to Allenby, 27 April 1925, FO 371/10880.
111. Sir G. Archer's proclamation on establishment of S.D.F., 17 January 1925, FO 371/10879; Allenby to Chamberlain, 25 January 1925, FO 371/10883; Archer to Allenby, 15 January 1925; Treasury to F.O., 4 February 1925, Minutes on Nimeyer to F.O., 17 February 1925; Ziwar pasha to Allenby, 12 March 1925, ibid.
112. Archer to Allenby, 27 March 1925, FO 371/10884; War Office to F.O., 18 December 1925, ibid., acknowledging cheque from Egyptian government for the evacuation.
113. Baily's diary, 7 December 1924, SAD/422/13/1.
114. Baily's diary, 11 December 1924, ibid.
115. Baily's diary, 27 February 1925, ibid., members of the committee were R. Davies, Baily himself and an intelligence officer, especially seconded from India.
116. Exchange of private telegrams between Chamberlain and Allenby between November 1924 and April 1925, FO 800/256; see also Henderson to Allenby (private & personal), 22 December 1924, ibid.; see also Wavell, pp. 119-126.

3

THE SINAI PENINSULA IN ANGLO-EGYPTIAN RELATIONS, 1906–1947

On 1 October 1906, the 'Separating Administrative Line' between the Ottoman province of the Hejaz, the governorate of Jerusalem and the Sinai peninsula was agreed upon, following nine months of military action and diplomatic activity which nearly brought the British and the Ottoman empires to the verge of war.[1] These so-called administrative lines remained unchanged despite the political upheavals through which this region had gone since the beginning of the twentieth century. The Sinai peninsula was consequently regarded as part of the British protectorate over Egypt from 1914 to 1922 and remained an Egyptian administered region ever since. However, the question of Egypt's sovereignty over Sinai remained unanswered and was raised frequently by British officials whenever Anglo-Egyptian relations were at a low ebb. It was as a result of the Sinai's strategic importance for Britain that its administration was entrusted to the governor-general of the Sudan and the *sirdar* (commander in chief) of the Egyptian army, who, at the time of the Taba incident of 1906 and the subsequent agreement, was Sir Reginald Wingate. This was the reason that the Frontier Administration Officer of the Sinai peninsula was a member of the Sudan Political Service and received his orders from Wingate. At the time of the Taba incident this post was filled by Wilfrid E. Jennings Bramly.[2]

A brief survey of the events leading up to the Anglo-Ottoman confrontation seems to be warranted, in order to understand later developments. The three major sources at our disposal seem to agree on the events leading to the Taba crisis, except on some minor details. Two of these sources are the accounts of the two men on the spot:

Rushdi Pasha, the Turkish commandant of 'Aqaba, and Jennings Bramly who, as frontier administration officer in Sinai, represented the Anglo-Egyptian side. Rushdi published a detailed account of the events as early as 1910–11,[3] while Jennings Bramly never published his memoirs but presented his papers, including his private correspondence relating to the incident, to the Royal Geographical Society in London in 1959.[4] The third source consists of the official correspondence of the British Foreign Office and the Cabinet papers of the years 1905–07 regarding the frontier dispute, as well as later references in the Foreign Office archives, especially during the Anglo-Egyptian negotiations of 1946–47.[5]

The events as related by Jennings Bramly were as follows: on 3 January 1906 by order of Sir Reginald Wingate, then governor-general of the Sudan and sirdar of the Egyptian army, which was transmitted to Bramly by his direct superior (R.C.R. Owen, director of intelligence), Bramly left his headquarters at Nakhl in the centre of Sinai and proceeded to Umm Rashrash (now Eilat) in Naqb al-'Aqaba to build up a small post for the Egyptian border police.[6]

The exact reasons behind this move were not stated either by Bramly or by Rushdi Pasha, the Turkish commandant of 'Aqaba.[7] It is, however, quite clear from the text of Wingate's telegram that he believed that 'Nakb el-Akaba ... is well within the frontier line settled upon between Turkey and Egypt after the El Wedg incident.'[8]

Bramly arrived at Naqb al-'Aqaba on 5 January and established a police station with the four Egyptian policemen accompanying him. On the same day he was visited by a Turkish *bimbashi* from 'Aqaba who questioned his right to remain in Umm Rashrash. After a long discussion the two officers agreed that it was not clear whether Umm Rashrash was within the Turkish or the Egyptian administrative boundaries, and Bramly was therefore allowed to stay where he was until the matter was clarified. Four days later Rushdi Pasha, who had in the meantime travelled to Syria, came back with new directives and ordered Bramly and his men to leave Umm Rashrash immediately.[9] Bramly therefore withdrew to Nakhl in order to avoid a direct confrontation. About four days later he was ordered by Owen, the director of intelligence, to proceed once again to the Gulf of 'Aqaba in order to meet the Egyptian coastguard boat, *Nur al-Bahr*, which had brought reinforcements. It was then that matters came to a head, according to Bramly's account:

I found the Turks occupying Taba so I lost no time in getting to Akaba in the Nur el Bahr to see Rushid [sic] Pasha and ask him on what grounds he had sent Turkish troops into Taba. Saad Bey Rafat [sic] the [Egyptian] commandant of Sinai had remained at Taba for some eight months after handing Akaba over to the Turks. Undoubtedly, it was in Egyptian territory then and I knew of nothing which had happened since, which could have altered this and made what was Egyptian then, Turkish now. Rushid Pasha's answer was that Turkey claimed Taba.[10]

Rushdi's account of these events differs in certain details, notably in that the Turkish occupation of Taba was undertaken under cover of darkness only after the Egyptian boat had arrived. Furthermore, according to Rushdi, he was ordered by telegram from the Ottoman grand vizier, Muhammad Farid Pasha, to oppose the Egyptian occupation of Taba even by force, if necessary.[11] Bramly, fearing an open confrontation and 'seeing that Turkey had now 1,000 men in Akaba besides reinforcements in the Wadi Yittem, I decided to put the 50 men of the Nur El Bahr on to the island of Faron'.[12]

The events in subsequent months brought about little change. A British gunboat was rushed to the gulf of 'Aqaba while Turkey further reinforced its troops in 'Aqaba. Britain retaliated in May by rushing additional forces to Egypt and by ordering its Mediterranean fleet to concentrate in Piraeus. In April a British attempt to land troops in Rafah, the northern tip of the Turco-Egyptian border, was opposed by the Turks and had to be abandoned.

Britain now resorted to diplomacy backed by force. The Turks first suggested that Egypt would administer two areas in the Sinai: the first, east of the Suez Canal up to a line leading from Rafah to Suez, corresponding to the area granted to Muhammad 'Ali in the *firman* of 1841; the second part was the southern section of the Peninsula up to a line in the north leading from a few kilometres west of 'Aqaba to Suez. Thus the central triangle of Rafah-'Aqaba-Suez was left in Turkish territory, enabling the Turks to extend the Hejaz railway from Ma'an to 'Aqaba and from there to Suez.[13] This suggestion was opposed by Britain as, according to Cromer 'the construction of a [Turkish] railway down to the banks of the Suez Canal could not but be regarded as a menace to the liberty of Egypt and to freedom of transit through the Canal'.[14] A second compromise was proposed by Turkey, dividing the peninsula into two, the separating line leading from El-Arish in the north to Ras Muhammad in the south. This proposal, which left the entire western half of the Sinai, including

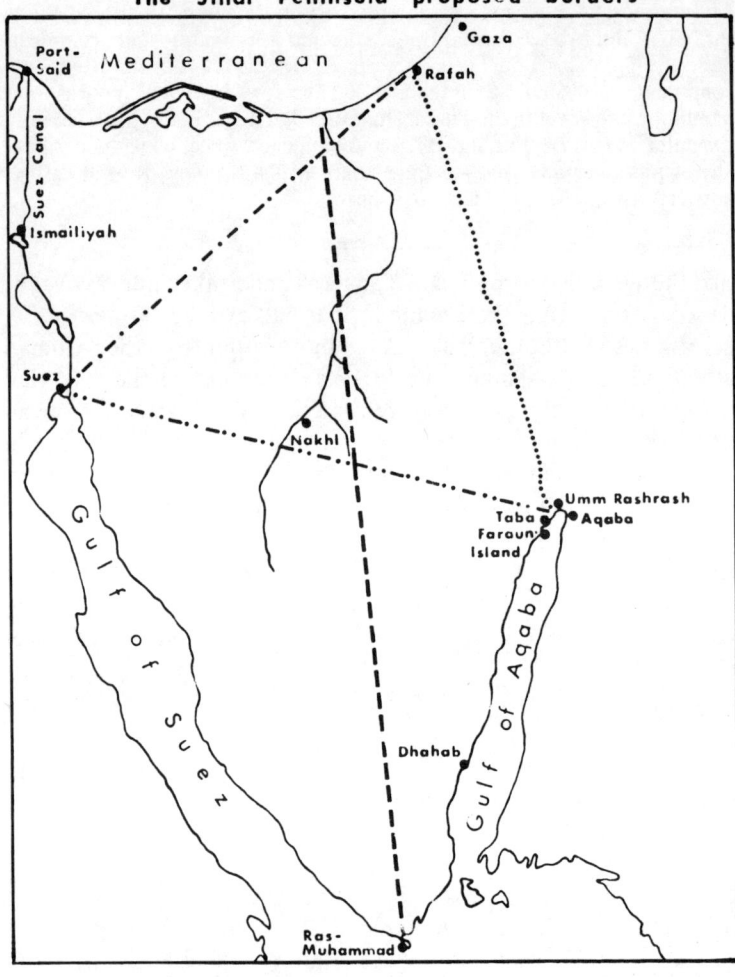

The Sinai Peninsula in Anglo-Egyptian Relations 93

the Suez Canal and its approaches, under Egyptian administration was also rejected by Britain on the grounds that the whole of the gulf of 'Aqaba would thus be in Turkish hands 'rendering the Gulf of Akaba a *mare clausum*, available for torpedo boats, which would lie on the flank of the route to India'.[15]

When, after further exchanges, it became clear that Turkey was adamant in pressing its rights to have at least a share in the Sinai, the British government resorted to more coercive measures and on 3 May 1906 handed an ultimatum to Sultan Abdulhamid II, warning him that unless he agreed within ten days to the proposed boundary leading from Rafah to the gulf of 'Aqaba and evacuated Taba, HMG would be forced to undertake stiff measures.[16] On 14 May the Sultan, realizing that without German, Russian or French support, he could not afford to resist, accepted the British demands and ordered the withdrawal from Taba and the delimitation of the administrative separating line between the Ottoman province of the Hejaz, the governorate of Jerusalem and the Sinai peninsula.

As Jennings Bramly rightly pointed out, the new separating line had little bearing on the geo-political realities of the Sinai. Bramly had suggested, as early as 1902, that Umm Rashrash and the wells in the Wadi Araba should be included in the Egyptian territory, as the Hiwat (Ahyawat) tribe owed allegiance to Egypt. On the other hand Bramly saw no reason for including the region south of Rafah and east of El-Arish in the Egyptian sector: 'inhabited as it is by the Terabin [Tarabin], a tribe belonging to Turkey, it might have been left to Turkey'.[17]

In an addendum to the above mentioned account, written after 1927, Bramly came to different conclusions. He stated that until 1927 the map annexed to the 1841 *firman* had not been available either in England or in Egypt. In that year Turkey gave a copy of the map to Ziwar Pasha, the Egyptian Prime Minister, who since 1925 had been negotiating with Italy regarding the Egyptian-Libyan frontier.[18] According to Bramly the map showed clearly that Turkey had never ceded southern Sinai to Egypt. All subsequent *firmans* referred to the same map and to the boundary drawn from Rafah to the northern tip of the Gulf of Suez. Hence the area south of that line remained under Turkish administration. Even when Turkey allowed Muhammad 'Ali and his successors to establish police posts at Nakhl, 'Aqaba, Wajh, etc., for the protection of the Egyptian *Hajj* (pilgrimage) to Mecca, he neither asked nor received the right to administer that region or include it within his boundaries.

When the Sultan Abdulhamid II decided in 1892 to reestablish his authority in the region belonging to Turkey, as drawn on the 1841 map, he did so on the advice of Marschall von Bieberstein, the German ambassador in Turkey.[19] According to Bramly, this justified demand would have brought several kilometres of the Suez Canal under Turkish control and hence Cromer reacted immediately: 'The line Rafah-Akaba was the invention of a moment, probably [by] Harry Boyle, it had never been heard of before.'[20] Bramly suggests that Cromer's ability to press the British government to agree to the new line and to achieve the reluctant support of 'Abbas Hilmi II, the Egyptian Khedive, for his demands, was based on the fact that neither the British nor the Egyptian governments had a copy of the 1841 map: 'And it was this loss that allowed Lord Cromer to claim Akaba-Rafah as the eastern boundary line'[21] instead of the Rafah-Suez line, drawn on the 1841 map.

Cromer's own account of the 1892 dispute differs in its interpretation and is rather misleading. The 1892 incident was caused, according to Cromer, by the suspicions of the Sultan with regard to planned Jewish settlement on the shores of 'Aqaba: 'The result was that the *firman* laid down the Egyptian frontier as drawn from Suez to El-Arish. The peninsula of Sinai, which had been administered by the Khedives of Egypt for the last forty years, would thus have reverted to Turkey.'[22] Cromer preferred to overlook the fact that the Suez-El-Arish line was the boundary laid down in the 1841 *firman* and restated in subsequent *firmans*, while the *de facto* administration of large sections of the peninsula had never been recognized as constituting a new boundary and was granted only as a security measure for the Egyptian pilgrimage to Mecca.

When, following British pressure, the Ottoman grand vizier sent a telegram to the Khedive recognizing the continued Egyptian administration in the interior of Sinai, he emphasized that this was not a new frontier, but a continuation of the administrative *status quo*.[23] Cromer's claim that the Sultan thereby recognized the line leading from El-Arish to 'Aqaba as the Turco-Egyptian frontier, had no foundation whatsoever.[24] But Cromer's misinterpretation of the 1892 *firman* and of the grand vizier's explanatory telegram served from then onwards as a basis for British claims in the Sinai. On 13 April 1892 Cromer wrote to Tigranne Pasha, the Egyptian minister for foreign affairs, that he accepted the grand vizier's telegram as proof that the El-Arish-'Aqaba frontier had been recognized by the Turks. This interpretation was not binding on the Ottomans, nor was it claimed by the Egyptians. But, throughout the 1905–06 conflict and even many years later, it was referred to continuously by Lord Cromer and the British government as proof that their claims were justified.[25]

With the dismembering of Turkey after the first world war the problem of the Sinai was no longer a Turco-Egyptian problem. It is true that at least since 1882, following the British occupation of Egypt, it was Britain who was pressing her own claims in the Sinai, doing so through the Egyptian official channels but in many cases against Egyptian popular feelings.[26] Following the declaration of a British protectorate over Egypt in December 1914, Britain could no longer disguise the fact that it was her own interests, namely the Suez Canal, the protection of her route to India and her general strategic policy, which were at stake, rather than the defence of Egypt's historic boundaries.

The old Separating Administrative Line between the three regions under ostensible Turkish suzerainty, now became a border between British-controlled Egypt, Palestine and later Transjordan. In the years 1918–1922 there were major discussions in the British government regarding the exact demarcation of this border, in which such experts as Lawrence, Toynbee and Vansittart played a prominent role. For the purpose of our discussion these deliberations, which remain buried in the foreign office archives, are unimportant, as the Egyptian government was never involved, and the final decision was to leave the 1906 separating administrative line intact while the question of sovereignty remained in abeyance. The question of Egyptian sovereignty over the Sinai along the dividing line, which had never been recognized as a frontier, now appeared primarily whenever Anglo-Egyptian relations were at a low ebb. The following are but a few examples indicating both official and unofficial British thinking on this question.

On 26 November 1926, Sir John Fischer Williams, one of the three legal assessors of the post-first world war Reparation Commission, raised the question as to whether or not 'the Sinai peninsula is to be considered Ottoman Territory on 1 August 1914 within the meaning of Article 6.1 (a) of the Convention'.[27] The Lausanne Treaty of 24 July 1923 specified in Article 17 that 'the renunciation by Turkey of all rights and titles over Egypt and the Sudan will take effect as from 5 November 1914'.[28] It therefore seemed that whatever the actual status of the Sinai prior to the first world war, it was legally under the Ottoman Sultan who was, at least nominally, the legal ruler of Egypt until Britain proclaimed a protectorate over Egypt on 18 December 1914. But even if one were to argue that the Ottomans were legally absolved from responsibility over Egypt proper, the same did not apply to the Sinai peninsula. The foreign office held the view that while the Turkish government recognized the administrative powers of the Egyptian Khedive up to the Rafah-'Aqaba line, as delimited after the Taba incident of 1906, the actual frontier between Turkey and Egypt ran from Suez to El-Arish, leaving most of the Sinai peninsula under Turkish suzerainty. Thus, the Foreign Office argued that while Egypt had administered most of the Sinai peninsula for many decades prior to 1906, up to the line drawn roughly between Rafah and 'Aqaba, Turkey had maintained its legal status in this area even after the 1906 agreement, following the Taba incident, along the same frontier drawn on the map which had been annexed to the 1841 *firman*.[29] In its official reply to the query raised by Sir John Fischer Williams the foreign office therefore insisted that 'the boundary thus established [from Rafah to 'Aqaba] was in effect an administrative division between two Ottoman provinces'.[30]

The question of Egypt's frontier in the Sinai, which had been raised in the context of a reparation claim of the Sinai Mining Company, remained in abeyance for the time being. It is, however, interesting to note that while the old separating administrative boundary was being put forward by Great Britain in international forums as the frontier between Egypt and Palestine, British foreign office officials, in their minutes, emphasized the fact that it had never been recognized as a frontier.

Following the second world war, nearly thirty years after Turkey had stopped playing a dominant role in the region, the boundaries of Egypt in the Sinai peninsula cropped up once again, though in a somewhat different context.

In July 1946, at the height of the Sidqi-Bevin negotiation for a new Anglo-Egyptian treaty, the question of the Egyptian boundary was raised by Jennings Bramly.[31] According to Jennings Bramly who, as will be remembered, was directly involved in the 1906 Taba incident as a Frontier Administration Officer of the Sinai peninsula, the agreement signed in 1906 did not settle the legal question of the Egyptian boundary in Sinai. He therefore sought to know whether this boundary had been legally fixed after the first world war and suggested that if the *status quo* of 1906 had remained in force, England should claim suzerainty in that area by right of conquest. Bramly's suggestion was made in the context of the anti-British 'outrages in Egypt fostered by the present Egyptian leaders'.

The foreign office reaction to this suggestion was, not surprisingly, negative. In its reply to the charges raised by Bramly the foreign office admitted that the legal status of the Sinai had remained in abeyance. However, it stated, 'the fact remains that since the 1914– 1918 war the whole of the Sinai peninsula has been accepted by us and by others as Egyptian territory'. Moreoever, in one document the administrative line drawn in 1906 was recognized as the Egyptian-Palestinian border. Hence, the foreign office concluded, Bramly's suggestion is 'entirely outside the bounds of practical politics'.[32]

The foreign office minutes to this correspondence shed further light on the rejection of Bramly's views. First, it was emphasized that any such move would jeopardize the Anglo-Egyptian negotiations. Second, it was admitted that neither the Treaty of Lausanne nor the declaration of a British protectorate over Egypt had in any way bound the Sinai peninsula legally to Egypt. The only document which might imply a change in the legal status of Sinai was a letter signed by Lord Lloyd in 1926 in which he gave an assurance to the Egyptian government that the delimitation of the borders of Palestine 'in no way concerned the Egyptian-Palestinian frontier as defined in 1906'.[33]

It was less than a fortnight later that the foreign office had to deal again with the Sinai peninsula, though in the framework of a more far-reaching proposal. Amery, in a letter to Sir Anthony Eden, suggested that Britain should demand 'a 99 years lease of the Sinai and in return let the Egyptians have the Arab-speaking Sudan up to Fashoda'.[34] In dismissing this idea the foreign office emphasized two facts: first, that the Egyptian prime minister, Sidqi Pasha, would not agree to a lease of the Sinai and second, that the Egyptians would never accept half the Sudan 'having regard to the progress they have now achieved in regard to the whole of the Sudan'.[35] Amery's proposal was therefore dismissed without further ado.

Jennings Bramly, however, returned to the Sinai question in February 1947. In a letter to Lord Tedder, Bramly restated his reasons for questioning Egyptian claims over the Sinai:

1. The 1841 *firman* allowed Muhammad Ali to administer the area south of a line drawn between Suez and Rafah, for the Egyptian pilgrimage, but did not concede this area as part of Egypt.
2. In 1902 Lord Cromer acknowledged Turkey's suzerainty over that area though he refused its claim to administer it.
3. In 1906 the new administrative boundary was drawn but Turkish suzerainty remained unchanged. In fact the Khedive Abbas Hilmi stated openly that Egypt had no claim to sovereignty over South Sinai.
4. Lord Lloyd's confirmation of the 1906 agreement, made to the Egyptian government in 1926, meant in effect that 'Turkey was suzerain of South Sinai and Egypt administered it'.
5. As England had never claimed this area by right of conquest 'South Sinai therefore still belongs to Turkey'.[36]

Bramly suggested that this was the right moment for Britain to establish its rights on the eastern side of the Suez Canal by building military bases: 'Egypt will say nothing as it knows it can only prove Turkey the owner. Turkey may say nothing as it knows we conquered this country.' Bramly did not, however, leave the matter with Lord Tedder alone, but succeeded at last in persuading James Bowker, counsellor at the British Embassy in Cairo and with considerable weight in the foreign office, to take up the Sinai boundary issue. In a long letter addressed to his colleagues in the Egyptian department of the foreign office, Bowker took up Bramly's case and concluded by saying: 'The territory can be only British (by conquest), Turkish or No Man's Land. It is certainly not Egyptian'.[37]

Consequently the Sinai peninsula border was at last treated more seriously and a series of research papers dealing both with the history and the legal aspects of the Sinai was produced. The first paper, produced by C. Howson on 29 May 1947, supported the line propagated since 1906 by Jennings Bramly. It documented the history of the Sinai peninsula borders proving clearly that 'the Eastern boundary of the "privileged" Egyptian Khedivate [was] a line running from Suez to El Arish'. Though Egypt enjoyed administrative rights over eastern Sinai – on account of the pilgrimage – Egypt never claimed sovereignty over the peninsula until 1947. According to Howson, Egypt's revived interest in the Sinai might be due to '(*a*) the falling-off of British prestige in the Middle East, (*b*) her desire to be responsible for her own defence when we withdraw, (*c*) her fear of a strong and active Zionist State in Palestine, and (*d*) her desire to discover mineral wealth'. In concluding his case, Howson stated that 'there appears ... to be no legal owner of Sinai' and he suggested that 'in

The Sinai Peninsula in Anglo-Egyptian Relations 99

negotiations over both the future of Palestine and the evacuation of our forces from the Canal Zone, we have in the undetermined status of Sinai a means of jolting the Egyptians sharply, countering their wild claims to the Sudan and indeed a reasonable case for claiming Sinai ourselves for strategic reasons'.[38]

Two other papers, produced in July and October 1947 respectively, stated exactly the opposite view. They argued that Egypt was in fact the legal owner of Sinai, along the administrative line drawn in 1906, at least since the Anglo-Egyptian Treaty of Alliance, signed in 1936.[39] In arguing the case for Egyptian sovereignty in the Sinai the legal counsellor of the British Embassy in Cairo stated the following: 'There is a presumption in law that on 22nd [sic] February 1922 and on 26th May 1937, Egypt had a defined territory and ... Sinai up to the 1906 line is part of Egypt.' The reasons leading to this statement are that Egypt's eastern frontiers, though not specified either in the declaration of independence in February 1922, or in the Anglo-Egyptian Treaty of 1936, were never challenged by any of the powers that recognized her. Furthermore 'Egypt was admitted to the League of Nations on 26th May 1937 without a dissentient voice in the Assembly'. Therefore

the U.K. by its own acts and admissions not only since 1922 but also since 1936 has deprived itself of any claim to it [the Sinai] which it certainly could have made and enforced during the protectorate (and possibly might have made after it until 1936), and did not choose to. A British claim to sovereignty over Sinai would be rejected by the International Court of Justice.[40]

With the legal question thus disposed of to the satisfaction of the British foreign office, there still remained the possibility of obtaining a lease for the Sinai in order to evacuate the military bases from Egypt and Palestine, and thereby facilitating a new Anglo-Egyptian Treaty. This suggestion was made on behalf of the foreign secretary to the chiefs of staff on 14 November 1947. The foreign secretary based his belief that such a solution would be acceptable both on American support and on 'a more amenable frame of mind' which he felt was developing in Egypt.[41] In rejecting the foreign secretary's proposal, the chiefs of staff based their argument on the lack of facilities in the Sinai and for that matter in any of the other adjacent territories: 'there is no practical alternative to the use of Egypt because neither ports, railway facilities, roads, oil pipelines or labour are available in Cyrenaica, Sinai or Transjordan'.[42]

In conclusion there are several points which emerge quite clearly and have a direct bearing on the problem of the Egyptian border in the Sinai. First and most important, it is certainly true to state that Sinai was never within the *privileged territories* granted to the Khedives of Egypt by their Ottoman rulers. The only part of the Sinai ever to be included in the privileged territories to which the Egyptian rulers had a hereditary title was the north-western corner, leading from Rafah to Suez.

Second, there is every indication that legally the Sinai peninsula became 'no man's land' following the Treaty of Lausanne in which Turkey renounced its claims over all her previous imperial possessions. England could have claimed the Sinai, in the wake of the first world war, by right of conquest, or annexed it to Egypt. But it did neither, thus leaving the problem of sovereignty over the Sinai in abeyance. The fact that the question of the Sinai border was raised again and again in the British foreign office indicates at least confusion. Even as late as 1947, less than a year before the establishment of Israel, there were diametrically opposing views within the foreign office itself, while in 1951 Mr. F. MacLean, M.P., questioned Egypt's right over Sinai, stating that 'the mere fact of administration does not confer sovereignty'.[43]

Finally, between 1906 and 1954, when the treaty for the evacuation of British forces from Egypt was signed between the British and Egyptian governments, the question of Egypt's eastern boundary was never officially raised. True there are numerous queries in the files of the British foreign office, as well as questions in Parliament and references in the press. But British policymakers refrained from acting both because they regarded the evidence itself as rather shaky and most probably because they feared that by raising this point Anglo-Egyptian relations would deteriorate even further. While legally the question of this boundary might still have been open to doubts, its political validity seems to have been established by default at least since 1937, when Egypt in its present borders was accepted into the League of Nations. Furthermore, political realities in the Sinai peninsula clearly indicated its connection with Egypt at least since the Wajh incident of 1892. This is probably one of the reasons why Egyptian politicians refrained from raising the question of this boundary, as they regarded it as an accomplished fact. However, knowing as they did that legally speaking this frontier had never been determined, they accepted the vague assurances as stated in Lloyd's letter of 1926, rather than disturb what might have become a hornets' nest. The Sinai was again mentioned by Nahhas pasha in July 1937, while he explained to Sir Miles Lampson his opposition to a Jewish State in Palestine, as suggested by the Peel Commission. The idea of a Jewish State on Egypt's borders was, according to Nahhas, unacceptable since 'the Jews might even later on advance some claim to Sinai'.[44] When the question of Sinai was raised once again by the Egyptian government in 1947, Britain was on her way out and the danger of a Jewish state in Palestine was about to become a reality.

NOTES

1. 'Agreement signed and exchanged at Rafah on 1 October 1906 between the Commissioners of the Turkish Sultanate and the Egyptian Khedivate concerning the fixing of a Separating Administrative line between the Vilayet of the Hejaz and the governorate of Jerusalem and the Sinai Peninsula', in *British and Foreign State Papers*, Vol. 99, pp. 482-84.
2. Wilfrid E. Jennings Bramly (Bramley), MBE, MC, served in the Sudan under Sir Reginald Wingate, from 1901–1905, when he was appointed Frontier Administration Officer of Sinai Peninsula. Following the Taba Incident he was recalled to the Sudan – ostensibly because of Turkish pressure – until 1914. From 1914 to 1918 he served in Cyrenaica in the campaign against the Sanusis. In 1918 he retired and settled in what he called Burg al-Arab, 30 kilometres west of Alexandria, which he believed would become the Capital of the Western Desert. He was expelled from Egypt in 1955 and died in Florence in 1960. (Bramly is sometimes spelt Bramley; however, except when quoting I have followed Bramly's own spelling of his name.)
3. Piyade Mirlivasi Rushdi, *'Aqaba Meselsei*, Istanbul 1910–11 [in Turkish]. Rushdi's book was the main source for U. Heyd, 'The Gulf of Eilat Crisis of 1906', in *Eilat*, Jerusalem 1963, pp. 194-206 [in Hebrew].
4. On the Jennings Bramly papers see J. Marshall-Cornwall, 'An Enigmatic Frontier' in *The Geographical Journal*, Vol. CXXV, 3-4 (September-December 1959): 459-62.
5. 'Memorandum respecting the Turco-Egyptian Frontier', printed for the use of the Cabinet, 26 April 1906, CAB/37/83. 'Correspondence Respecting the Turco-Egyptian Frontier in the Sinai Peninsula' in *Egypt*, No. 2 (1906) CD. 3006; for later references see below.
6. Wingate to Owen, 3 January 1906; 'A short account of the boundary dispute and of its probable effect on the tribes' by W. E. Jennings Bramly [n.d.] addressed to R. C. R. (Owen?) The Jennings Bramly papers, Royal Geographical Society, London [Hereafter: Bramly's *Account*].
7. In later British documents two reasons are given: first, the murder of two bedouins and the determination to bring security to the region; and second, the suspicion that Turkey, due to its desire to extend the Hejaz railway from 'Aqaba to Suez was attempting to alter the *status quo* in the Sinai; see 'Sovereignty over the Sinai Peninsula', the Legal Counsellor of the British Embassy in Cairo, 6 October 1947, FO 371/63080, J. 4940, see Appendix B, pp. 108-9.
8. Wingate to Owen, 3 January 1906, in the Bramly papers; the el-Wedj [al-Wajh]

incident, refers to the Turco-Egyptian controversy over the administrative line in Sinai in 1892; for details see below.

9. Rushdi's reason for travelling to Syria was that 'Aqaba had been cut off from telegraphic communication with the Turkish capital due to a flood. Rushdi's account of the above differs in certain details. He claims that he ordered Bramly to leave immediately following his arrival and does not mention the fact that he was cut off from telegraphic communication (see Heyd, op. cit. p. 196).
10. Bramly's *Account*; 'Rushid' is a misspelling of Rushdi.
11. Quoted by Heyd, pp. 196-97.
12. Quoted from Bramly's *Account*. The island referred to is Jazirat Far'un, about 14 kilometres south of Eilat.
13. Cromer to Foreign Office, 11 April 1906 (Telegram no. 97), quoted in 'Memorandum respecting the Turco-Egyptian Frontier' Cab. 37/83, p. 6.
14. Cromer to Foreign Office, 11 April 1906 (Telegram No. 98), ibid.
15. Ibid.; in his *Modern Egypt*, Vol. II, London 1908, p. 269, Cromer devotes only one sentence to the Taba incident while he deals at some length with the Turco-Egyptian frontier controversy of 1892; for proposed borders, see map, p. 92.
16. G. P. Gooch and H. Temperley, eds. *British Documents on the Origins of the War 1898–1914*, V, London 1928, pp. 190-91.
17. W. E. Jennings Bramly, 'A short account of the boundary dispute and its probable effect on the tribes' (1906); for the geographical elements of the settlement based largely on the Jennings Bramly papers, see M. Brawer, 'Geographical Elements in the Formation of the Egyptian-Palestinian boundary', in *Studies in the Geography of Israel* (new series), Vol. VII (1970), 125-37 [in Hebrew].
18. Lord Lloyd who at that time was British high commissioner in Egypt does not mention the map in connection with the negotiations with Italy; see Lord Lloyd, *Egypt since Cromer*, vol. II, New York 1970, pp. 149-50. Bramly's dates are confused, the negotiations took place in 1925 and the map was obtained in that year.
19. Adolf Freiherr Marschall von Bieberstein was from 1897 the German Ambassador in Turkey, who propagated an active German pro-Turkish policy. In 1896 he was behind the famous Kruger Telegram, which created an anti-German uproar in Britain. On the German interests in furthering Abdül Hamid's ambitions, see also G. Martel, 'The Near East in the Balance of Power: The repercussions of the Kaula Incident in 1893', *Middle Eastern Studies* 16/2 (1980), pp. 23-41.
20. Addendum to Bramly, 'A short account of the boundary dispute'; Harry Boyle was the oriental secretary to Lord Cromer, who was then Sir Evelyn Baring.
21. Ibid.; this map was published by the Egyptian Government as an appendix to the Egyptian-Italian Frontier Agreement of December 1925, in the *Green Book*, Document number 6 (Cairo 1926). In a note published recently in *Middle Eastern Studies*, G. Biger proved that the above was not the original map of June 1841. The latter was discovered in the Turkish Archives only in March 1934 at the request of the British foreign office and was then photographed and sent to London; see G. Biger, 'The first map of Modern Egypt, Mohamed Ali's firman and the map of 1841', *MES*, XIV, 3 (1978), 323-25; The Sinai borders, however, are identical in both these maps.
22. Cromer, II, pp. 268-269.
23. For details see L. M. Bloomfield, *Egypt, Israel and the Gulf of Aqaba in International Law*, Toronto 1957, p. 114. The grand vizier's cable was sent on 8 April 1892.
24. Cromer, II, p. 269; see also Bloomfield, pp. 114-15.
25. Ibid., 115-18.
26. On the opposition of Mustafa Kamil's *Hizb al-Watani* to British policy during

the Taba incident see for instance Arthur Goldschmidt, Jr., 'The Egyptian Nationalist Party: 1892–1919' in P. M. Holt, ed., *Political and Social Change in Modern Egypt*, London 1968, pp. 308-33.
27. Sir J. Fischer Williams to Sir C. Hurst, 26 November 1926, FO 371/11614, J. 3207.
28. Great Britain, *Parliamentary Papers*, 1923, Treaty Series No. 16, CMD, 1929; in article 16 of the Treaty Turkey renounced all rights and titles respecting territories outside her new frontiers.
29. Minute by J. Murray in Fischer Williams to Hurst, 26 November 1926, FO 371/11614, J. 3207; this map, which had not been found for many years in the Egyptian archives, was sent by Turkey to the Egyptian prime minister at his request, in 1925, see fn. 21.
30. Hurst to Fischer Williams, 16 December 1926, FO 371/11614.
31. F. H. R. Maclean, MP, to H. McNeil, MP, 22 July 1946, enclosing a letter from Colonel Jennings Bramly, FO 371/53433, J. 3264; MacLean persisted in his view that the Sinai was not Egyptian territory and raised this subject again in the House of Commons in February 1951; see below.
32. H. McNeil to F. H. R. Maclean, 12 August 1946, ibid.
33. Minutes by Brading, Grey and others in ibid., quoting file J 397/16 from 1926; I have not been able to locate Lloyd's letter in the above mentioned file.
34. Amery to Eden, 22 August 1946, FO 371/53433, J. 4503. Eden who was then in opposition, forwarded Amery's letter without comment.
35. Minutes by J. M. H. Riches, 8 November 1946, ibid; in a brief minute by Scrivener the latter agreed to the above but added also that it would be 'a breach of our pledge to the Sudanese', 8 November 1946, ibid. The idea to lease the Sinai peninsula and use it as a military base for British forces, was already raised in the MacDonald-Zaghlul negotiations of 1924; see Lloyd II, p. 396.
36. Bramly to Tedder, 22 February 1947, FO 371/63080, J. 1422.
37. J. Bowker to D. W. Lascelles, 17 April 1947, FO 371/63080, J. 1845.
38. C. Howson, 'The Status of the Sinai Peninsula', 29 May 1947, FO 371/63080, J. 1422; see Appendix A, pp. 104-5.
39. J. Mervyn Jones, 'The Sinai Question', 8 July 1947 in ibid.; the Legal Counsellor of the British Embassy in Cairo, 'Sovereignty over the Sinai Peninsula', 6 October 1947, in FO 371/63080, J. 4940, see Appendix B, pp. 106-15.
40. Ibid.
41. M. R. Wright to Lieutenant General Sir Leslie C. Hollis, 14 November 1947, Top Secret Personal, FO 371/62988.
42. Minutes on ibid. giving the views of the Chiefs of Staff, 1 December 1947, FO 371/62989, J. 5901.
43. *Parliamentary debates (Hansard)*, Vol. 484, Col. 1271, 20 February 1951; quoted in Bloomfield, op. cit. p. 143.
44. T. E. Evans (ed.) *The Killearn Diaries 1934–1946*, London 1972, pp. 83-84; see also Ralph M. Coury, 'Who "invented" Egyptian Arab Nationalism?' (part 2), *IJMES* 14/4 (1982) pp. 462-3; Coury quotes Nahhas but adds that the latter was also prompted by his fear of trouble spreading in the Jewish community in Egypt, as well as by his genuine concern for Palestinian Arabs.

APPENDIX A
'The Status of the Sinai Peninsula'
by C. Howson, 29 May, 1947*

The continuous attempts of Colonel Wilfred Jennings-Bramly of Burg-el-Arab to show that Sinai is not Egyptian but British (or possibly Turkish) territory have finally, after twenty-two years, stimulated a good deal of interest in Service departments, notably the Admiralty and the Air Ministry.

Now that the need has arisen for evacuating British troops eventually from the Suez Canal Zone as defined in the 1936 Treaty, it is possible that Sinai's doubtful legal status might be of considerable value to us in any bargaining in the future. Colonel Jennings-Bramly indeed suggests we should gradually move our camps to the country just East of Suez and present the Egyptians with a 'fait accompli' which they would hardly dare challenge. (Nor presumably does Sinai come within the 'Unity of the Nile Valley'.)

Here is an outline of the events leading up to the present position:

1. By the Firman of 1892 the Porte re-affirmed its sovereignty over the Sinai and defined the Eastern boundary of the 'privileged' Egyptian Khedivate as a line running from Suez to El Arish: but giving Egypt administrative rights over Sinai as far East as a line drawn from Akaba to Rafa, on account of the Egyptian pilgrimage route in that territory. Lord Cromer supported this settlement since he wished to put the Sinai between the Turks and the Suez Canal.

2. In 1904 [sic 1906] the Turks re-occupied Taba, just west of Akaba and tried to assert their sovereign rights over the Sinai in other parts – e.g. by removing the Rafa boundary stones sometime later. For strategic reasons Cromer supported the Egyptian protests with a British warship and by concentrating British troops in Egypt. He prevailed on the Turks to agree to the setting-up of a boundary commission.

3. In 1906, the Turkish-Egyptian agreement was signed, re-affirming Egypt's administrative rights over the Sinai as far as the Rafa-Akaba line. No mention was made of sovereignty over the Sinai.

4. In 1914, when the British protectorate was proclaimed over Egypt, no Egyptian frontier-limits were defined.

5. During the First World War the United Kingdom defended the Suez Canal and conquered Sinai from the Turks.

6. When Egypt became independent in 1922 no mention was made of Sinai. When the Palestine mandate was set up in the same year, no mention was made of Sinai.

7. By the Treaty of Lausaune, 1923, Turkey renounced in Article 16 all territories outside certain defined boundaries, amongst others Egypt, Sinai, Syria, etc. Outstanding questions of ownership were to be settled by the parties concerned. Yet no arrangement was ever concluded on Sinai, Egypt has never claimed it and ever since Turkey renounced it there has been a legal hiatus in sovereignty, though Egypt has continued to administer.

*FO 371/63080, J. 1422.

8. In 1925, in answer to a Parliamentary Question, it was stated that the boundary line of 1906 was still recognised as the administrative line between Egyptian and the former Turkish territories. However, a minute by Sir Lancelot Oliphant on the same paper shows that the Foreign Office did not wish then to clarify the position about sovereign rights over Sinai.

9. The Egyptians in 1926, when recognising the United Kingdom's special position as the mandatory of Palestine, 'fait cependant toutes réserves en ce qui concerne les frontières e l'Égypte avec la Palestine, qui ne sauraient être en aucune façon affectées par la délimitation des frontières Palestiniennes', – the first interest Egypt had officially taken in her Eastern frontiers since 1906. There is however no mention of the 1906 boundary in the Egyptian note of the 15 February, 1926; but Sir Neville Henderson in asking that we may reassure the Egyptians mentions the 1906 line and Lord Lloyd was authorised to give an assurance that the frontier as defined in 1906 was in no way affected – still with no mention of the ownership of Sinai (J 1477/397/16 of 5th June, 1926).

10. In the 1936 Treaty there is no mention of the status of Sinai: it is free to be used by British troops as a training area.

11. There appears therefore to be no legal owner of Sinai. The Turks renounced it by international Treaty; Egypt has never claimed it but has administered it since 1892 (till recently under British Governors); we conquered it in 1918 and have moved our troops freely in it since then, though we have never admitted that any one is sovereign over it. Indeed, till recently the Egyptian Customs on the Egypt Palestine Railway route were a Kantara on the Suez Canal.

12. Lately, however, the Egyptians have moved their customs barriers to the Sinai frontier, have disputed our occupation of a camp-site at Rafa, and, more obviously, Hadi Pasha, Minister of Finance, stated that Egypt regards the Sinai as Egyptian State land, not only because it is part of her strategic Eastern approaches but because of its mineral wealth and the necessity to keep Zionists from 'buying' land in it.

13. It is not unlikely that Egypt's recent interest in the Sinai is due to
(a) the falling-off of British prestige in the Middle East,
(b) her desire to be responsible for her own defense when we withdraw,
(c) her fear of a strong and active Zionist State in Palestine, and
(d) her desire to discover mineral wealth.

14. I submit therefore that in negotiations over both the future of Palestine and the evacuation of our forces from the Canal Zone, we have in the undetermined status of Sinai a means of jolting the Egyptians sharply, countering their wild claims to the Sudan and indeed a reasonable case for claiming Sinai ourselves for strategic reasons.

APPENDIX B

'Sovereignty over the Sinai Peninsula'
by the Legal Counsellor of the British Embassy in Cairo.
6 October, 1947*

By the Convention of London of 15th July, 1840, Austria, Great Britain, Prussia and Russia agreed with the Ottoman Porte on the terms of settlement with Mohammad Ali. These were incorporated in a separate Act annexed to the Convention. They provided that if Mohammad Ali submitted within ten days he should be given not only the hereditary pashalik of Egypt but also for his life the title of Pasha of Acre with the administration of the Southern part of Syria which was defined to include Sinai. Should he not submit within ten days the offer was to be restricted to the hereditary pashalik of Egypt. *In the event Mohammad Ali withdrew his forces from the whole of Syria including Sinai and the authority of the Sultan was legally established there.* It was thus that the first Firman of 13th February, 1841, conferred on Mohammad Ali only the hereditary pashalik of Egypt within the limits shown on the map sent to him and that by the second Firman of the same date he was given for life the administration of Nubia, Darfour, Kordofan and Sennaar. It appears that towards the end of Mohammed Ali's life he was given for life the administration of the Ports of Massawa and Suakin together with the province of Taka (all of which depended on Jeddah) in return for an undertaking to pay an annual tribute. In May, 1865, these two towns with the province of Taka were committed to the government of Ismail Pasha from March 1865, and in May 1866, they were included in the hereditary governorate of Egypt and the territories annexed to and dependent upon it. On 8th June, 1873, a Firman was issued to Ismail codifying, amending and superseding all previous Firmans. On 7th August, 1879, a Firman conferred on Tewfik and his male descendents in order of primogeniture, Egypt within its ancient limits and comprising the territories which had been annexed to it. There is nothing in any of these documents to indicate the grant to the Khedive of Egypt of any rights whatsoever over Sinai and unless there were other Firmans which have been lost the inference must be that any arrangement for the Khedive to police any part of the Ottoman territories outside those expressly mentioned must have been an informal arrangement.

2. The scope, however, of the authority conferred on Egypt is indicated in the telegram of 8th April, 1892, which reminds the Khedive that the Sultan had authorised the existence at El-Wedjh, Muellah, Daba and Akaba, on the coast of the Hedjaz, as also in certain places in the Tor-Sinai Peninsula, of a sufficient number of police zones (zaptiehs) established by the Egyptian Government for the passage of the Egyptian pilgrimage by land. The telegram refers to the fact that all these places, i.e. including those in the Sinai Peninsula, are outside the boundaries of Egypt as shown on the map sent to Mohammad Ali in 1841. The telegram states (and no one has denied) that in consequence

FO 371/63080, J. 4940.

of this El Wedjh had recently been re-absorbed into the Hedjaz by imperial decree as also had Daba and Muellah. The telegram also states (and it has not subsequently been contested) that Akaba at that time was equally annexed to the Hedjaz. As far as the Sinai Peninsula is concerned, the telegram says the *status quo* is maintained and the Peninsula will be administered by the Khedivate as it was administered in the time of Abbas Hilmi's grandfather, Ismail, and father Tewfik.

3. There is nothing in the telegram itself either to assimilate the status of the Sinai Peninsula to the privileged territory of Egypt confided to Mohammad Ali in 1841 and his successors or to commit the Turkish Government to any distinction between the Sinai Peninsula and the places re-absorbed into the Hedjaz so far as Turkish title was concerned. Lord Cromer's insistence over the Firman of 27th March, 1892, was due to the implication as he saw it:

> 'that the Sinai Peninsula would for the future depend administratively not on the Khedivate of Egypt but on the Vilayet of the Hedjaz.'

The anxiety so expressed was not that Sinai was being withdrawn from the privileged territory of Egypt (in which it had never been) but merely that the Khedivate of Egypt would no longer administer in the old *ad hoc* way this territory outside Egypt. However, Lord Cromer's letter to Tigrane Pasha of April 13th, 1892, described the line running from near El Arish to the head of the Gulf of Akaba leaving the Port of Akaba in the Hedjaz and then went on to say that H.M. Government consented to 'the definition of boundaries contained in the present Firman as supplemented, amended and expanded by the telegram of the 8th instant ... which they consider as annexed to and forming part of the Firman'. This statement might be taken to mean, and was probably intended to mean, that H.M. Government regarded Sinai as included in the territory conferred on the Khedive and his eldest male descendents. But I do not think this is a construction which would necessarily be adopted by an international tribunal. For one thing, Lord Cromer's letter went on to say that H.M. Government could not admit that any existing territorial rights or claims are in any degree affected by changes which have been introduced into the language of the Firman or by their acceptance thereof. That reservation while no doubt intended to accrue to the benefit of Egypt against Turkey is general enough to save equally the territorial rights or claims of the Ottoman Sultan and merely throws the inquiry back to whether the Firman of 1841 together with that of 1865 (Massawa and Suakin) included Sinai, which they clearly did not.

4. The question whether the administrative rights of Egypt over the Sinai Peninsula (and parts of the Hedjaz) were enjoyed by Ismail and Tewfik by virtue of the hereditary grant or by virtue of some other specific grant, i.e. whether these had in any way been incorporated in what was granted hereditarily must be answered in the negative. Even in 1892 the Khedive refused to make such a claim, and it was Britain that insisted on the maintenance of the *status quo*.

5. Moreover the description in the 1892 telegram of the permission accorded the Khedive to exercise certain powers in the Hedjaz and Sinai appears not to imply the grant of any general authority over those areas but

only an authority to maintain here and there for the protection of the pilgrimage police posts or zones and this, I understand, is all that Egypt had ever done up to that time and from 1892 to 1905 she did not even do that. It may be that there was no other manifestation of governmental administration in these areas and that the exercise of this authority being the only exercise of any authority might be extensively construed as complete administrative authority, but that does not appear to be the real meaning of the description in the telegram.

6. However that may be, the letter from Tigrane Pasha to Sir Evelyn Baring of 13th April, 1892 refers to the telegram of the 8th April as having entrusted to the Khedive as to his predecessors 'l'administration de la Péninsula du Mont-Sinai', and the language of the latter's reply of the same date implies that the Sinai Peninsula would continue to be administered by Egypt. Sir Evelyn Baring was at pains in his letter to describe what he meant by the Sinai Peninsula: 'that is to say, the territory bounded to the east by a line running in a south-easterly direction from a point a short distance to the east of El-Arish to the head of the Gulf of Akaba ... The Fort of Akaba, which lies to the east of the line in question, will thus form part of the Vilayet of the Hedjaz'.

7. My considered view of the events and documents of 1892 is that H.M. Government endeavoured to commit Turkey to the inclusion of Sinai in the hereditary Khedivate of Egypt, but failed. In other words Sinai remained a part of Turkish territory in a way that Egypt was not. In fact in my opinion, if the distinction is permissable, which I think it is, Turkey retained sovereignty over Sinai but had only suzerainty over Egypt. Britain's object was no doubt then as later in 1906 to insulate the Suez Canal from Turkish administered territory and she used her power as military occupant of Egypt to insist on the maintenance of such Egyptian licence in respect of Sinai as previously existed, without managing to turn that licence into an hereditary title such as the Khedive had to Egypt itself.

8. It was not until 1905–6 that the Egyptian Government took any steps really to administer Sinai and then they were very minor ones brought about by the desire to bring to justice the murderers of two Bedouin. Mr. Jennings-Bramly's mission for this purpose and to establish the beginnings of a local administration was regarded by the Turks as a threat and they began occupying places considered by H.M. Government to be west of the line described by Sir Evelyn Baring in his letter of 13th April, 1892, to Tigrane Pasha. The Turks occupied Taba on the west coast of the Gulf of Akaba and the Turkish Government indicated to the Khedive that it claimed as Turkish territory much if not all of Sinai outside the 1841 limits of Egypt. Britain, not merely from her military position in Egypt which she set about reinforcing, but also by the concentration of a fleet at the Piraeus and the despatch of warships to Rafah and the Gulf of Akaba, threatened Turkey with force and brought about the exchange of notes of May 14-15, 1906. Prior to this the Turkish Commissioner (Moukhtar Pasha) in Cairo had claimed that for the purposes of the 1892 telegram the Sinai Peninsula consisted only of the territory south of a straight line from Akaba to Suez and that as the Egyptian frontier was the 1841 line from Suez to Rafah, the intermediate

The Sinai Peninsula in Anglo-Egyptian Relations 109

portion of Sinai was fully Turkish territory and hence incidentally there was no need to delimit or demarcate the Rafah-Gulf of Akaba line mentioned by Sir Evelyn Baring to Tigrane Pasha in 1892. When this was rejected by H.M. Government (because it would bring Turkish administered territory up to the Suez Canal) Moukhtar Pasha suggested as a compromise a line from Rafah to Ras Mohamed (the southerly point of the Sinai Peninsula) which would bring the Turks within easy striking distance of Egypt. This too, Britain rejected.

9. The exchange of notes of 14th-15th May, 1906, between the British Ambassador at Constantinople and the Ottoman Minister for Foreign Affairs described more precisely the line of demarcation of the Peninsula of Sinai for the purpose of giving effect to the maintenance of the *status quo* assured by the 1892 telegram. And it provided for a joint demarcation commission. Moreover the Minister for Foreign Affairs stated that the evacuation of Taba had been decided and orders had already been given to that effect. This statement was enlarged upon by the British Ambassador who referred to the declaration of His Highness the Grand Vizier that orders had been sent for 'the withdrawal of Ottoman troops into *Turkish territory to the east of Rafah*, should any have crossed to the *Egyptian* side'. The words underlined might be interpreted to mean that the territory west of the line, i.e. Sinai, was Egyptian to all intents and purposes in the same way as the rest of the territory entrusted to the Khedive and no longer Turkish in any more real sense than that territory. But this phraseology would, I think be insufficient to conclude the Turks against maintaining that a significant difference still existed so far as their title was concerned between Sinai and the rest of Egyptian territory. However, as far as Britain is concerned, this exchange of notes is described in 'The Map of Africa by Treaty' (Volume III, 3rd edition page 1199) as being relative to 'the tracing of a line of demarcation *between Turkey and Egypt*'. Although this work is 'not an official publication' it was subsidised by H.M. Government and the words chosen by the Librarian and Keeper of the Papers of the Foreign Office as editor would be regarded by an international tribunal as some evidence of the British point of view. The inference that H.M. Government regarded the line as a boundary between Turkey and Egypt, rather than between Syria and Sinai would be consistent with the undoubted wish of H.M. Government that it should be definitely that.

10. This exchange of notes was followed by an agreement signed at Rafah on October 1st, 1906 between the Turkish and Egyptian Commissioners for the actual demarcation of 'the Administrative Separating Line between the Vilayet of Hedjaz and the Governorate of Jerusalem, and the Sinai Peninsula'. Apart from describing in detail the agreed line and providing for the erection of boundary pillars, the agreement while allowing Turkish soldiers and gendarmes to benefit from the water remaining west of the Separating Line, forbade armed Turkish soldiers and armed gendarmes crossing to the west of that line. This agreement has most of the characteristics of an international boundary agreement, but it is notable for the careful selection of words to describe what could have been much more simply described as 'the boundary' between 'Egypt' and the other territories mentioned. And it is a perfectly fair inference that the choice of the words 'Administrative Separating Line'

was intended (by the Turks at any rate) to show that the Sinai Peninsula was not severed from the Turkish territory to the east in the same way as the privileged territory of Egypt was. Had Sinai intended to be conceded or entrusted to the Khedive in the same way as the privileged territory presumably some sort of *quid pro quo* would have been asked as in the case of Souakin and Massawa and Egypt itself or some words would have been used to indicate that it was to be held and administered in the same way as the rest of the territory entrusted to the Khedive. The absence of such provisions is significant. The fact that Kenya has for a number of years policed part of the Sudan has not been and is not regarded as giving Kenya title to that Sudanese territory.

11. On the whole I think that up to 1906 and thereafter until with the war of 1914 the U.K. took Turkey's place in relation to the Khedivate of Egypt, it was open to Turkey to argue with some prospect of success that Sinai stood in a different relationship both to Turkey and to the Khedive from the rest of the territory entrusted to the Khedive, and was still subject to Turkish sovereignty, while Egypt's was subject only to Turkish suzerainty.

12. The next question is what construction should be put upon H.M. Government's acts after the outbreak of war with Turkey in 1914 when the U.K. was freed from its obligation to respect the integrity of the Ottoman Empire, and Egypt and everything controlled by Egypt came into the legally unfettered hands of the U.K. More particularly is it necessary to decide whether those acts show that H.M. Government regarded Sinai as an integral part of 'Egypt' as was their obvious aim in 1892 and 1906.

13. In the letter addressed to Prince Hussein by the British Acting Agent and Consul-General on December 9th, 1914, the circumstances preceding the outbreak of war between the U.K. and Turkey are described, and the following statement occurs (italics supplied):

> 'Hoping to the last wiser counsels might prevail, His Majesty and his Allies, in spite of repeated violation of their rights, abstained from retaliatory action until compelled thereto by *the crossing of the Egyptian frontier by armed bands* and by the unprovoked attacks on Russian open ports by Turkish naval forces under German officers.'

The letter went on to state the forfeiture to H.M. Government of the rights over the Egyptian executive of the Sultan and of the late Khedive, and to say that 'of the rights thus accruing to His Majesty no less than of those exercised in Egypt during the last 30 years of reform, His Majesty regarded themselves as trustees for the inhabitants of Egypt', the best means of fulfilling this responsibility being by the formal declaration of a British protectorate. The letter then gives the new Sultan the formal assurances that Great Britain accepts the fullest responsibility for the defence of *the territory under your Highness* against all aggression whensoever coming.

14. The British notification of December 18th, 1914, that Egypt would be henceforth under a British protectorate merely says 'Egypt' is placed under the protection of His Majesty and that the suzerainty of Turkey over 'Egypt' is thus terminated and H.M.G. will adopt all measures necessary for the defence of 'Egypt' and the protection of its inhabitants and interests. The

The Sinai Peninsula in Anglo-Egyptian Relations 111

reference to the crossing of the Egyptian frontier by armed bands may refer either to the crossing of the Separating Administrative Line of 1906 or to the line laid down in 1841, but almost certainly it refers to the crossing of the former and in that case this letter would be evidence of the adoption by H.M.G. of the Separating Administrative Line as the 'Egyptian frontier'. The Egyptians would almost certainly allege that this was so.

15. Apart from this it is necessary to consider what the 'territories under your Highness' were considered by H.M.G. to be. This phrase would almost certainly cover Sinai as it does not describe in any technical way the privileged territory. Moreover there is no doubt that one of the 'interests' of Egypt mentioned in the British notification of the protectorate which H.M.G. intended to protect was Egypt's administrative rights in Sinai. It seems probably incontrovertible therefore that H.M. Government regarded Sinai as part of Egypt for the purposes of the protectorate. We must now go on to the Treaty settlement at the end of the war to see how it affects Sinai.

16. Three articles of the Treaty of Lausanne of July 24th, 1923 (in force August 26th, 1924) are particularly relevant. By Article 16, Turkey renounced all rights and title whatsoever respecting territories outside her new frontiers – this means that Turkey renounced all rights and title over or respecting Sinai. Article 17 fixed the 5th November, 1914 as the date from which the renunciation by Turkey of all rights and titles over Egypt and over the Sudan, was to take effect. Article 19, provided that any question arising from the recognition of the State of Egypt shall be settled by agreements to be negotiated subsequently in a manner to be determined later between the Powers concerned and that the provisions of the present Treaty relating to territories detached from Turkey under it would not apply to Egypt.

17. With regard to Article 19, Turkey was no longer one of the Powers concerned. Egypt was not one, but the U.K. was. And the U.K. secured recognition by the other Powers of her arrangements with Egypt so the question of what was the territory of the State of Egypt must be decided by these arrangements and the actions of H.M. Government, and these include the termination in 1922 of the British Protectorate.

18. The British Government's Declaration of February 28th, 1922, declared 'Egypt' to be an independent sovereign state, and the only territorial reservation was that regarding the Sudan, with respect to which the *status quo* was to remain intact. The question of fact is whether H.M.G. then and from then on regarded Sinai as part of 'Egypt' or on the contrary regarded themselves as the successors to Turkish sovereignty over that territory as against Egypt. One indication might be whether martial law, proclaimed on November 2nd, 1914, extended to it and was withdrawn from it as from the rest of Egypt, as it almost certainly did and was. Another indication would be whether Egypt with H.M.G.'s acquiescence continued to administer Sinai. Certainly the Governor of Sinai had been appointed by the Egyptian Government for a number of years, and the fact is that Sinai was incorporated in Egypt for administrative, judicial and political purposes. Law No. 15 of 1911 (July 1st) provided that the administration of Sinai should continue under the Minister of War and it set up an administrative and judicial organisation. On May 4th, 1917 the military set up a Frontier Districts Administration which

was attached to the Ministry of War by a Decree of October 5th, *1922*, i.e. after the termination of the Protectorate. For the purpose of electing deputies and senators Sinai it is believed was attached to the Governorates of the Canal and Suez under the Constitution of *1923*. It certainly was under the Electoral Law of *1930* (No. 38 of 1930). Law No. 115 of 1946 applied the general judicial organisation of Egypt to parts of Sinai and refers several times to the Egyptian-Palestine frontier.

19. Lord Lloyd in 'Egypt since Cromer' Volume II, page 396 (Appendix B) in a comparison of the proposals put forward by H.M. Government in the various attempts to negotiate a treaty with Egypt gives as a proposal by Mr. MacDonald in 1924 the following:

> '(c) Leasing to His Majesty's Government, in consideration of an annual payment of £.--- the *territory situated between the Suez Canal and the south-western frontier of Palestine and comprising the whole of the Sinai Peninsula*. In order that the independence of Egypt may not be impaired, His Majesty's Government agree that, except in the circumstances and for the purposes defined above, no British forces or military establishments shall be maintained *on Egyptian territory other than that defined in (c) above.*'

There is no reason to doubt the accuracy of this statement of Mr. MacDonald's proposal and the passages underlined clearly describe the Sinai Peninsula as Egyptian territory without qualification. Such a proposal could hardly have been made if H.M. Government regarded Egypt merely as the administrator of Sinai on behalf of the U.K. and not as the Sovereign Power.

20. To this may be added the statement presumably made by Lord Lloyd to the Egyptian Government in 1926 in accordance with instructions to the effect that the delimitation of the boundaries of Palestine required by the Preamble of the Mandate 'in no way concerned the Egyptian-Palestine frontier as defined in the year 1906'. Moreover for what it is worth the Report of the Palestine Royal Commission of July, 1937 (Cmd. 5479) refers to the line established in 1906 as the 'Egyptian frontier' (page 383), while map No. 1 (War Office 1937) purporting to show pre-war Turkish administrative districts comprised in Syria and Palestine, shows the territory lying to the west of that line as 'Egypt'. On the other hand all the maps in the report of the Palestine Partition Commission of October, 1938 (Cmd. 5854) show the territory to the west of that line as 'Sinai' while at page 107 there is a reference to the Palestine-Sinai frontier. The latter, of course, proves nothing either way but the former report might be cited as evidence that in the view of H.M. Government Sinai was part of Egypt.

21. When the Egyptian-Italian accord of 6th December, 1925 regarding the Western Frontier of Egypt was printed in *1926* in Cairo as an official document of the Egyptian Government (M.F.A. No. 1 — 1926) there was included a reproduction of the 1841 map and also another map comparing the frontier of 1841 'avec la ligne frontière (ligne en vert) actuellement en vigueur' and the latter showed the 1906 line as the eastern frontier of Egypt. True this official publication was designed to show the western frontier just agreed with Italy but it must be assumed to have come to the notice of H.M.

The Sinai Peninsula in Anglo-Egyptian Relations 113

Government who made no reservation about the eastern frontier and it would certainly be considered by an international tribunal as some evidence of their having acquiesced in this statement by Egypt of her frontier.

22. Coming to the Treaty of Alliance of *1936* when all the reserved points were disposed of and it may be said that Egypt became fully independent, there is, in Article 8, a recognition that the Suez Canal is an integral part of Egypt. Now if the line on the 1841 map from Rafah to the Gulf of Suez when properly related to the terrain in fact cuts off from Egypt's 1841 territory five miles (or any other part) of the Suez Canal, as is stated by Mr. Jennings Bramly and as it seems actually to do, the acknowledgement in the 1936 Treaty that the Canal is an integral part of Egypt would, I think, conclude H.M. Government since 1936 from maintaining that Sinai or that part of it traversed by the Canal, was not part of Egypt. At this point it is worth going back to consider the inferences to be drawn from the Suez Canal Concession and the Convention of 1888.

23. A Firman of 19th March, 1866, definitively approved the final Convention between the Khedive and the Suez Canal Company signed in Cairo on 22nd February 1866. This Convention provides *inter alia* for (a) occupation by the Company of land in 'Asia' (i.e. to the east of the Canal) at the Suez end, including that required for the purposes of the deep water channel of the Port of Suez; (b) the Canal and all its appurtenances to remain subject to the Egyptian police; (c) the Egyptian Government occupying within the lands appurtenant to the Canal any position, strategic or other, 'nécessaire à la défense du pays'; (d) at the end of 99 years the termination of the Concession to the Company.

24. The negotiation of the Concession was conducted throughout between de Lesseps and the Company on the one hand and the Egyptian Government on the other and the obvious inference is that the territory through which it was to run and which was conceded to the Company was wholly within the limits of Egypt proper. At all events there is nothing in the Concession whereby any distinction is drawn between lands within the 1841 limits of Egypt and those outside those limits, e.g. Sinai. It is worth noticing too that the Concession approved by the Sultan was one with a Company in which the Powers were substantially interested and could not, therefore, be abrogated at any time as a purely domestic arrangement between the Sultan and the Khedive might have been, e.g. permission to the Khedive to administer Sinai.

25. On 27th May, 1866 (that is, two months later) a Firman was issued to Ismail modifying the Order of Succession to:

> 'le Gouvernement de l'Egypte avec les territoires qui y sont annexés et qui en dépendent, et avec les Caimacamats de Sévakin et de Moussawa.'

Whether or not up to this time it would have been possible to argue that any part of Sinai outside the 1841 limits was a territory annexed to or depending from Egypt (I think *not*), certainly it would seem reasonable to consider that part of Sinai included in the Suez Canal Concession as being so annexed or depending from Egypt from then on.

26. Moreover the Suez Canal Convention of 1888 imposed a régime which was not to be limited to the duration of the Concession, in other words a

régime unlimited in point of time. It also placed upon Egypt the obligation in the first place to see to the execution of the provisions of the Convention. One of these (Article X) expressly refers to the rights of the Sultan and the Khedive to assure the defence of 'Egypt' which surely must have inlcuded (in this context) the whole of the territory devoted to the Suez Canal. That same article provides that Articles IV, V, VII and VIII shall not interfere with any measures the Ottoman Government considers necessary to assure the defence 'de ses autres possessions situées sur la côte orientale de la Mer Rouge' which seems to distinguish these, quite naturally, from Egypt, i.e. Egypt including the Canal and thus a part of Sinai outside the 1841 limits of Egypt.

27. To round off this diversion to consider the implications of the international arrangements concerning the Suez Canal so far as they affect Sinai, it must be observed that the exchange of notes between the Earl of Perth and Count Ciano of 16th April, 1938, reconfirmed the intention of H.M. Government and the Italian Government always to respect and abide by the provisions of the Suez Canal Convention of 1888 and was communicated by both the same day to the Egyptian Minister in Rome as 'the representative of *the territorial power concerned*' who replied that the 'Egyptian Government, *as the territorial power concerned*, took note of the intention of the Government of the U.K. and the Italian Government and *associated themselves therewith*'.

28. These considerations seem to be conclusive that part of Sinai outside the 1841 limits of Egypt had ceased to be subject to the possibility of severance from Egypt proper by Turkey (or from 1914 on by Britain), even though the rest of Sinai was subject to that possibility.

29. To return to the 1936 Treaty, under paragraph 2 of the Annex to Article 8 of the Treaty the area within which the British Air Forces which Egypt authorises to be stationed 'in Egyptian territory in the vicinity of the Canal' may be stationed extends five miles East and West of the Port Said – Suez railway from Kantara in the North to the Suez Junction in the South and possibly, as the R.A.F. claim, also five miles North of Kantara and South of that junction. The R.A.F. in fact maintain east of the Canal within this area a bombing range at El Shatt and the location of El Shatt or part of it is almost certainly east of the 1841 boundary and British occupation of it is by Egyptian permission which means the area is Egyptian territory, unless it is to be supposed that we occupy some areas within the Treaty description by our own right, subject only to such permission as is required of Egypt having regard to the administrative rights she enjoys in Sinai by our sufferance as successors of Turkey.

30. Again the same paragraph in providing generally that areas suitable for air firing and bombing ranges may have to be placed east of the Canal certainly does not suggest that the only area East of the Canal which is 'Egyptian territory' is that which tapers off to nothing at the head of the Gulf of Suez.

31. Again, paragraph 10 of the Annex in specifying the area to be available for the training of British forces at all times of the year mentions quite generally '(b) East of the Canal as required', and the last sentence of that

paragraph says the areas of the localities referred to above are included in the map which is annexed to the present Treaty. True, that map ends at 33°E longtitude (about 30 miles East of Suez) and does not include all of Sinai, but it does include a very substantial part of Sinai which lay outside the limits of Egypt shown on the 1841 map, and the Treaty clearly means that Egypt consents to its use for training. It would be difficult to argue that this consent was necessary only because of Egypt's administrative rights, the territory in question really belonging to the U.K. all the time.

32. Again by paragraph 11 of the Annex, the Egyptian Government is to prohibit the passage of aircraft over the territories situated on either side of the Suez Canal and within 20 kilometres of it (subject to certain exceptions). This area certainly covers part of Sinai outside the 1841 limits of Egypt. Is Egypt to prohibit such passage over that part merely as the administrative agent of the U.K. or is it not rather as the territorial (meaning sovereign) Power that Egypt is to do this?

33. Finally one of the essentials of a State in international law is that it should have a defined territory. While this does not exclude recognition of a new State which may have some boundary question to settle with other States, nevertheless I think the presumption is that if other States make no reservations on such questions at the time of recognition of the new State, the boundaries of the new State are recognised. This qualification of a State was not specified in the provisions of the League of Nations Covenant regarding new members nor is it mentioned in the United Nations Charter, but under either it would certainly be a good reason for refusing admission to an applicant whose territory was not reasonably clearly defined and acknowledged by others.

34. No question of Egypt's eastern frontier was raised after the end of the Protectorate in 1922 by the Powers that recognised her, and Egypt was admitted to the League of Nations on May 26th, 1937 without a dissentient voice in the Assembly. Nahas Pasha speaking for Egypt then said:

> 'Moreover Egypt, firmly established *within her frontiers*, has no need to cast envious eyes beyond her horizons. While she is happy on *her own soil* she knows that today a nation's happiness is never sure unless there is general tranquility.' (italics supplied).

35. It follows that there is a presumption in law that on 22nd February 1922 and on 26th may, 1937, Egypt had a defined territory, and the evidence above adduced is, in my opinion, conclusive that Sinai up to the 1906 line is part of Egypt and that the U.K. by its own acts and admissions not only since 1922 but also since 1936 has deprived itself of any claim to it which it certainly could have made and enforced during the Protectorate (and possibly might have made after it until 1936), and did not choose to. A British claim to sovereignty over Sinai would be rejected by the International Court of Justice.

4

THE 'THREE-LEGGED STOOL': LAMPSON, FARUQ AND NAHHAS 1936–1944

England's informal and formal occupation of Egypt lasted for nearly a century and came to its end only in 1956, following the Suez debacle. Why then choose the years between 1936 and 1944 as a topic for a special study? It seems that while one could point to many events during those seventy-four years as being of importance in Egypt's history, the years forming the topic of this discussion were so crucial that a sound understanding is essential. This is true for a variety of reasons of which the following are the most important ones.

First, 1936 was the year in which the Anglo-Egyptian treaty was signed, following many abortive attempts since the end of the first world war to reach an accommodation. This treaty could have placed Anglo-Egyptian relations on a new and more healthy footing. Second, the Wafd, which had been one of the major obstacles to such a treaty since the Milner-Zaghlul talks in 1920, was the signatory of the 1936 treaty and hence became a potential ally. Thereby England seemed, for the first time since the occupation of Egypt in 1882, to have the collaboration of the most important and representative party in the Egyptian political spectrum. Third, in 1936 young King Faruq was making his first rather hesitant steps on the Egyptian political scene. Here was a king who had not been embittered by the defeat of 1919 or by the endless bickerings around the 1923 constitution. Moreover, having received part of his education in England he might have been expected to be more amenable to British interests than his father, King Fu'ad, had been. Last, in 1936 it was already quite clear that Mussolini was carving out an Italian empire touching on Egypt's borders, both in Libya and in Ethiopia. This new imperialist threat seemed to have enabled Egypt and Britain to forge an alliance against a common foe.

'The Three-Legged Stool': Lampson, Faruq and Nahhas

True, Egyptian nationalists were eager to rid themselves of the Westminster connection as soon as possible. And yet this desire hardly indicated a willingness to become part of a new Italian empire which did not mince words about its plans to turn its new possession into a permanent haven for Italian settlers in Africa.

The period chosen for this study is important from an additional point of view. It is dominated by three personalities, representing the three legs of the famous 'three-legged stool' of Anglo-Egyptian politics. The first of these personalities was Sir Miles Lampson, a recent (1934) arrival in the Nile Valley who, following the 1936 treaty, became Britain's first ambassador in Egypt. The second actor was Mustafa al-Nahhas Pasha, Sa'd Zaghlul's successor as the Wafd's leader who had engineered the 1936 treaty and was now looking forward to a long uninterrupted period as Egypt's Prime Minister. These hopes were based not only on the Wafd's unchallenged majority among the Egyptian populace, but on two additional factors. First, now that a treaty had been signed there seemed to be a good reason for HMG to keep the Wafd in power as the only representative party and its most effective ally and collaborator. And second, the young and inexperienced King Faruq hardly seemed capable of undermining the Wafd's supremacy, as his father had done. This brings us to the third of the above mentioned triumvirate, namely King Faruq. Of the three he was the youngest and most inexperienced, so much so that at the outset it seemed to Lampson that instead of the 'three-legged stool' England would in the immediate future be faced with only one contender, namely the Wafd. And yet within less than two years Faruq had rid himself of the Wafd and had proved that he was definitely assuming an important role in the political arena.

The following then is a study of Egyptian politics in the years 1936–1944, embracing the main period of the second world war and attempting to examine the role played by the three main contenders during these years. The result of this struggle for power and its ensuing political repercussions were not only crucial for the personalities mentioned above but undermined the traditional power structure to such an extent that by 1946 it seemed to be ripe for radical change.

THE ANGLO-EGYPTIAN TREATY AND THE WAFDIST GOVERNMENT 1936–1937

On 26 August 1936 the Anglo-Egyptian negotiations, led by Sir Miles Lampson and Mustafa al-Nahhas Pasha respectively, led to signing of a treaty between the two countries. Reflecting on this treaty eight years later, Lampson (since 1943 Lord Killearn) spoke of the treaty in the following terms:

> That date marked the beginning of a new era in relations between our two countries. For although Britain and Egypt had become friends many years before that, the treaty ... set the final seal on our friendship and gave the world a fine example of cooperation between two nations with common interests[1]

Isma'il Sidqi Pasha, describing the same treaty ten years later, accused the Wafd of having signed the 1936 treaty for one reason only, namely its obsession with achieving power. He maintained that far from gaining independence for Egypt, Nahhas had indeed signed away Egypt's sovereignty by allowing British troops to be stationed on Egyptian soil.[2] Another more recent view suggests that the treaty was the product of Egyptian political concerns to which Britain felt forced to respond in consideration of imperial security. A study published in Nazi Germany during the war described the treaty as a great success for Lampson and Britain and blamed Italy's crude imperialism as the major reason.[3] These views are rather partial and based either on political motives or on a superficial understanding of the events leading to the signing of the treaty.

It might be useful to state at the outset that the terms gained by Egypt under the 1936 treaty, though somewhat more advantageous, were not substantially different from those offered by England to Egypt in previous negotiations, especially with regard to the two major issues: the use of Egyptian military bases by British forces and the future of the Sudan. It would seem that Zaghlul could have achieved a not dissimilar treaty as early as 1924 following his negotiations with Prime Minister Ramsay MacDonald.[4] Why then was the Wafd more amenable to reach a compromise in 1936 than it had been previously? The Wafd under Nahhas had just emerged from a long period of futile opposition. Under the Governments of Sidqi and Mahmud, with an anti-democratic constitution and with Britain maintaining a neutral policy between the King and the Wafd, Nahhas realized that unless he came to an agreement with H.M.G. his chances of governing Egypt

"The Three-Legged Stool": Lampson, Faruq and Nahhas

were rather slim. Indeed, a recent study of the Wafd explains Britain's tolerance of the palace-dominated regime in 1930–1935 as an attempt to show the Wafd that a more reasonable frame of mind, leading to compromise, was highly commendable.[5] This hope seems to have been fulfilled in 1936 with the contribution of two major additional factors. First, the demise of King Fu'ad, (who had always been a disrupting element in previous negotiations due to his desire to overcome the danger of an alliance between the Wafd and England) had for the first time enabled the Wafd to play its cards without palace interference. Second, the Ethiopian crisis and the growing menace of an impending war, in which Egypt was bound to be of crucial importance, made a treaty more urgent than ever. In stressing this point during his talks in London in June 1936, Lampson agreed with Anthony Eden that 'the inclusion of Egypt in the British Empire ... [was] the only true solution of the problem'. However, this solution had to be shelved for the time being due to the Ethiopian crisis and to the emergence of the Wafdist led 'united front' in Egypt.[6]

Lampson's 'cautious optimism' was confided to his diary when he wrote on 2 March 1936, following the inaugural opening of the negotiations at Za'afran palace in Cairo:

So here we are, well and truly launched. Who would dare say how it is going to eventuate? I suppose the betting is distinctly against success, but personally I would not be so sure. Contrary to all probabilities I have a 'hunch' that the chances of success are greater than reason dictates.[7]

However, in a somewhat more sombre tone Lampson expressed some doubts about the outcome:

as the Egyptians are by nature foolish people and as in addition the delegation is composed entirely of self-seeking politicians.[8]

The treaty signed in August 1936 was therefore neither a British nor an Egyptian victory. On the Egyptian-Wafdist side, it was the result of twelve years of frustration in which the party, despite its undisputed overwhelming majority, had never been allowed to hold power for any length of time. With the death of its arch-rival, King Fu'ad, and the newly signed treaty with Britain, the Wafd looked forward to a long and undisputed period of power. On the British side it was viewed as a long overdue recognition by Egypt of Britain's unique role and predominant interest in the Suez Canal and the Nile Valley. True, it promised British military evacuation from Egypt's population centres and opened the way for further British concession within ten or twenty years. Yet in the meantime it provided England with the collaborative atmosphere it had sought in vain in the Nile valley since the end of the first world war. This became even more important in the face of the new challenges in Africa and Europe emanating from fascist Italy and Nazi Germany respectively.

'Abd al-'Azim Ramadan enumerated several reasons for the Wafd's collaboration with the British authorities in the years 1936–1939: first, the King's attempt, aided by 'Ali Mahir and Shaykh Mustafa al-Maraghi, to rid himself of constitutional government and to exploit Islam in order to strengthen his position; second, having just engineered the Anglo-Egyptian treaty, Nahhas realized that he needed Lampson's backing in order to remain in power; third, the King was trying his utmost to gain the support of the army, through promotions, increases in officers' pay and the like. Nahhas, on the other hand, introduced a new law creating a Supreme Defence Council in order to sever the direct link between the King and the army high command. Last, the dissension within the Wafd, which culminated in the expulsion of Ahmad Mahir, Mahmud Fahmi al-Nuqrashi and their supporters in 1937, was instigated by the King's men, especially 'Ali Mahir, and thus weakened the Wafd and called for closer collaboration with Lampson and the British authorities. In fact, Nahhas was already contemplating the deposal of the King, and for this he required the British Ambassador's backing.[9]

ALL THE KING'S MEN: 1937–1941

The Wafd, and its leader Nahhas, were the first to be rebuffed, as in December 1937, a little over a year since they had signed the treaty and assumed power, they were ousted from government in what was one of young Faruq's first demonstrations of power. Thus it seemed that Faruq, who was not yet twenty, had decided to follow in his father's footsteps rather than cooperate with the governing majority of the Wafd, as suggested by his mother, Queen Nazli.[10] His reasons for doing so were probably the result of his resentment of Nahhas Pasha's demonstrated paternalism coupled with his belief that with the help of the cunning 'Ali Mahir and the support of the Rector of al-Azhar, Shaykh Mustafa al-Maraghi, he would be able to undermine the Wafd's support and enhance his own popularity. The reasons selected for the ensuing conflict between the King and the majority party, were not really important. However, the bitter argument involved the two personalities mentioned above, 'Ali Mahir, as Faruq's choice to lead his Royal Cabinet, and Shaykh al-Maraghi, as Faruq's ally in his quest for a grand religious coronation ceremony.[11] In selecting these allies Faruq was gaining the support of such populist movements as the Muslim Brethren and Misr al-Fatah, who had already begun to undermine Wafdist support, especially among the students and the lower middle classes. In November 1937, a member of Misr al-Fatah, even attempted to assassinate Nahhas. The large landowners and the urban bourgeoisie, represented in the Liberal Constitutionalist party and the *Kutla Sa'diyya* respectively, were also happy to join in any anti-Wafdist crusade. Likewise there is no doubt that ever since 'Ali-Mahir's appointment, Faruq was even further alienated from the Wafd and every suggestion or request made by the Wafd was either held up by Mahir in the *diwan* or rejected outright. The final dismissal of Nahhas in December 1937 was therefore largely instigated by 'Ali Mahir with the young and inexperienced King falling into the trap of the 'slippery old schemer'.[12] The extent of Mahir's influence over the young King became even more apparent when in February 1939 Faruq bypassed his new Prime Minister, Muhammad Mahmud, and sent 'Ali Mahir and 'Azzam Pasha to represent Egypt at the London conference on Palestine. The slogans calling for an 'Islamic order' and for 'fundamental reforms' emanated from Faruq's new mentors and from their close associate Mustafa al-Maraghi. Very soon Mahir moved again, this time to get rid of Muhammad Mahmud, the new Prime Minister, who received a surprising phone call on 11 August 1939 requesting his resignation so as to make place for a new government headed by 'Ali Mahir himself.[13] While this intriguing was going on, Lampson and the British embassy continued to regard 'Ali Mahir as both efficient and trustworthy.[14] If one takes into account the fact that in the rigged elections of 1938 the Wafd was defeated by such slogans as 'a vote for the Wafd is a vote for the Copts', and that the moving spirit in this propaganda was none other than Mustafa al-Maraghi, 'Ali Mahir's and Faruq's close associate, the complacency of Lampson is even more surprising.[15] There are two possible explanations of this willingness to tolerate Mahir's ascendancy. First, a genuine ignorance as to Mahir's real motives; and second, a reluctance to intervene in Egypt's internal affairs now that a treaty had been signed. Indeed, a senior official in the foreign office regarded the very idea of Britain's intervention in order to restore the Wafd to power as incredible.[16]

It seems that Nahhas was much more realistic in his assessment of Britain's future requirements in Egypt. He guessed that sooner or later Britain would require a real ally in Egypt and hence would restore him to power even if it meant a row with the King. In an interview with Lampson in January 1940, he warned him that by avoiding an immediate crisis he would be held responsible for a political explosion which was bound to happen.[17]

'Ali Mahir's replacement of Muhammad Mahumud as Prime Minister had taken place while Lampson was on home leave. He was, however, surprised when, upon his return on 1 September 1939, he was told by Mahir that while Egypt would do anything to help Britain's war effort, he saw no need to declare war. Lampson regarded 'Azzam and Faruq, who were known for their pro-Italian leanings, as the real culprits. Realizing that short of dictation there would be no declaration of war, Lampson hesitated whether to force the issue.[18] However, following talks with Nuqrashi and Sirri, both of whom suggested strong action, Lampson asked London for authority to use force with 'Ali Mahir. His request was turned down, on Kelly's advice, stating that a declaration of war by Egypt was inessential and that the present situation held certain advantages for Britain.[19] Lampson was however, not convinced. In two further telegrams, addressed to Halifax, he described the pro-Italian atmosphere both in the palace and its entourage as well as in the army, and warned that Britain's influence in Egypt was being undermined.

Lampson singled out 'Aziz al-Misri, 'Abd al-Rahman 'Azzam and Salah al-Harb as the major culprits, and warned that sooner or later he would have to confront Faruq and even depose him, unless the King promised full cooperation. Both Kelly and Rose advised Halifax to support Lampson on this issue even if it meant the forcing of a Nahhas-led government on Faruq. However, Lampson's colleagues at the British foreign office dismissed the three personalities mentioned by him, as nonentities who should not be taken too seriously.[20] Furthermore, while al-Misri was described as 'a half witted doctrinaire', Kelly suggested that there were definite advantages resulting from his presence, since a weak and ineffective Egyptian army enhanced Britain's force and influence.[21] Lampson, however, continued to press for al-Misri's removal which he achieved in February 1940.[22]

Under these circumstances, the following episode seems to shed some light on the personalities involved. In May 1941 'Aziz al-Misri was arrested upon trying to fly from Egypt to Lebanon on his way to

"The Three-Legged Stool": Lampson, Faruq and Nahhas 123

Iraq, with two of his colleagues. In the ensuing trial, the British authorities were greatly embarrassed, since al-Misri proved that his whole trip was planned and executed with the blessings of British intelligence but without Lampson's knowledge. Lampson cursed the 'infernal military' and complained that it was 'really intolerable that an incident of that kind should occur in one's own parish completely behind one's back'.[23] The final exposure of al-Misri, in August 1942, as being connected with German espionage must therefore have come as a relief to Lampson. The two German spies who were caught by British counter intelligence exposed al-Misri as well as Capt. Muhammad Anwar al-Sadat and F/Lt. Hasan Izzet, and some civilians, as their Egyptian collaborators. One of their plans was to cross the lines in the Western desert in order to join Rommell's forces.[24] So much for 'Aziz al-Misri. As for 'Azzam Pasha, also one of 'Ali Mahir's supporters, Lampson reported that J. Heyworth-Dunne, of London University, 'a Muslim married to an Egyptian lady' had held long talks with 'Azzam who was then Minister of Social Affairs in Mahir's government and Commander of the Territorial Force. 'Azzam stated that if Lampson tried to depose 'Ali Mahir's government there would be an outcry throughout Egypt and the Arab world. He even warned of an armed uprising which he himself would lead with the Territorial Force, if Britain tried to restore power to the 'old gang of Pashas and Beys'. Lampson, however, dismissed 'Azzam as an idealist with half-baked ideas on Arab unity who constantly jumped from one ill-conceived plan to another, without seeing either through.[25]

Britain's ambivalence and her determination to stay out of Egyptian politics were therefore part of her policy even after the outbreak of the second world war. On 1 April the Wafd published its manifesto in which it enunciated its demands from Britain after the end of the war. While affirming its loyalty to the 1936 treaty and its support for democracy, the Wafd demanded an immediate end to martial law, the full evacuation of all British troops from Egypt after the war, and a recognition of Egypt's rights in the Sudan. The British foreign office regarded this as a clear confirmation of its views on Nahhas's irresponsibility.[26] Faruq, as might have been expected, expressed his satisfaction that Nahhas had played into his hands and told Lampson that it was time he realized how irresponsible the Wafd's leader was.[27] This view of Nahhas, which was shared by many in the foreign office, resulted in a letter to Lampson ordering him to inform

'Ali Mahir of Britain's total rejection of the Wafd's manifesto.[28] Lampson, though forced to act against Nahhas, resented the foreign office's attitude, which alienated the Wafd — which in his view still controlled between sixty and eighty per cent of the population — and made Britain a captive of 'Ali Mahir, who had no popular support and hence leaned exclusively on the palace.[29] Indeed, while Lampson agreed that Nahhas had to be rebuked, he was opposed to a harsh British reaction and suggested that Nahhas might have been misunderstood.[30]

On 16 June 1940 the Secretary of State for Foreign Affairs at last authorized Lampson to inform King Faruq that 'Ali Mahir had to be removed and replaced by a Prime Minister who would comply both with the letter and the spirit of the 1936 treaty. But even at this stage several of Lampson's colleagues at the foreign office still regarded his accusations against 'Ali Mahir 'to be too prejudiced to be worth printing'.[31] Following Lampson's interview with Faruq the latter protested to King George VI against what he called Lampson's interference in internal Egyptian affairs and warned that such interference would cause complications.[32] This brought about an even stronger reaction from the British War Cabinet which decided as follows:

> King Farouk must either fall in with our wishes or vacate the throne. The latter alternative would be welcome to us ... If Nahhas Pasha were unwilling to form Government on the conditions which we thought essential, the British authorities would have to govern Egypt under martial law.[33]

Thus the use of force leading, if necessary, to Faruq's deposal was already contemplated in June 1940, though some of the members of the Egyptian department regarded this as premature and dangerous as it was 'in effect a threat to break the Treaty of Alliance when we are hardly in a position to say that the Egyptians have themselves first broken it'.[34] Two days later Lampson was able to inform his colleagues, following his meeting with the King, that 'we may possibly turn the present corner without a change of monarch here'. True, Faruq had not yet agreed to send for Nahhas, as requested, but had stated his willingness to form a government on lines which were regarded by Britain as 'good for both countries'.[35] In the meantime Faruq exploited Lampson's apparent hesitation to force the issue of Nahhas and called upon Hasan Sabri, an independent politician who was known for his friendliness to Britain, to form the new government. There are conflicting views as to the reasons for Lampson's not forcing the issue despite his conviction that a Wafdist government was essential. Al-Tabi'i claims that the anti-Wafdist plot was engineered by Ahmad Hasanayn, the new chief of the Royal Cabinet, who, having replaced 'Ali Mahir wanted to enhance his own position in Faruq's eyes. He realized that sooner or later the Wafd would indeed return to power but he wanted to manipulate it in such a manner that it would occur on the King's terms and not under British pressure.[36] Lampson himself complained that while he had been willing to force Nahhas on the King, General Archibald Wavell, who had previously backed him, retreated at the crucial moment. Yet the main reason was probably a misunderstanding between the Ambassador and Nahhas since the latter, having been led to believe that Britain was supporting Sabri, refused to become Prime Minister if it implied the use of force by Great Britain.[37] Faruq thus gained another period of grace in which he was helped once again by the British foreign office, which advised Lampson to move with caution. When in August 1940 Lampson once again toyed with the idea of forcing a Wafdist government on the King, he was advised by his colleagues in the foreign office that this 'would not only be undesirable but also, in all probability a failure'. Indeed, both Lampson and Wavell were warned against any intervention unless public security or the prosecution of the war required it.[38] Hence, while Lampson could not openly object to the new Prime Minister, Hasan Sabri, or, after his death in November 1940, to Husayn Sirri's government, it became quite clear that with a pro-Axis Monarch, surrounded by an anti-British entourage, the Wafd presented the only acceptable alternative.

Following Antony Eden's visit in Cairo in October 1940, Lampson felt that he was now on much safer ground regarding the possible deposal of King Faruq. Eden sympathized with Lampson's ordeal in dealing with 'that boy' and even reached the conclusion, following a discussion with Egypt's major political leaders, 'that the only thing to do is to kick the boy out'. Lampson regarded this as a most opportune moment and asked the British Commanders in Chief, headed by General Wavell, to join him in proposing Faruq's deposal to H.M.G. However, following Wavell's objection, due to his fear of extremist reactions, Lampson decided to act on his own and asked Lord Halifax for permission to force Faruq's abdication when the time seemed opportune.[39] Vansittart in his minutes commented rather cynically: 'Unfortunately in the handling of this matter, as in others, Sir Miles Lampson has been only too prone to the tendencies of *une soupe au lait*, which boils up, over and down very quickly.' Vansittart's suggestion was to 'eject Faruq' and the sooner the better. Halifax in his reply was rather more cautious. He authorized Lampson to handle Faruq as he saw fit, provided the Egyptian government collaborated and Faruq could be proved to have contravened the 1936 treaty.[40]

By April 1941 the British foreign office, which had hitherto vehemently rejected any pro-Wafdist intervention by the British ambassador, began to have second thoughts. In a minute titled 'An Approach to the Wafd', Bateman and Seymour, both of the Egyptian department of foreign office, suggested that Lampson undertake 'a careful approach to Nahhas'. Their argument went as follows:

It would be a dangerous combination ... were the Wafd, representing 80% of the people of Egypt, to combine with the palace against us. In theory a combination between palace and people should be ideal; but we know perfectly well that any such combination would ... be most hostile to us. The whole of Egyptian history over the past sixty years has shown that the only combination which bids fair to work at all is one whereby the palace would be faced by the Embassy and the majority of the people.[41]

It was quite clear that while Sirri Pasha abided by the terms of the 1936 treaty and was therefore quite acceptable to the British, he lacked any popular support and hence was dependent on Faruq's whims. The return of the Wafd was thereafter only a matter of time.

The basic difference in the relations between Britain and the Wafd between the pre-treaty years and those after 1936 lay, according to Deeb, in Britain's willingness to support the Wafd against the palace. Young King Faruq, in those early years, possessed the popularity his father had lacked and thus was able to unite the anti-Wafdist opposition, as he did in 1937. Indeed it became quite clear that Faruq, having become the centre of the opposition, containing not only 'Ali Mahir or Mustafa al-Maraghi, but also Muhammad Mahmud and, after the Wafd's split in 1937, Ahmad Mahir and Nuqrashi, was less dependent on Britain and hence increasingly dangerous.[42] Another reason for Britain's willingness to support the Wafd may have been the latter's decline and hence increased dependence on collaboration with the British authorities. With the departure of large sections of the urban bourgeoisie, who had left the Wafd with Nuqrashi and Mahir in 1937–1938, the Wafd's power base had shrunk. To this one should add the fact that throughout the 1930s both Misr al-Fatah and especially the Muslim Brethren had already undermined Wafdist support among the *effendiyya*. Hence the Wafd, though still capable of winning in any freely conducted elections, could no longer be identified as *the* national movement of Egypt.[43] The third and probably dominant factor in Britain's gradual shift to a pro-Wafdist posture ever since 1939 was the realization that the Wafd was the only power in Egypt both capable and willing to support the Allies' war effort. With a pro-Axis King surrounded by a nationalist-Islamic anti-British leadership, the Wafd became the only effective and reliable alternative. True, the Sa'dists had openly declared their support for Britain and, unlike the Wafd, had even demanded that Egypt declare war against Italy and Germany. However, the Kutla Sa'diyya had no grass-root support and hence, with little parliamentary backing, had to depend on Faruq. The view which, according to al-Tabi'i, prevailed in both London and Cairo was that the Wafd would have to be brought back to power under British auspices so as to make its dependency on the British authorities as complete as possible.[44]

LAMPSON'S ULTIMATUM TO FARUQ, 4 FEBRUARY, 1942

The ultimatum submitted by Lampson to Faruq, on 4 February, 1942, has come to be regarded as a landmark in Egypt's political history. It humiliated the palace, and brought the Wafd back to power after more than four years in the political wilderness. Yet the Wafd's return was made in unfortunate circumstances, as it resumed power by threat of British military intervention, and not by its own power. Thus the following two years, during which Nahhas was Prime Minister heading a purely Wafdist government, witnessed a further decline in the Wafd's popularity and a parallel rise in the fortunes of anti-parliamentary movements headed by the Muslim Brothers. It may be useful to recall some of the comments made on this topic by historians and politicians in the past. John Marlowe dismissed the events in a few lines, substituting 'urgent request' for ultimatum. He concluded, however, that Nahhas's circumstances of assuming power 'presented his opponents with a deadly weapon to use against him as soon as British protection is withdrawn'.[45] A more detailed, but by no means accurate, evaluation is given by Z.M. Quraishi in his history of the Wafd. Following a description of the events leading up to the ultimatum and of the Lampson-Faruq confrontation that followed, Quraishi stated: 'This was the first time when the British Government intervened in favour of a popular movement in Egypt. The people welcomed it with a demonstration of enthusiasm and happiness.' However, Quraishi continued that despite the so-called demonstrations of enthusiasm, the circumstances of the Wafd's assuming power enabled the King to mobilize the support of all the anti-Wafdist elements and, by accusing the Wafd of betrayal, to save both his throne and his prestige.[46] In another study, assessing the impact of the 4th February 1942 events on Egyptian history, Mahmud Mutawalli tried to find rational grounds for Nahhas's willingness to serve under these circumstances. In his view, the unholy alliance which had hitherto existed between the palace, the minority parties and the British Embassy, had robbed the Wafd, the only representative party, of its true share in governing Egypt. Indeed, he stated that between 1878 and 1952 there were 70 governments in Egypt. Yet of all the Prime Ministers who served during that period, only Nahhas was dismissed by the King four times.[47]

Observers of Egyptian politics know only too well that a united anti-Wafd front was not a unique achievement and did not require a British ultimatum to bring it about. Furthermore, the Wafd had already been branded as traitor, in certain political circles, following the 1936 Anglo-Egyptian treaty. As for Faruq's regaining his prestige, B. St. Clair McBride, Faruq's biographer, takes a more careful and probably more realistic attitude when he describes the far-reaching consequences of Faruq's humiliation. He states that 'Lampson's action brought down the very Party the British had installed; it was the final inspiration and confirmation of their cause to those forces in Egypt working to rid themselves of Farouk and the British'.[48]

In his *Modern Egypt* Tom Little goes even further when he claims that 'Lord Killearn [Lampson] had wrecked the triangle of forces within which the political life in Egypt was evolving by creating an implacable enmity between Britain and the King'. He states, secondly, that 'the gross insult of February 4, 1942' widened the gulf between the King and the people. And finally, Little feels that the events of February undermined the popularity of the Wafd, which lost its militant nationalist wing to the Muslim Brothers.[49]

It is probably even more interesting to recall some of the comments made by Egyptians, both politicians and army officers, about the 1942 events. Dr. Muhammad Husayn Haykal, the deputy leader of the Liberal-Constitutionalist party and an intellectual of the first rank, played an active role in the events and described them ten years later in his memoirs.

Devoting a whole chapter to this one memorable day, Haykal stated:

February 4, 1942 is one of the darkest days in Egyptian history and in the history of England in Egypt. It is a day to be recorded in Egyptian history alongside the day of Dinshiway, or the battle of al-Tal al-Kabir, or the bombardment of Alexandria, or any of these days in Egyptian history, the memory of which cannot be erased throughout the generations.[50]

Haykal admitted, however, that despite his efforts he had not succeeded during the ten years that had passed since the events in uncovering all the details leading to February 4 and its historic happenings.

Three of the leading members of the 'Free Officers', Muhammad Najib, Jamal 'Abd al-Nasir (Nasser) and Anwar al-Sadat, mentioned the 1942 events in their writings after the 1952 revolution. Najib stated that Faruq's surrender to the ultimatum was his own breaking point and constituted one of the main factors leading to the officers' revolt in July 1952. Though Najib had been a keen supporter of the Wafd, he regarded their willingness to serve in government, under the threat of British bayonets, as an act of treason.[51] Nasser wrote in a similar vein when he defined the ultimatum as a catastrophe: 'Henceforth officers spoke not of corruption and pleasure, but of sacrifice and of their willingness to give up their lives to save their country's dignity.'[52] Sadat went even further when he described the February 1942 events as 'one of the crucial incidents in contemporary Egyptian history' and stated: 'the result of the British coup of February 4, 1942, was to impose upon Egypt two years of dictatorship by the Wafd – two years of nepotism, jobbery and speculation which thoroughly discredited the major nationalist party in Egypt'.[53]

The views mentioned above and many others besides, leave no doubt as to the impact of the February 1942 events on Egyptian history. However, a somewhat more detailed examination of the events leading up to the February 1942 crisis seems to be warranted.

Not surprisingly the intermediary between Nahhas and the British Embassy was Amin 'Uthman Pasha, who had been awarded a KBE for his services to Britain during the 1936 treaty negotiations. Amin 'Uthman had acted in a similar capacity on previous occasions and was regarded by the Embassy as 'very pro-British' and trustworthy.[54]

In an interview held in June 1941, with Mr. (later Sir) W. Smart, the British Embassy's oriental secretary, Amin 'Uthman conveyed Nahhas's views on Egypt's internal situation. Nahhas offered three solutions to the crisis in Anglo-Egyptian relations, all of which involved the dismissal of the government and the dissolution of the chamber of deputies in which the Wafd was in a minority. The three proposed solutions were '(1) A purely Wafdist Cabinet under his own premiership. This he considered the best solution; (2) A United Front Cabinet under his premiership; (3) A non-party Cabinet under, if desired, the Premiership of Hussein Sirry Pasha, with a United Front to support it'.[55] But Amin 'Uthman went even further and warned Britain that unless the Wafd returned to power he could not 'exclude the possibility of anti-British action on the part of the Wafd'. Therefore, he openly suggested British intervention in order to help Nahhas in achieving his aim, stating 'that the Wafd were quite convinced that we [the British Embassy] could do what we liked in Egypt and that a slight intervention on our part would result in their [the Wafd's] return'.

It is quite clear that the Wafd had timed its approach very carefully, as it closely followed the German invasion of the Balkans in the spring of 1941. It was also bound up with the growing feeling among the Egyptian ruling class and intelligentsia, which was further strengthened after the German invasion of Russia in June 1941, that a German victory was not only more likely than a British triumph, but was also the lesser of two evils. To use Lampson's words, the Wafd was 'using the present danger to facilitate their return to power'.

Lampson was quite willing to admit the desirability of strengthening Husayn Sirri's government, through Wafdist participation. However, both Lampson and the British service chiefs whom he had consulted were of the opinion 'that it was neither desirable nor practical politics for us at present to intervene to bring about such a solution ... Moreover, we could not be sure that a Wafdist Government would be amendable to our point of view'. Hence he concluded that the only practical measure was 'to continue to encourage the parties to come to some agreement that would ensure greater political unity'. This unrealistic wish was described by one of the foreign office officials as 'fantastic'.[56] However, it is absolutely clear that the idea of British intervention in Egypt's internal politics emanated in June 1941 from the Wafd and not from the British Embassy. In July and August there were additional approaches by the Wafd to the Embassy. Lampson maintained the position that due to the 1936 treaty, which Nahhas himself had negotiated, Britain had no right to intervene in internal Egyptian politics. In a message delivered to Nahhas through 'an intimate friend', Lampson asked Nahhas whether he seriously suggested that Britain 'impose on King Farouk a Government which he seemingly does not want'.[57]

A number of events which took place between June 1941 and January 1942 brought about a complete change in British attitudes. As the 4th February ultimatum was prompted largely by Lampson's assessment of the situation, it would be most useful to follow his reasoning as presented in a confidential memorandum to Eden, written after the events.[58] The first factor leading to the crisis was the gradual weakening of Husayn Sirri's position as Prime Minister, especially vis-à-vis the Palace. This was brought about gradually by 'Ali Mahir, who succeeded in persuading Faruq that

Hussein Sirry's loyalty to us [Great Britain] constituted subserviency to British interests ... Once assured of Royal support, all the reactionary anti-British elements inside and outside the palace, Watanists, Young Egypt, Moslem Brethren, the Azhar, Aly Maher Pasha's creatures scattered through the Administration, and his student organisation in the university, were marshalled in a continuous campaign against Sirry Pasha as the tool of the British.

This in turn weakened Sirri's position in Parliament, where, lacking a majority, he had to rely on other parties' support. With the Sa'dists, the Liberal-Constitutionalists and the Wafd, each clamouring for power, Sirri Pasha's position became intolerable.

Lampson, who regarded the internal political situation as the crucial point in Sirri's downfall summarised the position as follows:

No Government under the late régime could hope to cooperate with us and retain the King's support, without which, in the absence of popular backing, it could not handle the unrepresentative Parliament, on which the Government's continuance depended.

It was, however, Eden who took the initiative in October 1941 and asked Lampson to look into the possibility of bringing the Wafd back to power through the holding of free elections. Lampson, at that stage, had several reservations about forming a Wafdist government. Chief among them were the reluctance of the British military forces to use force, if necessary, and Lampson's fear that Nahhas might withdraw at the crucial moment as he did after the 'Ali Mahir crisis.[59]

Numerous internal problems added to Sirri's difficulties. The poor grain harvest in 1941 brought about a government order, emanating from the British authorities, to limit cotton acreage, aiming to bring about an increase in the supply of cereals. In addition measures were taken to prevent hoarding and to fix cereal prices. As most members of parliament were landowners, who could only be adversely affected by these measures, Sirri was forced to compromise, which in turn made his policy ineffective and brought about a constant rise in the cost of living. Still in the internal field, Lampson accused Sirri of being too conciliatory towards 'Egyptian mischief-makers', such as the Muslim Brothers 'whose continued internment was obviously to our mutual advantage'. If one adds to this the problems connected with censorship, which owing to Lampson's insistence was introduced into parliamentary proceedings, the unpopular and unstable position of Sirri's government was self-evident.

To complete the picture one would have to take a brief look at occurrences outside Egypt, both military and political. First there was the Rashid 'Ali uprising in Iraq, which created a feeling of unrest in Egypt. Then came British military set-backs in Libya with expectations of a successful German invasion of Egypt running high. Finally, in the sphere of external relations, came the 'Vichy Crisis' which served as a pretext for mass political demonstrations against the Government and its so-called British overlords, instigated by the Palace through 'Ali Mahir and Shaykh Mustafa al-Maraghi. The Vichy crisis was prompted by British insistence that Egypt suspend diplomatic relations with Vichy. The matter was delayed for several months owing to the reluctance of Faruq to comply with British wishes. When Sirri Pasha finally decided to act, in January 1942, he did so without consulting or acquainting Faruq with the proposed action, and hence was accused of violating the Royal prerogative. The King, fearing a direct confrontation with the British authorities, refrained from dismissing Sirri's government and chose the Egyptian Foreign Minister as a scapegoat. To quote from Lampson's memorandum once again:

> At this point I felt obliged to enter on the scene. I was compelled to point out to both Sirry Pasha and Hassanain Pasha that we could not acquiesce in this sacrifice of a Minister for Foreign Affairs and his Cabinet at the reiterated and urgent request of His Majesty's Government based on the treaty.

Consequently the dismissal of the Foreign Minister was not accepted. But the open confrontation between Sirri's government and the Palace, the mass demonstrations organised against him and the British authorities under the slogan 'Long Live Rommel', and his awareness that he could not muster parliamentary support, forced Sirri to tender his resignation to the King on February 1, 1942. In his diaries, Lampson recorded the events leading to Sirri's resignation in some detail. Lampson then asked for Sirri's advice as to who should form the next government. Sirri first suggested Haykal, Ahmad Mahir, or Barakat, and only when pressed by Lampson did he reply: 'send for the Wafd'. Lampson then met with Amin 'Uthman and received a promise that Nahhas was 'perfectly prepared to play if I would back him'. Nahhas however, refused to accept Lampson's idea of heading a coalition, because of his fear of Palace intrigues. On the same day Lampson prepared 'a cut and dried plan for dealing with King Farouk'. The plan included the King's abdication or deposal, in case he refused 'legitimate British demands', and his replacement by Prince Muhammad 'Ali or some other prince. Faruq would then be removed to another British territory.[60] In the investigation which followed Amin 'Uthman's assassination in 1946, Nahhas denied any knowledge of the Embassy's plans leading up to the February 1942 events. He denied having had any direct or indirect contacts with the Embassy while in opposition.[61]

A brief summary of Lampson's relations with the young King, some forty years his junior, may be helpful in understanding the subsequent events. When Lampson first met Faruq, in October 1935, he commented on his excellent English and wrote the following in his diary: 'I was frankly impressed by him – a nice honest lad I should say.'[62] Yet, while this first impression continued for some time, Lampson started to treat the young King in a paternalistic manner. He continuously rebuked Faruq for not devoting enough time to his studies and urged him to 'improve his mind' and his character. Lampson admitted that his 'lectures' to Faruq sounded rather 'governessy', but insisted that in fact the relationship remained friendly.[63] Even after Faruq had dismissed Nahhas and installed a non-Wafdist government, in December 1937, Lampson continued for a while to regard the King as 'a nice lad' who, he felt 'was essentially English in his outlook'. Hence, Lampson ascribed the difficulties he had with Faruq to the bad influence of 'Ali Mahir and his ilk.[64] However, by the end of 1938 Lampson had already changed his views about Faruq: 'no one ... has the guts to stand up to the boy. Indeed he is becoming a fair pickle and the latest reports show that even Aly Maher is losing what little influence he had over him'.[65] Lampson already foresaw the possibility that Faruq would be asked to abdicate and even wrote of a possible officers' coup which would end the dynasty.[66]

Since the beginning of 1939 Lampson increasingly regarded Faruq as a nuisance and, as time went on, believed with ever growing conviction that it would be desirable and wise to get rid of the King. To begin with, Lampson explained to his colleagues in London that, unlike King Fu'ad, Faruq, as a result of the 1936 treaty was 'very much the first independent King of an independent Egypt' and hence did not like advice from anyone, least of all from the British ambassador. Lampson had the following to say regarding Faruq's view of himself: 'In his own estimation he is very much of a man, very much of a Jimmy-know-all ... very omniscient.'[67] Two months later Lampson expressed his desire to 'deliver the strongest admonition' to the king, whom he now defined 'as an overgrown, overdeveloped boy ... [who] is getting badly out of hand'. However, Lampson was still reluctant to cause an open rupture and suggested reserving Britain's 'heavy artillery' for an opportune moment.[68] A contemporary report from Upper Egypt stated that Faruq's popularity had decreased considerably among the educated class, due to his autocratic tendencies, and among the Copts, as a result of his 'Islamic stunts'.[69] Lampson's reports on Faruq's declining popularity and low morals evoked the following positive response from some of his colleagues in the foreign office:

> The latent danger to our position lies not in Egyptian politicians, who we can always play off one against the other by exploiting their fears, hopes, and vanity, but rather in the possibility of a strong stand being taken against us by a King backed by an army with modern weapons.[70]

Hence, Faruq's loss of popularity was viewed 'with a certain satisfaction'. However, the danger of the army's entering politics in support of the King was also raised early in 1939 when, following the King's support for a pay-rise for officers, the latter cheered him, crying 'long live the Caliph' during the Friday prayers.[71] As far as Lampson was concerned the die had been cast against the King, and it was quite clear that he would have to be removed either by the British authorities or by an Egyptian revolution. Lampson regarded Faruq as 'uncontrolled, headstrong and irresponsible' and prophesied that the King 'was heading for an abyss just as Abbas Hilmi did'.[72] There was behind this resentment not only the political assessment that Faruq endangered Britain's position, but also the resentment of an older and experienced British diplomat, who felt himself slighted by an 'oriental boy' who was not yet twenty. This resentment was constantly expressed by Lampson both in his diary and his correspondence and may be illustrated by the following lines:

> Isn't it curious how history has a habit of repeating itself? Abbas Hilmi and Lord Cromer and now once more Farouk and the Embassy (far be it from me to compare myself to Cromer). I fear there is something not quite normal in the stock.[73]

A few months later Lampson again warned the foreign office of the possible need to force Faruq's abdication. This time his suggestion was backed by members of the Egyptian department while Sir Robert Vansittart, who was then chief diplomatic adviser to Halifax, wrote in the minutes: 'I have said for years that King Farouk will have to be liquidated and the sooner the better.'[74] But Lampson had to wait patiently until his chance arrived at last.

On 4 February 1942 at 3.00 p.m., the day of the British ultimatum, Faruq summoned a meeting at the palace, attended by seventeen leading politicians, including Nahhas, in order to reach a consensus which would enable him to remain in power without complying with British demands. The meeting and its results have been described by one of the participants, Muhammad Husayn Haykal, who clearly blamed Nahhas both for the British intervention and for its outcome. In his view British intervention could have been avoided had Nahhas agreed to head a national coalition government, instead of insisting on one composed purely of Wafd members. Even after the ultimatum had been submitted, Haykal felt certain that the British embassy would have agreed to a coalition headed by Nahhas. But the latter was unwilling to compromise and turned down all the suggestions made by the participants of that meeting. Nahhas consistently maintained the position he had taken right at the beginning, namely, he ignored the ultimatum and insisted that he would be willing to form a government only if directed to do so by the King, knowing only too well that this was tantamount to the King's submission to the British ultimatum. This was rejected by all the other leaders and consequently the only result of the meeting was a resolution signed by all of them (including Nahhas) protesting against British intervention in Egypt's internal affairs and condemning the undermining of Egyptian sovereignty and independence. This resolution, which was submitted to the British Embassy, on the King's orders, at 6.15 p.m. (fifteen minutes after the termination of the ultimatum) was regarded by Lampson as a rejection of his 'advice' and hence he demanded an immediate audience with the King. The following is Lampson's account of this historic meeting.[75]

At 9.00 p.m. I arrived at the palace accompanied by General Stone [G.O.C. British troops in Egypt] and an impressive array of specially picked stalwart military officers armed to the teeth ... Whilst we waited upstairs I could hear the rumble of tanks and armoured cars, taking up their positions around the palace.

The meeting between Lampson and Faruq was curt, and again among the many accounts written or told about this meeting Lampson's is probably nearest the truth first, because it was written immediately after the event and by one of the two main participants, and secondly because it does not glorify Lampson in any way but is rather a matter-of-fact statement. Lampson first read to the King an oral statement listing Faruq's shortcomings over the last few years and concluded that these misdeeds 'make it clear that Your Majesty is no longer fit to occupy the throne'.[76] Following the statement, Lampson handed to Faruq a letter of abdication 'saying that he must sign it at once or I should have something else and more unpleasant with which to confront him'. Lampson stated quite clearly that what he really wanted was Faruq's abdication and what is more 'Farouk would have signed the letter had not Hassanain intervened in Arabic' (which Lampson did not understand). The suggestion to summon Nahhas and to entrust him with forming a government of his own choosing was not mentioned by Lampson as an alternative to abdication. It was proposed by the King and Lampson reluctantly agreed. To use his own words once again:

It was sorely tempting to have insisted on King Farouk's abdication which I believe I could have extracted. But the course of wisdom seemed on the balance (very reluctantly I admit) to lie in allowing him to send for Nahhas. After all if he had agreed at 6.00 p.m. we should be glad to have accepted this solution: the fact that his acceptance came three hours later would hardly have justified a different sanction of ejection however tempting ... It was a difficult decision but I hope that all in all you will think it was right.[77]

This statement makes Lampson's position quite clear and helps to understand the less detailed and accurate versions told many years after the events by two of the participants in that drama, King Faruq and General Stone.[78] Lampson's sincerity, in this case, is again apparent at the very end of his statement, when he writes: 'So much for the events of the evening which I confess I could not have more enjoyed.' These rather flippant words, written as they were immediately after the meeting, tend to suggest that Lampson, though he would have preferred Faruq's abdication, was proud of what he had achieved and was in no way trying to hush up or re-write any of the day's events. However, Lampson failed to mention in his report to Eden that the possibility of the King's giving in to British demands after the ultimatum had expired had already been discussed over dinner at the embassy earlier that evening. The question had been raised by Oliver

"The Three-Legged Stool": Lampson, Faruq and Nahhas

Lyttelton, who had suggested that in such a case Lampson should not insist on Faruq's abdication. 'So I made up my mind then and there', Lampson wrote in his diary, 'that if the King caved in I should be wrong, taking the long and wise view, not to agree.'[79]

It was hardly surprising that Nahhas was bitterly attacked by Egyptian political leaders for his part in these events, though it is unlikely that they knew that it was Nahhas who had first proposed British intervention. Following a strongly worded letter of protest from Ahmad Mahir, president of the Chamber of Deputies, Nahhas pleaded with Lampson for an exchange of letters affirming British adherence to the terms of the 1936 treaty 'with assurances of non-intervention in internal affairs'.[80] Letters were accordingly exchanged on February 5, emphasizing that Nahhas agreed to form a government at the invitation of 'His Majesty the King in the exercise of his constitutional powers' and without any outside intervention 'in the internal affairs of the country and in particular in the formation or resignation of the Ministry'. These letters were duly published with the intention of rehabilitating Nahhas.[81] But, according to Muhsin Muhammad, the Wafd was the real loser since it lost the support of most of the *effendiyya*, the students, and young army officers while the bourgeoisie became even more anti-Wafdist. Faruq, on the other hand, received a new lease of life and became the hero of Egypt's independence. Lampson thus achieved the opposite of his original aim, since through the use of force Britain brought about the discreditation of the Wafd while enhancing the power of Faruq, whom it had wanted to depose. Had it insisted on Faruq's deposal, as planned, Britain would have taken a much wiser step.[82]

As for Amin 'Uthman, the initiator of the rapprochement between Nahhas and Lampson, he was advised by Lampson 'to decline ministerial office and to receive appointment as Secretary-General to the Cabinet where he could be more influential and far more useful to us as immediate shadow to Nahas Pasha'. A few weeks later, a royal decree was published appointing Amin 'Uthman to the post of auditor general, which was regarded 'as a cloak for position of liaison officer between Prime Minister and Embassy'.[83] Amin, who had been knighted by Britain, was assassinated in January 1946, probably for his assumed pro-British services.[84]

Lampson is quite outspoken on yet another point, namely who was responsible for distorting the truth about his historic meeting with Faruq:

to spare His Majesty's feelings, I had concurred in his request that our proceedings of that night should remain within those four walls, an undertaking which had been scrupulously respected on our side; but not so on theirs. For there was now talk among Egyptians of the Wafd having been imposed by British bayonets ... that was a distortion of the facts: British bayonets had been present for quite another purpose which we on our side had loyally not disclosed.[85]

Even more explicit was Lampson's letter of March 12, where he reviewed the Egyptian political scene: 'The public cannot, unfortunately, be told the true story. King Farouk, it will be remembered, particularly asked, in my interview with him on February 4, that the abdication issue should remain a secret between the four people present at the interview.'[86]

NAHHAS'S DEPENDENCY ON LAMPSON: 1942-1944

Looking back on the Wafd's first six months in office, Lampson felt that the party had fully repaid Britain for bringing it back to power. The central theme in Lampson's appraisal was his appreciation of the Wafd's courageous pro-British stand in the crucial months when it seemed likely that Rommel would conquer the Delta and the Egyptian countryside, while the Cairo mobs as well were openly expecting their salvation. The Wafd was steadfast not only in its sentiments but also in its actions, neither of which added to its popularity. Nahhas started off by banning 'Ali Mahir to his country home and did likewise with Salah Harb. He dissolved 'Azzam's Territorials and arrested their pro-fascist commander, Tahir Pasha. Furthermore the pro-Axis Royal Automobile Club, one of Faruq's favourite haunts, was closed by order of Nahhas, while its president Prince Omar Faruq was arrested alongside Nabil 'Abbas Halim, the labour union leader. The only political leaders who were willing to support the Wafd during these months were Ahmad Mahir, Muhammad Husayn Haykal and some other Sa'dists and Liberals, none of whom had any fear of losing their grass-root support, since they had none to begin with.[87]

But these first six months also witnessed the Wafd's recurring weakness on a larger scale than ever before. Favouritism, nepotism and politicization of the administration, swept the countryside. The Wafd was 'digging in', to use Lampson's words, and trying to make up for the five lean years it had spent in opposition. However, the most worrying aspect was the Wafd's attempt to gain a foothold in the army. The army, on the whole, had remained loyal to the King, and a secret association of Egyptian army officers, founded at about that time, called for sweeping reforms in the army and warned the government that unless it cooperated, the officers would act on their own.[88] The first real clash between the Wafd and the King also centred on the army and on the Wafd's demand to remove 'Atallah Pasha, the chief of staff. The latter's sole sin, according to Smart, the Oriental Counsellor, was that he was loyal to the King and referred everything to him and not to the Wafdist minister of defence, Hamdi Sayf al-Nasr. Smart was therefore opposed to British interference on the Wafd's behalf. He warned Lampson that while both King Fu'ad and Faruq had kept politics out of the army, the Wafd was trying to 'permeate the higher branches of the Egyptian army with Wafdist sympathisers'.[89] Lampson, however, decided to intervene and have 'Atallah Pasha removed from his post since he was too weak and could not keep discipline. The Wafd later agreed to compromise and to leave 'Atallah in his position in return for the appointment of a Wafdist undersecretary for military affairs.[90] The Wafd's success in penetrating the army's high command was limited primarily to the air force and constituted a cause for continuous clashes throughout the period.[91]

Al-Azhar also remained an area of constant friction between the Wafd and the Palace regarding the matter of new appointments. The reforms carried out under Shaykh Mustafa al-Maraghi's rectorship left all important appointments in the hand of the King but in consultation with the council of ministers. Here was a sphere for constant misunderstandings since the definition of 'important appointments' was rather vague and when the Government recommended to Faruq the appointment of a new *wakil*, the King insisted that the appointment was his sole responsibility. Clashes also occurred around the allocation of jobs to Azharite graduates in government schools, with the Wafd trying to incite the students against their Rector, al-Maraghi.[92] One is of course reminded of the 1937 crisis which had been ignited by the intended religious coronation ceremony of King Faruq. The ceremony had been proposed by the same Shaykh al-Maraghi and was bitterly opposed by Nahhas as unconstitutional.

If one had to choose a single issue, during the Wafd's period in government, which undermined its position and helped Faruq to regain the initiative it was the split resulting from Makram 'Ubayd's dismissal from the government, in May 1942, and his expulsion from the party two months later along with some fifteen Wafdist members of parliament. Makram had for fifteen years been the number two man in the party's leadership. He was intellectually far above his colleagues. But, most important, his position represented the historic alliance between Muslims and Copts in the Egyptian national movement which had started under Mustafa Kamil and continued through Sa'd Zaghlul to Mustafa al-Nahhas. Indeed, under Nahhas, Makram 'Ubayd had become the 'power behind the throne' and was regarded as the driving force within the Wafd both while in opposition and in power. Muhsin Muhammad lists the following as the reasons for the Nahhas-'Ubayd rift: first, the emergence of Fu'ad Siraj al-Din, a relative newcomer, as the number two man in the Wafd. Second, Nahhas overruled Makram 'Ubayd when the latter objected to irregular promotions and other financial benefits offered to Wafdist representatives and high ranking officials who demanded 'compensation' for the five 'lean years' during which the party had been in opposition. Last but not least, Makram clashed with Zaynab al-Wakil, Nahhas's wife, when he refused to bend the rules, as applied to her and her relatives. Once out of the Wafd, Makram 'Ubayd unleashed his legal training and his intellectual abilities against the Wafd. The famous *Black Book*, in which Nahhas and his entourage were accused of corruption and nepotism on a scale unparalleled even in Egyptian politics, was 'Ubayd's next venture. It was officially submitted to Faruq, as a petition for the dismissal of Nahhas, in March 1943, and received its main publicity in the British press, due to the censorship rules applied to its publication in Egypt.[93]

This was the situation when Lord Killearn (Lampson was made a Baron in the 1943 New Year's Honours List) returned to Egypt from his South African vacation early in April 1943. As might have been expected, the question of dismissing the Wafdist government on grounds of corruption was raised almost immediately by King Faruq. Killearn felt that Faruq wanted to have his revenge on Nahhas, as 'Public Enemy No. 1', so as to be 'better in a position to tackle Public Enemy No. 2 – to wit myself whom he obviously can never forgive for what happened on 4 February last year'.[94] Killearn was therefore prepared to back Nahhas to the hilt, but within the Embassy as well as within the British military authorities and the cabinet itself, there were different views. Killearn had himself warned Eden of the weakening of the Wafd as a result of the split in its ranks. He had written that there remained very little 'governing talent' in the Wafd, and had even implied that: 'the throne is still the most permanent native power in the land, and its cooperation with us, amidst the instability of Egyptian politics has been in the past and might be in the future most valuable'. Nonetheless, he firmly believed that the Wafd, which had proved its loyalty to Britain and was still the most formidable force in the country, should remain in power.[95] Killearn's position was endorsed by the foreign office which stated that Great Britain would not drop its friends – the Wafd – 'once we have sucked them dry', while it was quite willing to bear the charge of 'condoning corruption'.[96] An analysis of the *Black Book*, made by His Majesty's Crown Advocate, came to the conclusion that the evidence presented therein against Nahhas and his Ministers was inconclusive.[97] Another attempt at explaining the *Black Book* was even more far-reaching. While the author admitted that the charges made regarding the Wafd's corruption, even if inaccurate in detail were probably true in substance, he suggested the following explanation. First, corruption in Egypt was endemic and its extent was not surprising if one took into account that the Wafd, unlike its rivals, was a popular party of relatively poor men and hence required more 'public monies' than rich parties such as the Liberals or Sa'dists. Second, it was as wrong to judge corruption in Egypt according to British standards as it would be to judge British drunkenness by Muslim-Egyptian standards. Last, the outcry against the Wafd, from the Palace as well as from Egyptian poltiical circles and from Egypt's sizeable and wealthy foreign community, was politically motivated. The foreigners had always regarded the nationalist-popular Wafd as the main threat to their privileged position. The *Black Book* was therefore a 'heaven sent opportunity for getting rid of an enemy' under the convenient cover of 'moral disgust'. The author's conclusion was therefore in line with Killearn's but he also suggested that Hasan al-Banna and the Muslim Brothers whom he defined as the 'second most representative group in Egypt', should not be underestimated.

Killearn's view was first challenged by Smart, who suggested that in backing the Wafd England might repeat its mistake of 1937 when it had antagonized the King but had not been able to keep the Wafd in power.[99] Smart next suggested that the Embassy's intervention should be limited to a request that Nahhas be allowed to refute the charges made against him and the Wafd in the *Black Book*. But, he concluded:

The Wafd are on a downward grade and, whatever may be the result of this crisis, it will have accentuated their decline ... We do not want to appear as making a bargain with a corrupt Government, particularly as its lasting powers are not very great.[100]

Smart was therefore dismayed by the foreign office telegram of 21 April in which official preference was given to 'condoning corruption' over 'letting down our friends'. He cynically defined it as a 'theory novel in our imperial history'. Smart therefore suggested that the foreign office experts should study the facts before jumping to conclusions so as not to endanger 'the legend of British honesty' which had survived in Egypt since Cromer.[101] Smart's position received unexpected support from Sir Winston Churchill who preferred 'to let things crash and reserve our intervention for a later stage', since it was wrong to shield a corrupt government.[102] In a further note Churchill also opposed Lampson's suggestion that Nahhas be enabled to hold so-called 'free elections' and repeated his view that Nahhas should be left to his fate.[103] Killearn's suggestion that Nahhas be supported to the hilt was further undermined by the three commanders in chief who opposed any use of force should the King reject British advice. While this enabled some of Killearn's critiques at the foreign office to join the anti-Wafd camp, the ambassador was not swayed and insisted that 'weakness does not pay and never will in Egypt'.[104]

It was Eden who saved the situation as far as Killearn and Nahhas were concerned. In a minute addressed to Churchill, Eden repeated the belief that 'it would be more damaging to us to have to face the charge of dropping our friends than one of "condoning corruption"'. Eden added that corruption had not been proved and that in his view Nahhas should get a fair deal. Eden insisted that should Nahhas ultimately lose popular support and hence his power, Britain and the Wafd should 'part on good terms' since the Wafd was bound to come back.[105]

Thus the die was cast and General Wilson, commander in chief Middle East, was ordered by Churchill to back Killearn in implementing his policy of tendering 'formal advice to the Palace', even if it implied the use of force.[106] While this enabled Killearn to act as he had suggested, some of his colleagues at the foreign office were still trying to limit him so that the use of force or the deposal of King Faruq would not be left to his discretion.[107] In two further telegrams sent to Eden after he had secured the Wafd's remaining in office, Killearn insisted that the Wafd, regardless of the support it had lost,

"The Three-Legged Stool": Lampson, Faruq and Nahhas 143

would still win in any free elections with a comfortable majority of some sixty per cent. While it was true that the upper classes and the intelligentsia were largely anti-Wafd, it still enjoyed overwhelming support among the lower classes, who constituted the absolute majority. Hence Killearn had suggested to Amin 'Uthman, who continued to act as his 'confidence man' and as Nahhas's representative in his dealings with the Embassy, that the Wafd should change its role and, instead of flirting with the upper classes, become concerned with the poorer people and with their problems of health, housing and education.[108]

The final scene in this extended crisis, was played by Killearn and Faruq when the latter reluctantly agreed to maintain the Wafd in power. In summing up the *Black Book* crisis, Killearn insisted that the palace was deeply involved in it since is inception. Faruq and his supporters had helped Makram in gathering his evidence and in preparing his case against the Wafd. Moreover, the King had boycotted Nahhas and his ministers ever since the crisis started and hence both the opposition leaders and the public at large were certain that the Wafd's fate was sealed. Faruq and Hasanayn even cultivated the Embassy and promised to install a pro-British government once Nahhas was removed. It was only when they realized that the Embassy was adamant in its support of the Wafd, basing itself on 'Treaty rights' and 'security needs', that Faruq realized that he had to give in.[109] Smart's conclusion, while loyal to his superior, was somewhat different in its implications. He suggested cultivating the opposition leaders, since 'among them are many friends of ours who have collaborated with us at different times in the last quarter of a century and may quite well collaborate with us again'.[110] Scrivener of the Egyptian department wrote in a somewhat different mood when he suggested that 'the more we can return to the role of spectators the better. It will be impossible for Egypt to work out her own destiny until we have done so'. The Ambassador's comment was that the British authorities had never been and would never become 'mere spectators in Egypt'.[111]

One of the most important results of the *Black Book* crisis was a further strengthening of King Faruq's position. The King had submitted, under protest, to the Ambassador's pressure. But throughout the crisis he had maintained a pro-British stance and had conveyed a very clear message, namely that 'governments are transient features while the Monarchy is permanent and therefore more worthy of support'.[112] Killearn, though critical of Faruq, admitted quite frankly that the King's attitude to him and to the British authorities had become both friendly and supportive. Faruq's policy was, in Killearn's view, dictated by his belief that as long as he maintained friendly relations with the Embassy, he would sooner or later be allowed to get rid of the Wafd and then he would reign supreme. This was so since the *Black Book* crisis had again proved the total dependence of all the opposition parties on the Palace. Thus once Faruq had decided to submit to British pressures, all opposition to the Wafd had suddenly ceased, since without the King there was no one to carry the anti-Wafd campaign.[113]

It was therefore no surprise that some six months after the *Black Book* crisis, relations between Faruq and Nahhas reached a new low ebb. The excuse was the King's refusal to approve the appointment of several military commanders and of three new judges, nominated by the Wafd to the Court of Cassation. Killearn, who realized that Faruq was 'deliberately working to provoke a rupture', reiterated once again his firm support for the Wafd as the only possible government for Egypt as long as the war lasted.[114] Moreover, while he freely admitted the Wafd's increasing corruption, Killearn agreed with Amin 'Uthman that what was at stake was not just a conflict of personalities but 'democracy versus Palace autocracy'. His opening statement for the new year of 1944 was that 'the boy [Faruq] was definitely bad' and that a show-down was almost inevitable. A few days later he assured Amin 'Uthman that he would use pressure in order to force the King either to stop interfering or to let the Wafd hold new elections in order to prove its majority.[115] But Killearn's colleagues in the foreign office were far from happy with the new developments. They reiterated their belief that the Wafd had become extremely unpopular and that 'in contrast to the situation in 1942 there is neither the military necessity nor the political calculation to maintain Wafd in power at all costs'. While Killearn was therefore empowered to demand from Faruq that he live up to his undertakings, he was not allowed to use pressure, let alone force, without further consultations with London.[116] Though the crisis blew over without further complications, it may be worth noting that Smart once again warned his superiors both in Egypt and London not to side with the Wafd whose reputation had deteriorated even further. Moreover, Smart stated that in order to stop the Wafd's administrative manipulations, it was essential to uphold the power of the King.[117]

But the Killearn-Nahhas alliance was clearly on a downward grade. Grave food shortages and hunger in the Upper Nile, developing later into a malaria epidemic, were admitted by Killearn to have been brought about by the government's follies. Although he still insisted that Nahhas should be kept in office, he admitted reluctantly that once the war situation improved, the Wafd might have to be replaced. The only other ground for dropping the Wafd even earlier, according to Killearn, was that 'by their follies they so undermine their position that they no longer are of use to us'.[118] But some of his colleagues saw no reason to wait, since the British authorities were constantly being blamed for all the Wafd's shortcomings. Hence, the sooner Great Britain disengaged herself from internal Egyptian politics, the better it would be for both parties concerned, even if there were an 'ultimate risk of some slight and transient political upheaval'.[119] This feeling was, not surprisingly, shared by Faruq who submitted to Killearn a memorandum in which he explained his reasons for dismissing the Wafd as being dictated by his duties to Egypt and its people. Killearn, however, was not swayed and recommended, once again, that the King's plan be prevented, even if it meant the use of force.[120] Describing his meeting with the King in his diary, Killearn admitted that Faruq's memorandum was 'not at all badly drawn up'. But when the King accused Nahhas of royal ambitions, stating that 'there really could not be two Kings in Egypt', Killearn agreed saying: 'God forbid, we have found one quite enough.'[121] In a 'most personal and secret' telegram to Eden, Killearn went even further and stated his belief that it might be advisable that Great Britain assume more direct control of Egypt, so that these 'perpetual embarrassments' could be overcome.[122] Churchill, who was then in charge of the foreign office, decided to discuss the new crisis at a special meeting of the cabinet, and warned both Faruq and Nahhas against any hasty action. He stated that 'His Majesty's Government would almost certainly range themselves against whoever strikes first'.[123] The crisis was thus postponed while deliberations continued.[124] It was however quite clear that Killearn was losing ground both among his colleagues at the foreign office and among the British civilian and military staff in Egypt. The foreign office minutes were unanimous in rejecting his suggestion to use force. One of them suggested rather cynically 'I fear Lord Killearn is hankering after tanks again', while another claimed that the King's case was rather stronger than Killearn had suggested.[125] But even stronger opposition came from all British service chiefs who, in a special meeting of the defence committee, convened to discuss Killearn's proposed use of force, rejected his suggestion unanimously. Their reason, as conveyed by Lord Moyne, then Minister Resident in Cairo, was that the likely results of the use of force 'would constitute a greater threat to the security of our base in Egypt ... than any disturbances which might arise from the Wafd being out of office'.[126] While the meeting of the defence committee on 18 April was still discussing the alternatives, Faruq decided to sack Nahhas without waiting.

Killearn demanded an immediate audience with the King and warned him of the consequences, although he was not yet sure whether the war cabinet would in fact support his proposal to use force or would be swayed by Moyne and the service chiefs. He succeeded, however, in persuading Faruq not to act before the cabinet had reached a decision.[127] Consequently, despite considerable opposition, Killearn succeeded in saving Nahhas once again. The special meeting of the war cabinet, convened to discuss the 'Egyptian Crisis', decided to support Killearn's suggestion even if it implied the use of force. In explaining the resolution to Moyne and the service chiefs, Churchill reminded them that in the *Black Book* crisis they had also been opposed to the strong line suggested by Killearn, but that the latter had been proved right, the implication being that Faruq would cave in under pressure.[128] Indeed this is what happened and once again the rupture was avoided. But judging by the elaborate plans prepared by the Embassy under the heading: 'Procedure to be adopted in the event of King Farouk dismissing the present Government', the mood among senior British officials was far from optimistic. The procedure suggested for the event of a showdown was that the Wafd would remain in power, under British protection, while Faruq would either abdicate or be removed by force. The plan, which had been prepared by three senior members of the Embassy, headed by Smart, in collaboration with Amin 'Uthman, proved quite clearly that the Wafd's survival was totally dependent on British support. Even Nahhas's letter to the King, in which he was to insist on the Wafd's retaining power against Faruq's wish, was written in the Embassy. Moreover, this letter was not entrusted to Nahhas himself but to Amin 'Uthman and the whole plan was to be executed by him and Nahhas only if he received explicit instructions from the British authorities.[129] Killearn's doubts regarding the outcome of his policy were confided to his diary: 'I hope to heaven that I am right ...

"The Three-Legged Stool": Lampson, Faruq and Nahhas

personally I think that I am but I am once more surrounded by many doubting Thomases.'[130]

To Killearn's great relief the King once again gave in, on 24 April, and Nahhas remained in power. But Killearn was hardly complimentary in his attitude to the Wafd's leader: 'My intention is to have Field Day with Nahas once he has had his interview with Farouk ... In this I should tell him squarely that we have saved his face and saved his bacon now three times and that we cannot continue the process indefinitely.'[131] In a 'most personal' telegram, addressed to Eden, Killearn added that the whole crisis had been induced by Hasanayn Pasha, who was seeking the post of prime minister for himself. According to Killearn, Hasanayn had been 'very stupid' in planning the Wafd's dismissal, without first consulting the Embassy.[132]

Nahhas's audience with King Faruq, as well as Killearn's 'Field days' with the King and the Prime Minister, took place in the first week of May. The issues raised by Faruq in these audiences had, according to Killearn, no bearing on the recent crisis. They were: British policy in the Sudan, Churchill's reference to British protection of Egypt, and Britain's dictating the resolutions to the Arab delegates who were gathered in Cairo for a financial conference. All these instances were regarded by Faruq as proof of Britain's intention to dominate the Nile Valley in the foreseeable future and hence he requested Nahhas to protest against them. Nahhas, however, was unwilling to be drawn into another conflict, this time with Britain, having just been saved from the previous one by British intervention. But he warned Killearn that the Wafd's cooperation with Britain would soon be used by Faruq as an excuse for dismissing the government and accusing them of betraying Egyptian interests. Scrivener, of the Egyptian department, was rather uneasy about Faruq's intentions, feeling that the King was probably going to challenge both Britain and the Wafd for their threat to Egypt's independence.[133]

The opposition parties, as may have been expected, launched a bitter attack against British interference in internal Egyptian affairs. They regarded Killearn's policy as a renewal of the protectorate and as contravening the 1936 Anglo-Egyptian treaty. Moreover, Britain, who was fighting against Fascism in Europe, was, they claimed, supporting a Fascist regime in Egypt. In a manifesto signed by all the major opposition leaders and sent to the Ambassadors of the Allies in Cairo, these and other accusations were levelled against Killearn, while the King was praised for defending Egypt's democratic rights.[134]

Of the four party leaders who signed the manifesto, only Makram 'Ubayd was arrested, ostensibly for inciting his supporters to revolt. However, his arrest on 9 May 1944 may have been brought about by the resolutions passed by the Independent Wafdist bloc a few days earlier, in which anyone agreeing to serve in the Wafdist administration under Nahhas was defined as a traitor. More specifically, the Wafd was accused of having sold out on the question of Sudan's sovereignty while Nahhas was branded for his part in preparing the foundations of the Arab League, not in order to serve Arab interests but because 'he has been commissioned by the English to favour and execute Arab unity under British patronage'.[135]

When the next manifesto of the National Front was issued, on 13 June, it centred on three issues all concerned with Egypt's grievances against British policies. These included the demand for the evacuation of all British troops from Egypt after the end of the war; Egyptian control of the Suez Canal; and the realization of the unity of Egypt and the Sudan.[136] But while Killearn dismissed the opposition and their propaganda as ineffective, he warned Eden that there were real economic grievances in Egypt, as a result of the war, and that an armed uprising, as in 1919, was a definite danger.

It is in this connection that one should view the Wafd's attempts to marshal public support in the rural areas and among the workers. Fu'ad Siraj al-Din, who was strengthening his position as the Wafd's deputy leader, realized that Wafdist domination of labour syndicates was of crucial importance, especially among the railway workers. Killearn expressed some doubts as to whether the Wafd, in its present post-revolutionary mood, resembling 'Tammany Hall in its later stages', was still able to gain popular support, especially since repeated British interventions to save the Wafd had without doubt damaged its nationalist prestige.[137]

Killearn's clear ambition, however, was to undermine the power of the throne through a reform in Egypt's constitution, so that the King would be confined within 'workable, constitutional and democratic limits'. This, he knew, could only be achieved by the Wafd who, however, had no chance of succeeding without British support. Killearn used his influence with Eden as well as the good services of 'Abbud Pasha, a leading Egyptian industrialist, to convey this message to the British government. When no positive response came, Killearn, who was about to leave for a South African holiday, sent another personal plea to Eden in which he was even more outspoken:

"The Three-Legged Stool": Lampson, Faruq and Nahhas 149

I don't believe we shall ever have real peace or quiet in this country until either (a) the young man loses his job, or (b) his wings are effectively clipped ... I rather hope — selfishly perhaps — that this may happen in my time here. For I should like, as a matter of pure personal sentiment and romance, to see this drama played out to its final act.[138]

But Killearn's plea remained unanswered and one can only guess from the minutes to his 'personal and secret' telegram to Eden that the prevailing mood in the foreign office was against any further intervention in Egyptian politics. In fact Scrivener warned that the adoption of Killearn's policy would convince the Egyptians that Britain intended to control Egypt once again.[139]

Killearn's last few days before he left for South Africa were determined by his realization that a new crisis between the Palace and the Wafd was a likely possibility. However, he hoped that even if a crisis should occur the British government would uphold the Wafd despite his absence. He promised as much to both Amin 'Uthman and Nahhas, whom he met before his departure. He warned Amin 'Uthman against having another row with Faruq, especially over al-Azhar, but made to Nahhas the following promise:

British policy in Egypt as elsewhere was corporate and not individual and in an emergency His Majesty's Government would act with the same promptness and firmness whether I was at the local helm or not.

It seemed, however, that the prevailing belief in the circles close to the Ambassador was that Faruq had decided to wait for a rift between Nahhas and the British authorities which the King hoped was bound to come over the Sudan question. Indeed, Nahhas's parting words to Killearn were that Faruq had accused him of not being firm enough in his demands regarding the Sudan.[140]

On 12 September 1944, Lord and Lady Killearn left for South Africa, and less than a month later while they were still on leave Faruq finally had his way and dismissed Nahhas from office. The crisis which brought about the final rift between Faruq and Nahhas was defined by Terence Shone, the chargé d'affaires, as even more childish than previous ones. It started on 16 September, the last day of Ramadan, while Faruq was heading for the 'Amr Mosque. Near the Mosque streamers had been put up bearing the inscriptions 'Long live King Farouk', and 'Long live Nahhas Pasha'. The King ordered the director of public security, Ghazali, to have the streamers mentioning Nahhas removed immediately. Nahhas thereupon retaliated by having Ghazali suspended from office, pending an investigation. Shone tried to find a compromise, seeking the help of Amin 'Uthman, who was then on holiday in Palestine, as well as that of Hasanayn and other moderate personalities, but to no avail.[141] While he realized that Britain should not interfere in this matter, Shone was rather reluctant to be at the helm at such a critical moment without doing his utmost to save Nahhas. He tried, therefore, to persuade the foreign office to act as 'honest brokers' and press the two sides to accept a compromise. He warned Eden that 'if we stand back altogether ... Nahas Pasha is likely to say that we have let him down completely and he may seek to make considerable capital out of this'. But the foreign office, which had given in under Killearn's pressure on previous occasions, was adamant that he should keep aloof.[142] Even Shone's suggestion to seek Killearn's views met with the foreign office's refusal. They stated that since 'events must now take their course, the sooner the better'.[143] It had previously been agreed by the King (who, according to Hasanayn, realized the importance attached by Nahhas to the Arab unity talks, which were about to be inaugurated by the Wafd's leader in Alexandria), that the show-down should be postponed until after that event.[144] But even after Shone had informed Hasanayn that Faruq was now free to act and that there would be no British intervention, the King still hesitated and asked for a direct talk with Shone. 'Hassanein explained that King Farouk after his experiences of black book crisis ... no longer trusted Hassanein's versions of what we said to him.' An interview was therefore arranged for that same day and Nahhas was dismissed immediately afterwards.[145]

Two of the main actors had bitter feelings as a result of this development. Nahhas, who was now once again in opposition, was so antagonized by what he regarded as his betrayal that he refused to meet Shone or even talk with him over the phone. His message, conveyed once again by Amin 'Uthman, was that:

if he feels sorry about anything it is that he has incurred the King's displeasure because he stood by your side when you Britishers had very little chance. He is sorry that all this will shake the confidence of the Egyptian people in Great Britain and [in the] policy which for two years he was trying to build.[146]

Killearn, who read the news of Nahhas having been sacked in the South African papers, noted in his diary:

If it had to happen ... I am greatly relieved that it has been during my absence ... cannot be charged either by Nahas or the Wafd with having let them down ... Nahas did us well and one must stand by one's friends. That I have done

— up to the hilt: indeed many people think too much so. But if there had to be a change — and I reckon there had — better, ever so much better, whilst I was away.[147]

But clearly Killearn had lost the last round to Faruq since his aim, as he freely admitted, had been to either depose the King or 'have his wings clipped'. With a King whose authority was limited through an amendment in the constitution, and a Wafd dependent on the Embassy for its remaining in power, Killearn had in reality hoped for indirect British control over Egypt. But instead, one of the major results of his long interference in internal Egyptian politics had been the discreditation of the Wafd, Britain's most reliable ally since 1936.

In 1942 Campbell, who was to replace Killearn as Ambassador in Egypt, in 1946, composed a 'Note on the habitual sequence of political change in the Government of Egypt'. He viewed the changes in Egyptian internal politics as moving in a regular cycle, as follows:

These changes consist of three 'stock movements':
(1) A P.M. who is acceptable to both Palace and ourselves is stabbed by King — because he has become too dependent on us — on some trivial matter.
(2) A P.M. who is purely a Palace man, does not enjoy popular support and causes graft and discontent. We reluctantly interfere.
(3) A P.M. who is either Wafdist or at least enjoys Wafdist popular support. British interests and influence are threatened and in cooperation with Palace we interfere again and go back to stage 1.[148]

Killearn had been the first British representative in Egypt to break this so-called 'regular cycle' in order to cooperate with the Wafd against the King. This Anglo-Wafdist 'honeymoon' had survived despite numerous crises since 1936. Now, political leadership moved back to stage one in Campbell's cycle. However, with a strengthened King and a discredited Wafd, political power was shifting gradually from its constitutional pattern, with the ex-parliamentary forces gaining in popularity as a result.

NOTES

1. Speech by Lord Killearn, R. Cairo, 26 August 1944, FO 371/41332.
2. Bowker to Foreign Office, 11 October 1946, FO 371/53314.
3. Charles D. Smith, '4 February 1942: Its Causes and Its Influence on The Future of Anglo-Egyptian Relations 1937–1945', *International Journal of Middle East*

Studies, 10 (1979), pp. 456-457. See also, Conrad Oehlrich, *England's Hand in Ägypten*, Berlin 1940, pp. 57-58.
4. For details see Mahmud Y. Zayid, *Egypt's Struggle for Independence*, Beirut 1965, pp. 95-98; see also Lord Lloyd, *Egypt Since Cromer*, London 1933/34, Vol. 2, pp. 396-399.
5. Marius Deeb, *Party Politics in Egypt: The Wafd and Its Rivals 1919–1939*, London 1979, pp. 238-240.
6. Trefor, Evans (ed.), *The Killearn Diaries 1934–1946* ..., London 1972, (in future references *KD*), pp. 71-78.
7. *KD*, pp. 63-64.
8. Lord Killearn's unedited Diaries are deposited at the Middle East Centre, St. Antony's College, Oxford, (hereafter *KDSA*) entry for 9 March 1936; it is from these diaries that Trefor Evans selected the text which he included in the edited version of the diaries.
9. 'Abd al-'Azim Ramadan, *al-sira'bayn al-wafd w'al-ursh 1936–1939*, Beirut 1979, pp. 3, 36-37; see also Lampson to F.O. 30 Jan. 1939, FO 371/23304, Lampson reported that Faruq was inciting army officers against the government and that they greeted him crying 'long live the Caliph'.
10. Muhammad al-Tabi'i, *Min Asrar al-Sasa w'al-Siyasa, Misr ma Qabl al-Thawra*, Cairo 1970, pp. 177-79; according to Tabi'i the queen asked her brother, Husayn Sabri, to 'deliver' Faruq to the Wafd, so as to save him from the old court establishment which was instrumental in alienating King Fu'ad from the Wafd.
11. For details see al-Tabi'i, pp. 184-187.
12. Al-Tabi'i, 192-201; see also J. Berque, *Egypt Imperialism and Revolution*, London 1970, p. 561.
13. Ibid., p. 563.
14. *KD*, 1 September 1939, pp. 108-110; see also Bateman to F.O. 20 August 1939 and 25 August 1939, FO. 371/23306; yet in a letter sent to Halifax earlier in that year, Lampson suggested that 'Ali Mahir had been 'kicked out' of the Palace because of his intrigues during the St. James Conference on Palestine, Lampson to Halifax, 12 May 1939, FO 371/23305.
15. Deeb, p. 399; see also E. Kedourie, *The Chatham House Version*, London 1969, pp. 199-201.
16. Kelly's minute, 5 April 1939, in Lampson to Foreign Office 31 March 1939, FO 371/23305; Lampson reported that the Wafd was conducting a bitter anti-British campaign, exploiting Muslim feelings with regards to Palestine; see also minute by Kelly, 25 September 1939, on Lampson to F.O. 19 September 1939, FO 371/23306.
17. Lampson to F.O., 13 January 1940, FO 371/24622.
18. *KD*, pp. 108-110; Lampson to Oliphant, 14 September 1939, FO 371/23369.
19. Lampson to F.O., 16 September 1939, ibid.; see also Minute by Kelly, 18 September 1939; and F.O. to Lampson, 19 September 1939, ibid.
20. Lampson to Halifax, 20 September 1939, and 2 October 1939, FO 371/23307; Minute by Rose 7 October 1939, Minute by Kelly 9 October 1939, ibid.; see also al-Tabi'i, pp. 205-210, who confirms the view that Azzam was behind the opposition to a declaration of war.
21. Lampson to Halifax, 5 October 1939, ibid., Minute by Kelly 17 October 1939, ibid.
22. Lampson to F.O., 3 February 1940, FO 371/24623.
23. *KD*, pp. 170-171, 185-186; see also Lampson to F.O., 9 August 1941, FO 371/27431; the intelligence officers concerned wanted to use al-Misri's good offices in undermining the Rashid 'Ali revolt in Iraq.
24. 'Note on Aziz el Masri Pasha and his connection with the two German spies now in custody in British hands', n.d. [12 August 1942?] FO 141/852; see also:

"The Three-Legged Stool": Lampson, Faruq and Nahhas 153

'Report of arrest of F/Lt. Hassan Ezzet and Capt. Mohd. Anwar El Sadat, Commander Wireless Section, Jabal Asfar', 12 August 1942, ibid; see also Anwar el-Sadat, *In Search of Identity*, New York 1978, pp. 28-40; Sadat who was also involved in al-Misri's first attempted flight apparently did not know that it was engineered by British intelligence.

25. Lampson to Halifax, 5 February 1940, FO 371/24623.
26. Lampson to F.O., 1 April 1940, FO 371/24624 and Minutes to above, 3 April 1940, ibid.
27. Lampson to F.O., 3 April 1940, ibid., in his interview with Lampson Faruq dismissed the Wafd as an insignificant group.
28. F.O. to Lampson, 4 April, 1940, ibid.
29. Lampson to Horace Seymour (personal), 8 April 1940, FO 371/24624; see also Lampson to F.O., 6 April 1940, ibid., in which he writes of 'Ali Mahir's satisfaction with the Wafd having been rebuked.
30. Lampson to Halifax, 15 April 1940, FO 371/24624; see also Lampson to F.O. 6 April 1940, ibid., where he reports on his interview with Nahhas in which the latter reaffirms his and the Wafd's loyalty to the treaty and to Britain.
31. Minutes on Lampson to Halifax, 2 July 1940, ibid., see also Extract from Cabinet Conclusions, 170 (40), 17th June 1940, FO 371/24625.
32. Minute by C. J. Norton, 19 June 1940, FO 371/24625; see also Lampson to F.O., 17 June 1940, ibid.
33. Extract from War Cabinet Conclusions, 175 (40), 22 June 1940, F.O. 371/24625.
34. Minute by C. J. Norton, 21 June 1940, ibid.
35. Lampson to F.O., 23 June 1940, FO 371/24625.
36. Al-Tabi'i, pp. 185-193.
37. *KD*, 119-122; see also Lampson to F.O., 29 June 1940, FO 371/24625.
38. Minute by Thompson on Cairo Telegram No. 946, 25 August 1940; and Secretary of State to Lampson, 26 August 1940, FO 371/24626; Lampson denied any desire to intervene but reiterated his conviction that sooner or later it would be unavoidable, see Lampson to F.O., 31 August 1940, ibid.
39. *KD*, pp. 129-135, 15-24 October 1940; see also Muhsin Muhammad, *Al-Tarikh al-Sirri li-Misr*, Cairo 1979, pp. 145-146. The meeting with the Commanders in Chief took place on 23 October 1940; see also Lampson to Halifax (Most Secret) 27 October 1940, FO 371/24626.
40. R. V.'s [Vansittart] minute, 30 October 1940, ibid., Halifax to Lampson (Most Secret), 2 November 1940, ibid.
41. 'An Approach to the Wafd' by Bateman, 28 April 1941, and minute by Seymour, 28 April 1941, FO 371/27431.
42. Deeb, pp. 330-335.
43. Smith, pp. 458-459.
44. Al-Tabi'i, pp. 248-258.
45. J. Marlowe, *Anglo-Egyptian Relations 1800–1956*, 1959; 2nd ed. Frank Cass, London 1965, p. 318.
46. Z. M. Quraishi, *Liberal Nationalism in Egypt*, Delhi 1967, pp. 141-142.
47. Mahmud Mutawalli, *Hadith 4 Febrayir Sanat 1942 fi al-Tarikh al-Misri al-Mu'asir*, Cairo 1978, pp. 221-223, 235-249; see also Muhsin Muhammad, pp. 190-192.
48. B. St. Clair McBride, *Farouk of Egypt*, Cranbury, N.J. 1967, pp. 123-4.
49. T. Little, *Modern Egypt*, New York 1967, pp. 91-2.
50. Muhammad Husayn Haykal, *Mudhakkirat fi al-siyasa al-Misriyya*, Cairo 1951, p. 227.
51. Mohammed Neguib, *Egypt's Destiny*, London 1955, p. 14; see also Muhammad Najib, *Kalimati l'il-tarikh*, Cairo n.d. [written after 1972] pp. 11-13.
52. Gamal Abd El-Nasser, *The Philosophy of the Revolution*, Cairo n.d., p. 14.

53. Anwar El Sadat, *Revolt on the Nile*, New York 1957, pp. 44-5.
54. Lampson to Halifax, 10 July, 1939, enclosing revised list of Egyptian personalities (Confidential) FO 371/23362.
55. Lampson to Eden, 20 June, 1941, FO 371/27431; the following, unless otherwise stated, is from Lampson's letter.
56. Ibid., minutes by Seymour, 14 July, 1941.
57. Memo signed: M.W.L. [Lampson] 16 August 1941; Memo signed: M.W.L. [Lampson] 21 August 1941, FO 371/27432; in the second memo Lampson reported on a meeting with Amin 'Uthman; see also Smith, pp. 464-465.
58. Lampson to Eden, 12 March 1942, FO 371/31570; the following, unless otherwise stated, is based on Lampson's memorandum; see also Lampson to Eden, 23 September 1941, FO 371/27433 in which Lampson indicated that with both Faruq and the Wafd opposing Britain, he might be forced to intervene against the King and even bring back a Wafdist government, a suggestion he had rejected a month earlier.
59. Eden to Lampson, 24 October 1941, FO 371/27432; Lampson to Eden, 31 October 1941, FO 371/27434.
60. *KD*, pp. 197-206; see also Lampson to F.O., 2 February 1942, FO 371/31566; in the minutes all agreed with Lampson's plan, in case Faruq refused to cooperate. One suggestion was to send Faruq to Canada 'to indulge in winter sports'.
61. Muhsin Muhammad, pp. 217-223.
62. *KD*, p. 59.
63. Ibid., pp. 79-81.
64. Ibid., pp. 91-94; though in a note to the F.O. Lampson was already describing Faruq as the 'typical oriental despot'. Lampson to F.O., 29 November 1937, FO 407/221.
65. *KD*, p. 101.
66. Lampson to Oliphant, 23 July 1938, FO 371/21948, as quoted by P.J. Vatikiotis, *Nasser and his Generation*, London 1978, p. 40.
67. Lampson to Oliphant, 6 January 1939, FO 371/23304.
68. Lampson to F.O., 7 March 1939, FO 371/23304.
69. Lampson to F.O., 17 March 1939, FO 371/23305.
70. Lampson to Halifax, 2 December 1939, FO 371/23307.
71. Lampson to F.O., 30 January 1939, FO 371/23304; see also above.
72. Lampson to Halifax, 9 January 1940, FO 371/24622.
73. Lampson to Sir Horace Seymour, 29 January 1940, FO 371/24623; *KD*, pp. 113-114.
74. Lampson to F.O., 22 July 1940, FO 371/24626.
75. Lampson to Eden (highly secret telegram) 5 February 1942 (No. 491) FO 371/31567.
76. Lampson to Eden (highly secret telegram) 5 February 1942 (No. 492) FO 371/31567.
77. Lampson to Eden (highly secret telegram) 5 February 1942 (No. 491) FO 371/31567.
78. McBride, pp. 120-21.
79. *KD*, p. 212.
80. Lampson to Eden, 5 February 1942, FO 371/31567.
81. Ibid. In the Foreign Office the exchange was regarded as 'inconvenient' but unavoidable. 'Actually', wrote Mr. Scrivener, 'they alter nothing. If internal political developments appear to threaten the security of our base in Egypt we shall continue to give advice − letters or no letters'. Minutes to above, ibid.
82. Muhsin Muhammad, pp. 236-240.

"The Three-Legged Stool": Lampson, Faruq and Nahhas 155

83. Lampson to Eden (highly secret) 7 February 1942, FO 371/31567; Lampson to Eden, 26 March 1942, FO 371/31570.
84. Little, op. cit., p. 97. On Sadat's role in this assassination and his subsequent arrest, see *In Search of Identity*, pp. 59-61.
85. Lampson to Eden (highly secret) 11 February 1942, FO 371/31567.
86. Lampson to Eden, 12 March 1942, FO 371/31570.
87. Lampson to Eden, 28 September 1942, FO 371/31574.
88. Jenkins, Defence Security Office, to Tomlyn, Embassy, 23 July 1942, FO 141/841.
89. Memorandum by W. S. [Smart] 13 August 1942, FO 141/841.
90. Lampson to F.O., 25 August 1942, and 28 August 1942, FO 371/31574; Lampson to Eden, 28 September 1942, ibid.
91. Review of Political Developments in Egypt ... during the year 1942, Cairo n.d., FO 371/41326.
92. Ibid., see also 'The Azhar Crisis', Cairo, 5 January 1944, FO 371/41326.
93. Muhsin Muhammad, pp. 325-332; since the police were raiding the houses of 'Ubayd and his supporters in order to suppress the evidence, Hasanayn Pasha agreed to store the material in the Palace, for safe keeping, ibid., pp. 330-1; for a slightly different version, in which Hasanayn features as the main culprit, see al-Tabi'i, pp. 261-269.
94. *KD*, 8 April 1943, pp. 248-250.
95. Lampson to Eden, 31 January 1943, FO 371/35529; see also Lampson to Eden, 28 September 1942, FO 371/31574.
96. Lampson to Eden, 14 April 1943, FO 371/35531; Lampson to F.O., 18 April 1943, FO 371/35532; F.O. to Lampson, 21 April 1943, FO 371/35531.
97. 'Analysis made by H.M. Crown Advocate in Egypt of the Black Book Charges' (J. 1888, n.d.) FO 371/35532.
98. Kellar to Scrivener, 7 June 1943 'The Black Book and its Moral' (most secret) FO 371/35536; it is interesting to note that the experts of the Foreign Office Egyptian department dismissed Kellar's assessment of the Brothers as 'ridiculous' and defined them as 'ignorant pretenders'.
99. Memorandum by W. Smart, 30 March 1943, FO 141/855.
100. Memorandum on Political Situation, by W. Smart, 13 April 1943, ibid., relations between Killearn and Smart became rather strained when Tomlyn, of the Oriental Secretariat joined the discussion and was snubbed by Killearn who wrote: 'I think that junior members of the staff had better avoid discussions on matters of high policy'; see Memorandum by Tomlyn, 23 May 1943, ibid.
101. Memorandum on Political Situation, by W. Smart, 22 April 1942, FO 141/855.
102. Prime Minister's personal Minute, (J. 2222) addressed to Eden signed W. C., FO 371/35534.
103. Personal Minute by W. C. [Churchill], 28 April 1943, ibid.
104. Killearn to Eden, 29 April 1943, FO 371/35532, and minutes by E. A. Chapman-Andrews and R. Campbell; even Moyne, then Minister of State in Egypt, objected to Killearn's suggested use of force in backing Nahhas, Moyne to Eden, 5 May 1943, FO 371/35533.
105. Minutes by A. E. [Eden] addressed to Prime Minister, 1 May 1943, FO 371/35534.
106. Churchill to Gen. Wilson, 1 May 1943; F.O. to Lampson, 5 May 1943, FO 371/35532.
107. Minute by C. [R. Campbell] to Secretary of State, 5 May 1943, FO 371/35533.
108. Killearn to Eden, 6 May 1943, 8 May 1943, FO 371/35533.
109. Killearn to Eden, 16 June 1943, FO 371/35536.
110. 'Political Situation' by W.S. [Smart], 23 June 1943, FO 141/855.
111. Departmental Review of Political Developments in Egypt, by Scrivener, 25 October 1943, FO 371/35540; Shone to MacKereth, 21 November 1943, ibid.

112. Departmental Review ... by Scrivener, 25 October 1943, FO 371/35540.
113. Killearn to Eden, 29 November 1943, FO 371/35541.
114. Killearn to F.O., 24 December 1943, 31 December 1943, FO 371/41326.
115. Killearn to F.O., 30 December 1943, ibid.; Killearn to F.O., 5 January 1944, ibid.; see also *KD*, 1-3 January 1944, pp. 375-377.
116. Minutes by Scrivener, 14 January 1944; and F.O. to Killearn, 20 January 1944, FO 371/41326.
117. Memorandum by W.S. [Smart] 7 January 1944, FO 141/937.
118. Killearn to F.O., 2 March 1944, FO 371/41327.
119. Egyptian politics, Minute by Scrivener on Killearn to F.O., ibid.
120. Killearn to F.O., 12 April 1944 (top secret) ibid.; Killearn to F.O., 13 April 1944, ibid.
121. *KD*, 12 April 1944, pp. 286-287.
122. Ibid., p. 289 (I have not been able to locate this telegram in the F.O. archives).
123. F.O. to Killearn, 16 April 1944, FO 371/41327.
124. Killearn to F.O., 18 April 1944, ibid.
125. Minutes on King Faruq's Memorandum and on Killearn's telegram of 14 April 1944, ibid.
126. Moyne to F.O., 18 April 1944, ibid.; General Paget, Commander in Chief Middle East, was according to Killearn, the spokesman of those opposing the use of force, *KD*, pp. 289-291.
127. Ibid., pp. 291-294.
128. Memo by P.M. to members of War Cabinet, W.P. (44) 19 April 1944, FO 371/41328, Egypt W.M. 52 (44) War Cabinet Minutes 19 April 1944, Cab/65/42; see also Churchill to Moyne and three C.I.C.s, 19 April 1944, ibid.
129. Note by Shone [?], *Top Secret*, 20 April 1944 [?], FO 141/937.
130. *KD*, 19 April 1944, pp. 295-298.
131. Killearn to F.O., 25 April 1944, FO 371/41328; see also *KD*, p. 303.
132. Killearn to Eden, *Most Personal*, 27 April 1944, FO 371/41329.
133. Killearn to F.O. (Telegrams No. 888 and No. 889), 2 May 1944, FO 371/41328; Minutes to the above, 3 May 1944, ibid.; Killearn to F.O., 4 May 1944, ibid.; Nahhas to Killearn, 6 May 1944, ibid.; Killearn to Eden (*Personal*), 4 May 1944, FO 371/41329.
134. Killearn to Eden, 13 May 1944, FO 371/41329; Killearn to Eden, 28 May 1944, ibid.
135. Killearn to Eden, 6 May 1944, transmitting letter of Makram Ebeid and Resolutions of Assembly of Wafdist Bloc, FO 371/41328; Killearn to Eden, 11 May 1944, ibid.
136. McLean to Ravensdale, 22 June 1944, FO 371/41329.
137. Killearn to Eden, 27 June 1944, ibid.
138. Killearn to Eden, (Most Personal & Secret), 17 August 1944, FO 371/41331; see also Killearn to Eden, (Most Personal & Secret) 14 July 1944, ibid.
139. Minute by Scrivener on Killearn's above letter to Eden, dated 29 July 1944, ibid.
140. Killearn to F.O., 24 August 1944, FO 371/41331; Killearn to Secretary of State, *Personal*, 29 August 1944, ibid.; Killearn to F.O., 6 September 1944, FO 371/41332.
141. Shone to F.O., 16 September 1944 (No. 1826); 16 September 1944, (No. 1829); 16 September 1944 (No. 1831), ibid.; Shone even sent Hamilton on a secret mission to Palestine in order to get Amin 'Uthman's help in persuading Nahhas, see Shone to F.O., 19 September 1944, ibid.
142. Shone to F.O., 18 September 1944; Eden to Shone, 20 September 1944; Shone to F.O. 19 September 1944, FO 371/41322; see also Shone to F.O., 27 September 1944; Minutes by Scrivener and F.O. to Shone, 28 September 1944, FO 371/41323.
143. Shone to F.O., 5 October 1944 (No. 1959), 5 October 1944 (No. 1960), and Minutes by Price; F.O. to Shone, 6 October 1944, FO 371/41333.

144. Shone to F.O., 25 September 1944, ibid., apparently Nahhas had neither invited nor informed Faruq about the 'Arab Unity Conference', Shone to F.O., 29 September 1944, ibid. The Alexandria protocol for the foundation of the Arab League, was signed on 7 October 1944.
145. Shone to F.O., 8 October 1944, (No. 1991), ibid.
146. Shone to Eden, 14 October 1944, FO 371/41334.
147. *KD*, 9 October 1944, pp. 314-315.
148. 27 January 1942, FO 371/31566.

PART TWO

REGIONAL AND POLITICAL CONSIDERATIONS

5

EGYPT'S REGIONAL POLICY IN THE NINETEENTH AND TWENTIETH CENTURIES

THE NINETEENTH CENTURY

When Muhammad 'Ali assumed power in 1805, Egypt re-emerged as a dominant factor in regional politcs both in the Eastern Mediterranean and in East Africa. Though Egypt remained, *de jure*, an Ottoman province until World War I, its foreign policy during most of the nineteenth century was formulated and executed from Cairo and not from Istanbul.

Hence any attempt to examine Egypt's foreign policy, following the European penetration into this area, will have to start with the turbulent period of Muhammad 'Ali's reign in the first half of the nineteenth century. Such an examination will yield the following conclusions:

1. Modern Egypt, based on its strategic position, was set on playing a leading role in regional politics.
2. Geopolitical factors suggested two major trends. First, the Nile Valley as a natural area for Egyptian expansion; and second, the recognition of the North-East as an area from which potential enemies might penetrate into Egypt and which consequently should be under Egyptian influence.
3. Remembering the Napoleonic experience in Egypt (1798–1802), Muhammad 'Ali and his successors realised their limitations as semi-independent rulers. In other words, they had to limit their ambitions in accordance with the constraints of the 'Eastern Question', namely to British predominance in the Eastern Mediterranean. Britain ruled the seas, as had been adequately proved

both in the annihilation of Bonaparte's navy by Nelson at Abukir (1798) and in the battle of Navarino (1827), when the combined Turco-Egyptian navy was destroyed. Hence, any new venture in Egyptian regional politics could only be viable if it received at least the tacit blessing of Whitehall.

The highlights of Egypt's regional politics in the nineteenth century can therefore be illustrated in the following manner. The centrality of the African hinterland and in particular of the Nile Valley was a dominant and constant factor throughout the century. The conquest of the Sudan in 1820–1821 and the expansion of Egyptian rule into Equatorial Africa, as well as into Bahr al-Ghazal and Dar Fur in the 1870s, are clear indications of the importance of these regions for Egypt's new rulers. The discovery of the sources of the Nile in the 1860s and the opening of the Suez Canal in 1869 add another dimension to this area, and shed light on the Khedive Isma'il's abortive venture into Ethiopia (1875–1876). There is an additional reason for focusing on Africa rather than on the Middle East in the second half of the nineteenth century. Egypt had been rebuffed in Syria and hence had to relinquish its conquests in the north-east. Thus, following the Treaty of London (1841), Africa became the only area for legitimate expansion, especially since Egypt had become a reluctant, though active, partner in the Anglo-Egyptian treaty for the suppression of the slave trade (1877). When, in 1881–1885, Egypt was forced by Britain to evacuate the Sudan, following the Mahdist revolt, it did so under protest. The 'Unity of the Nile Valley' remained a dominant feature both in Egypt's evolving nationalist ideology and in its regional politics throughout the nineteenth and twentieth centuries.

Egyptian conquests in the east and the north-east in the first half of the nineteenth century illustrate Egypt's determination to play a leading role in the region, on the one hand, and its perception of the north-east as an area of potential danger, on the other hand. First came the destruction of the Wahhabi state and the conquest of Najd and the Hejaz, including Mecca and Medina, in 1811–1818. From Egypt's point of view this venture had the following advantages. It proved Egypt's military power vis-à-vis the Ottoman Sultan, who had not been able to overcome the Wahhabi challenge with his forces stationed in Syria and Iraq. Secondly, by bringing the holy cities under Egyptian suzerainty, Muhammad 'Ali's prestige within the Islamic world had been considerably enhanced. Thirdly, Egypt's pacifying

Egypt's Regional Policy 163

role in the Red Sea and her ability to renew the pilgrimage to Mecca was also a clear demonstration of her power and good-will as far as the Muslims under British rule were concerned. Hence Britain's first attempt to cooperate with Ibrahim Pasha goes back to this period. Lastly, the conquest of the Hejaz and later of the Sudan brought both the eastern and the western coasts of the Red Sea under Egyptian control. Even after its expulsion from Syria in 1841, Egypt retained at least part of its influence in the Arabian peninsula, especially along the Red Sea coast, where several harbours in northern Hejaz remained under Egyptian administration until the 1890s.

The Syrian campaigns (1831–1840) of Ibrahim Pasha provide the sole example of Egyptian expansion in the north-eastern direction in the nineteenth century. In contrast to the campaigns in the Arabian peninsula and the Sudan, undertaken under Ottoman auspices, this was a direct challenge to the Sultan and an abortive attempt to link Egypt with British interests, as interpreted in Cairo. Muhammad 'Ali tried to convince the British authorities that the shaky Ottoman Sultan could no longer guarantee the safety of British imperial communications and hence a strong Egyptian government in the Fertile Crescent would be an asset as far as H.M.G. was concerned. Muhammad 'Ali's own ambitions went far beyond those linked to British interests, for there is little doubt that Egyptian forces could and would have conquered Anatolia itself if the Russians had not intervened with the treaty of Hünkar Iskelesi in 1833.

Egyptian rule in Syria lasted for an additional seven years. However, when following the London 'Convention for the pacification of the Levant' (July-September 1840) the Egyptian army was forced to retreat, the sole gain of Muhammad 'Ali's dynasty in the north-eastern region was a right granted in the *firman* of 1841 to administer a narrow section of Sinai west of a line running from Suez toward Rafah. This brought an end to Egyptian expansion in that region during the nineteenth century. The opening of the Suez Canal (1869) and the British occupation of Egypt (1882) created a new situation with regard to the Sinai peninsula. However, when Great Britain forced the Ottomans to accept Egyptian administration of the Sinai in 1892 and 1906, it did so out of concern for its own imperial interests, while the Egyptian Nationalist party of Mustafa Kamil defended Ottoman sovereignty over the peninsula.[1]

THE SUDAN IN ANGLO-EGYPTIAN RELATIONS

Egypt's dependence on England remained a dominant factor in its foreign policy throughout the first half of the twentieth century. Despite its *de jure* independence since February 1922, Egypt was in no position to determine its own foreign relations as long as the British army occupied Egypt and the so-called 'advice' of H.M.G., granted through the British high commissioners (later ambassadors) in Cairo, was binding.

Its active venture into regional politcs was until World War II primarily limited to the Sudan. No Egyptian king, government, or political party ever recognised the legitimacy of the Anglo-Egyptian condominium leading to British predominance in the Sudan from 1899. Hence the 'Unity of the Nile Valley' remained a constant and central issue of controversy throughout the period. In fact a close look at the numerous attempts to reach an agreement undertaken by the British and Egyptian governments, both before the signing of the Anglo-Egyptian treaty of 1936 and after World War II, demonstrates that they foundered on the Sudan question. The two governments succeeded in reaching tentative agreements with regard to the eventual evacuation of British forces from Egyptian territory. But the gap in their respective positions regarding the Sudan was so great that no compromise could be found. England regarded its trusteeship over the Sudan as one which would ultimately lead to Sudanese independence. This desire was based primarily on two assumptions. First, that the Sudanese revolted against Egyptian rule, in 1881–1885, for good reasons and hence had no desire to come once again under Egyptian domination. Second, that Egypt's nationalist anti-British fervour, as demonstrated in the revolt of 1919, would sooner or later force Britain to relinquish its direct hold over that country. Therefore, British presence south of Wadi Halfa, leading to an independent, pro-British Sudan, would facilitate the safeguarding of H.M.G.'s interests in Egypt and the Suez even after the evacuation.

Egypt's position could be summarised under similar headings. First, that the Sudan was part of Egypt and any attempt to grant the Sudanese independence was an imperialist plot aimed at creating artificial divisions against the natural aspirations of the people of the Nile Valley. Second, while Britain was bound to relinquish its hold over Egypt sooner or later, its presence in the Sudan was of much greater concern as its separatist policy was irreversible and every

Egypt's Regional Policy

additional year of British administration and education in the Sudan would further diminish the chances of eventual unity.

This gap was finally bridged in 1953 when, following the 'Free Officers' coup and the deposal of King Faruq, the Revolutionary Command Council under President Muhammad Najib decided to grant the Sudanese the right of self-determination. This was based on a better understanding of the Sudanese on the one hand and, on the other, the belief that Ismail al-Azhari and his National Unionist party would ultimately lead the Sudan to unity with Egypt. However, the Sudanese opted for independence and thus, since January 1956, the 'Unity of the Nile Valley' ceased to be a realistic political aim.[2]

ACTIVE PAN-ARABISM

World War II and its aftermath was a turning point in Egypt's foreign and regional policy. First there was a beginning of renewed interest in the north-east. Second, the gradual exit of Britain from the Middle Eastern scene and the emergence of the superpowers as the main actors created a new situation.

The two are of course interrelated, for even before the world war Britain attempted to involve Egypt in its broader Arab policy, both in order to counteract Jewish ambitions in mandatory Palestine and to withstand the growing tide of Arab nationalism. The claim that Anglo-Arab interests are in harmony and that by acting in concert with Britain and with each other the Arabs would serve their own interests, was first officially aired by Sir Anthony Eden in 1941. Egypt's leading role in the founding of the Arab League in 1945 was, in a large measure, the result of British initiative on the one hand, and the fear of Hashemite ambitions on the other hand. The unity of Greater Syria and a Hashemite federation of the Fertile Crescent were regarded as a threat by both Egypt and Saudi Arabia. The Arab League thus provided Egypt with a convenient vehicle with which to withstand prospective challengers for supremacy in the Arab Middle East. While there had been strong ideological currents since the 1930s in quest of greater Egyptian involvement in the Arab and Islamic arenas, politically there had been no serious move in that direction. The Muslim Brothers had been involved in the Arab Revolt in Palestine in 1936–1939, while King Faruq's close associates, 'Ali Mahir and 'Abd al-Rahman 'Azzam, took part in various pan-Arab ventures, such as the Palestine Round Table Conference, convened in

London in 1939, and tried to serve the King's pan-Arab ambitions whenever possible. However, the major political parties, including the Wafd, paid little more than lip-service to these efforts. Only after the war, when it became clear that Britain and France were on their way out and hence the vacuum left in their wake might be filled by undesirable opponents, did Egypt venture once again into the northeastern region, with the 1948 war in Palestine as its first real manifestation. But while the Muslim Brothers and their *Jawwala* (Rovers) were enthusiastic fighters and martyrs for the Palestinian cause, the Egyptian government was reluctant in committing the army to full-scale fighting.[3] Even when Faruq gave the order for the Egyptian army to invade Palestine on 15 May 1948, he did so both in order to fight the new Jewish state, and to stop the Hashemites from annexing Arab Palestine.

The next phase in Egypt's regional and international relations started in 1955 and came to its end following the 1967 debacle. It was characterised by an aggressive leadership role played by Nasser which ultimately led Egypt to a fiasco not unlike the one suffered by Muhammad 'Ali following his Syrian venture. Four major events, all of which occurred in 1955, symbolize the opening of this new chapter: the decision of the Sudan to opt for independence rather than unity with Egypt; the Baghdad pact; the Bandung Conference; and the Soviet inspired arms deal with Czechoslovakia. The fact that the Sudanese opted for independence rather than unity was, as mentioned, a great disappointment for the Egyptians. However, it enabled Nasser to shift the focus of his regional politics from the south, where it had been centred for over a century, to the north-east. The Baghdad pact symbolized Britain's last attempt to retain a foothold in the region following its reluctant agreement to evacuate Egypt and Palestine. Moreover, it proved to Nasser that in a divided Arab world Iraq, his main rival for Arab leadership, could still play an important role with imperialist backing, and thereby frustrate Egypt's regional ambitions. The Bandung Conference, Nasser's first venture into the international arena, proved that with the support of prominent leaders such as Chou En-Lai, Tito and Nehru, Nasser could assume the mantle of leadership of the Arab Middle East and independent Africa. To do so he had to create conditions in which he could challenge the West openly and force his fellow leaders of the Arab states to fall into step. The announcement of the arms deal with the Soviet bloc in September 1955 was such an event, and the nationalization of the Suez Canal in 1956 was yet another. Here was an aggressive, independent Arab leader, ruling the biggest and strongest Arab state in the Middle East, commanding a well equipped army trained in modern warfare, who had achieved all this without submitting to the dictates of the superpowers. Through positive neutralism as formulated in Delhi, Belgrade and Bandung, Nasser hoped to succeed where Muhammad 'Ali had failed, namely to bring the Arabs under Egyptian control without firing a single shot and without outside interference.

His success lasted for less than six years. Its major manifestations were the Suez War and the final humiliation of Britain and France at the hands of the United States and the Soviet Union. The fact that at the height of the cold war and despite the Soviet arms deal and Soviet financing of the high dam at Aswan, Nasser succeeded in maintaining for most of that period cordial relations with the United States too, and in receiving from both superpowers massive aid for his five-year development plans and his armed forces, convinced him that his regional supremacy and his so-called positive neutralism were his major political and economic assets. Arabism thus became the dominant feature of Egypt's regional politics. Through it Nasser aborted the Eisenhower doctrine and in February 1958 came to the rescue of Syria in creating the United Arab Republic. When in July of that year the Hashemite Kingdom of Iraq was toppled by what appeared to be a Nasser-type military coup, it seemed that Egypt was well on the way to achieve the paramountcy which had eluded it a hundred years earlier.

However, within a year the dream of Arab unity and Nasser's aggressive Arabism were both challenged. Opposition stiffened within the traditional monarchies of Saudi Arabia and Jordan. In the latter, as well as in Lebanon, Nasserist attempts to topple the regime had been successfully resisted with western aid. But even more discouraging was the attitude of fellow-revolutionaries in Iraq, who, having assumed power, had no intention of succumbing to the Egyptian embrace. In March 1959 an Egyptian-inspired and backed coup in Mosul was crushed and all known pro-Nasserists were either annihilated or put behind bars. Even in Syria, the Ba'th party, which had been the main instigator of unity, was seeking a greater role in running the state and hence had to be brought under strict control. With Field Marshal 'Abd al-Hakim 'Amer in charge of Syria, and Egyptian officers replacing Syrians in the army, relations within the U.A.R. were under considerable strain long before the unity finally broke down in 1961. Thus the only modest manifestation of Nasser-style Arab unity, and his attempt to dominate the Fertile Crescent, came to its untimely end, exactly one hundred and twenty years after Muhammad 'Ali had failed in a similar adventure. The 'Unity of Ranks', coined by Nasser to embrace his Arab unity plans, had to be discarded following this debacle.

Nasser's involvement in the war in Yemen (1962–1967) and his growing commitment to the conflict with Israel, culminating in the June 1967 war, were probably the two major elements in the final failure of his regional ambitions. When, under the banner of 'the unity of purpose', Nasser decided to back the Yemenite revolutionaries against the traditional Imamate and its Saudi Arabian ally, he entered into direct confrontation with the United States. This was connected with the decline of the Afro-Asian positive neutralist bloc through internal strife and the inherent weakness of its members. The failure to convene a second Bandung conference in 1965, combined with the Sino-Soviet conflict, forced many of the weaker members of this bloc to become clients of one or the other of the superpowers. Nasser opted for Soviet patronage and by 1966 President Johnson came to the conclusion that there was no longer any logical reason to pour American aid into the Soviet-dominated economy of Egypt.

By 1966 Egypt's power in the region had also declined considerably. The revolutionary regimes in Syria and Iraq were openly challenging Nasser's supremacy, using his own revolutionary jargon refined by Ba'thist ideology. The stalemate in the Yemen was proving Egypt's military weakness in the face of growing resistance from the traditional, conservative camp. Nasser's attempt to revive his regional leadership in the Arab Summit Conferences in 1964–1965, under the banner of 'unity of action', ended in a fiasco. It only proved that even the Palestinian issue, as symbolised in the creation of the P.L.O., was not enough to create unity in the Arab camp where suspicions and open hostility were the order of the day.

It was under these circumstances that Nasser decided to take the gamble which ultimately led to the June 1967 war. The instigators were the Syrians, who had again and again challenged his leadership and questioned his willingness to commit the Egyptian army against the main foe, namely Israel. Ever since the Suez War of 1956, Nasser had claimed that he was preparing his armed forces, with Soviet aid, for the final battle against Israel. But when in May 1967 he ordered the U.N. emergency forces out of the Sinai and closed the straits of

Egypt's Regional Policy

Tiran to Israeli shipping, he believed that Israel would submit without battle. It was an Israel which, as in 1956, did not have the backing of England and France, without which, as Ben Gurion had declared, he would not have dared to challenge Egypt. Now Israel was standing alone against three well-equipped and Soviet-trained armies and with a prospective fourth ally in King Hussein. Moreover, Israel itself was in the midst of a severe economic crisis which seemed to have weakened its political leadership and undermined its ability to reach critical decisions. Hence, Nasser's gamble was based on the assumption that even if Israel decided to fight it could be overcome by the combined Arab forces. Had the gamble succeeded, Nasser's leadership role in the 'Arab Circle' would have gained a new lease of life. Having failed and been humbled by Israel's complete and fast victory in the Six-Day War, Nasser had lost his last shred of credibility as *the* regional leader. It was also the end of Nasserism, the creed which had been cultivated by Nasser's followers in the belief that it would lead the Arab world to modernism and enable the Arabs to assume their rightful position within the advanced nations of the world. All that remained of this messianic belief, which Nasser had successfully evoked, was the promise made by Nasser that 'what had been taken by force shall be returned by force'. However, following Egypt's failure in the war of attrition in 1969–1970, even that announcement seemed to have become an empty slogan.

It may be an irony of history that Nasser's last attempt in Arab politics and unity was in north-east Africa. Having been humiliated and crushed in the Fertile Crescent, first by his Arab compatriots and then by Israel, and having been forced out of the Arabian Peninsula after a long and protracted war in the Yemen, the military coups in Libya and the Sudan in 1969 suddenly provided Nasser's Arabism with a new ray of hope. It was symbolical because of the fact that this new prospect of Arab unity followed Nasser's final humiliation at the Rabat Summit conference, in December 1969, where all his requests had been bluntly turned down by his fellow Arab leaders and he had walked out empty-handed.

In Tripoli, whence he travelled from Rabat, Nasser was welcomed by his new protégés Qadhafi of Libya and Numayri of the Sudan, and signed with them an agreement for the coordination of political, economic and military action. Here was what seemed to be a new area for action and a new lease of life for Nasser's dwindling prestige. A possible revival of the 'Unity of the Nile Valley', providing a prospective solution for Egypt's population explosion, combined with unity with Libya, where recent oil discoveries had boosted the economy and hence could provide aid for Egypt's development. It seemed a much more realistic approach to Arab unity than the failures of the past and it shifted the focus of Egypt's regional politics in the direction from which it had been diverted by Nasser since 1955. Nasser's last act in this direction was to sign an agreement of economic unity with Libya and the Sudan in April 1970. But when he died in September of that year, having just accepted the 'Rogers Plan' in July – a clear admission of Egypt's failure in the so-called war of attrition – Nasser's standing as a regional leader was in ruins.[4]

PREPARING THE GROUND FOR A NEW POLICY

President Sadat's approach to regional politics cannot be separated from his overall view of Egypt's internal problems on the one hand and, on the other, her crucial involvement in international relations. To put it more bluntly: Egypt's economy was a shambles with no solution in sight; the continued conflict with Israel consumed all Egypt's energy and resources; moreover, its dependence on the Soviet bloc on the one hand and on the complexities of inter-Arab relations on the other, created the magic circle within which Nasser had gambled and lost.

Several steps were required in order to break out of what seemed a hopeless situation. In order to arrive at a settlement with Israel, on terms acceptable to Egypt, the post-1967 status quo had to be broken. This in turn would serve to convince both Israel and the United States, her major protector, that a compromise was essential. The steps leading to an Egyptian solution of its conflict with Israel started with Sadat's hesitant initiative in February 1971, led to the October 1973 War, which brought about the Sinai disengagement agreements of 1974–1975 and ultimately led to the peace initiative in November 1977. By 1982 Egypt had regained all of her territories, had improved her image both internally and internationally and had been able to move economically from near stagnation to economic growth. This growth was made possible by a considerable growth in capital imports, primarily from the United States (nearly $1 billion per annum in 1977–1979) and other western sources. Even the unilateral transfer of some $2 billion per annum from Egyptian workers in the Arab oil states, was not interrupted despite the economic sanctions decided upon at the Arab Summit in Baghdad in 1978. If one adds the foreign loans received by Egypt from other sources, such as the International Development Association of the World Bank (in 1980 $215 million for infrastructural projects), or the Gulf Organization for the Development of Egypt, the pressing economic hardships of the pre-1977 economy had been somewhat eased. However, none of the serious economic problems facing Egypt have been solved. These include a large foreign debt, which has to be serviced, growing inflation, heavy expenditure on armaments and an enormous inefficient bureaucracy. When Robert McNamara, president of the World Bank stated, in February 1981, that due to its improved economic performance Egypt was no longer eligible for soft loans, this certainly signified an improvement in Egypt's economy but not a solution to its problems. In the long term Egyptian economists hope to transform the economy with increased foreign investments, lured by the 'open door' policy, growing revenues from crude oil, and the 1978–1982 development plan, which in its first year envisaged an investment of nearly $4,5 billion.[5]

One can discern several stages in the process which led Egypt from complete dependence on the Soviet Union to a pro-American orientation. When Sadat was forced to sign the Treaty of Friendship with the Soviet Union, in May 1971, he still hoped that Soviet aid on a massive scale would enable him both to boost Egypt's stagnant economy and to re-equip his armed forces. Neither of these hopes was fully realised and while the Soviets fulfilled some of their promises as far as equipment was concerned, they did so, according to Sadat, on a selective and humiliating basis. Moreover, the Soviet-inspired abortive coup in the Sudan, in July 1971, as well as growing Soviet involvement in other parts of Africa and the Middle East, convinced Sadat that there was a Soviet master-plan to dominate the region.

Furthermore, the Soviet Union, despite its military and economic aid since 1955, had neither been able to modernise Egypt's economy, nor to help it in regaining its lost territories in the Sinai. The answer clearly lay in Washington and not in Moscow, as the Americans had the money, the technology and the leverage over Israel required to satisfy Egyptian needs. The steps leading to the shift in Egypt's superpower alliance started with the expulsion of Soviet military personnel from Egypt in July 1972 and culminated in the exclusion of the Soviets from the post-1973 settlements and in Sadat's open objection to a future Soviet role in the negotiations.

Hostility reached a further peak following the Soviet Union's open rejection of Sadat's peace initiative and the subsequent Camp David accords. Sadat accused the Soviets of trying to topple his regime, through aiding fanatic opposition groups to commit acts of sabotage in Egypt, and of attempting to undermine his regime through the good offices of Soviet puppet states in Libya, Ethiopia, and the People's Democratic Republic of Yemen. Even in the Sudan, Sadat suspected the Soviets of attempting once again to topple his closest ally, in the Libyan-backed Ansar revolt of July 1976. Attempts at rapprochement undertaken during 1978 failed completely and only strengthened Sadat's conviction regarding Soviet intrigues and hostility.

The shift towards the United States was therefore based on the belief that the U.S. would be able and willing to aid Egypt both politically and economically, as well as on anti-Soviet sentiments and suspicions. Economically, as mentioned above, Egypt's reliance on the U.S. and its allies has already borne considerable fruit, far beyond what the Soviet bloc would have been willing to deliver. Politically, Sadat set out to prove that while he appreciated the U.S. special relationship with Israel, Egypt, the Horn of Africa and the Persian Gulf were also cardinal western interests and had to be treated accordingly. In other words, while Egypt needed American economic aid and technology, Egypt could guarantee for America the stability of the region and its security as well as provide a barrier against the Soviets, once the Middle East conflict was brought to a satisfactory end. Sadat's success in conveying this message both to the administration and to the American public, especially during the hostage crisis in Iran, clearly indicates that the bilateral relations between Egypt and the U.S. have moved according to his original plans.[6]

INTER-ARAB RELATIONS

In examining the shift in Sadat's regional policy, which is our major topic, it is advisable to examine this policy in relation to the Arab Middle East and to assess its implications in Africa, especially in relation to Libya, the Sudan and the Horn of Africa.

When Sadat assumed power in September 1970, Egypt's standing in the Arab world was, as mentioned above, at a very low ebb. Even the two youngest and weakest so-called revolutionary regimes, in Libya and the Sudan, who had sought protection under Nasser's umbrella, were not so sure whether Sadat could provide them with similar services. Sadat's own preferences and personal friendships were among the so-called 'reactionary' rulers such as King Hasan of Morocco, King Faysal of Saudi Arabia, the Sabah ruling family of Kuwait, president Franjieh of Lebanon, and others. Although he did pursue the planned federation with Libya, the Sudan and later also Syria, he did so primarily for reasons connected with internal Egyptian politics, and especially as part of his fight for survival against the Nasserist power centres. In May 1971, with the internal battle won, the quest for unity could therefore be discarded.[7] Thus, by 1972, Sadat's earlier adherence to Arab unity had become subordinate to what he regarded as the values of true Egyptian patriotism. Two observers of the Middle East scene have described this shift in the following terms. Fouad Ajami has stated:

The idea that has dominated the political consciousness of modern Arabs is nearing its end ... It is the myth of pan-Arabism ... Slowly and grimly, with a great deal of anguish and of outright violence, a 'normal', state system is becoming a fact of life.[8]

Burrell and Kelidar have phrased it somewhat more critically:

Sadat has sought ... to extricate Egypt as far as possible from the labyrinth of inter-Arab politics and rivalries; but in doing so he has rendered Egypt dependent upon the goodwill of the conservative states of the Arab world. The result of this has been to reduce the number of policy options open to the Egyptian leadership, a position Nasser would have striven to avoid.

In fact, Sadat had gambled his future on this policy and his survival was thus questionable.[9]

Mohamed Hassanein Heikal, one of the main exponents of Nasserism, went even further when he stated that since Egypt was culturally, linguistically and religiously part of the Arab nation and could never lose its identity, Sadat's mistaken foreign policy had alienated the Arabs. This led, according to Heikal, to Sadat's losing his real constituency and with it his regional and internal standing.[10]

Sadat's premise when determining his new regional policy was based on the following components. Egyptian interests made a political solution of the Middle East conflict essential; such a solution could be arrived at, on Egyptian terms, only with American backing; American backing could only be marshalled if the U.S. was convinced that a shift away from Israel leading to a more 'balanced' Middle East policy would serve its own interests; to convince the Americans Sadat needed the backing of the conservative pro-American states, primarily Saudi Arabia and Iran; lastly, there was an acute danger of a Soviet pincer movement starting from Afghanistan, through Iran or Iraq, to the Persian Gulf, and from there through Oman to South Yemen, the Horn of Africa, Ethiopia and Libya. To Sadat it seemed clear that only a pro-American alliance, headed by Egypt and including all possible anti-Soviet regimes, could, with American aid, stop this danger. Hence his choice of allies was quite obvious. Iran, Saudi Arabia and Morocco seemed more reliable allies against the Soviets than the Fertile Crescent, let alone the Palestinians. Therefore, after the October 1973 War, when Asad and 'Arafat became obstacles to Sadat's political programme, he all but discarded them and concentrated on the traditional rulers, who continued to back him, at least tacitly, until the Camp David accords. Sadat's regional policy was therefore based on areas of possible cooperation, which would benefit Egypt, rather than on ideological principles or pan-Arab considerations.

By 1975–1976 Syria was accusing Sadat of betraying the Arab world and although a temporary reconciliation was reached, under Saudi auspices, it lasted for less than a year and disappeared with Sadat's trip to Jerusalem. The fate of Egypt's relations with other radical Arab states and with the P.L.O. was similar. In the case of Libya, relations deteriorated even earlier and in the summer of 1977 military conflict broke out along Egypt's western border. Sadat branded Qadhafi as a fanatic lunatic and regarded him as a menace, not only to his own people, but to the whole continent. Libyans, and Libyan-paid Egyptian agents, were accused of numerous acts of sabotage in Egypt, and Qadhafi's regime was accused of financing the anti-Sadat opposition and its propaganda machine both in Egypt itself and in the diaspora.[11] More dangerous were Libya's continued attempts to overthrow the regime in the Sudan, both in an abortive coup in July 1976 and later. In March 1979 Qadhafi declared his willingness to sign a treaty of defence with the Marxist regime in Ethiopia aimed against the Cairo-Khartoum axis.[12] Later in that month Libyan and Syrian forces were again accused of massing on the Egyptian border.[13] In June 1979, Qadhafi asked through Moscow, for Iraqi troops to come to his aid against Egypt. According to Iraqi sources there were at that time some 5,000 Cubans and 2,000 Hungarian troops in Libya while there was no proof of Egyptian military presence on the Libyan border.[14] In June 1980 Egypt imposed martial law on its border regions with Libya in response to

Egypt's Regional Policy

Qadhafi's threats against Egypt and the Sudan.[15] In November 1980 Libyan troops invaded Chad and 'liberated' its northern province. Tripoli accused Egypt and the Sudan of aiding the separatist forces in Chad under Hisseine Habre.[16] In December the Libyan attack reached a new peak with the conquest of Ndjamena, the capital of Chad. On 6 January 1981, a communique was issued in Tripoli announcing the unification of Libya and Chad into one people's republic (*Jamahiriyya*). While the Chadian delegation tried its utmost to resist, Qadhafi was set on extending his rule into black Africa. But opposition to what was branded as Libyan imperialism soon embraced the whole Organization of African Unity whose committee on Chad, composed of twelve member-states, declared the merger illegal and on 14 January 1981 demanded an immediate withdrawal of Libyan forces from Chad.[17] The Sudan, which feared that it might become Qadhafi's next target for forced unity, asked for French military help while its own troops, supported by Egyptian forces, were concentrating on the Chadian border.[18] Although Qadhafi continued to boast that he and his Syrian allies would spread the 'Islamic Socialist Revolution' in Africa through military and subversive means,[19] pressure was beginning to build up, and in November 1981 Libyan forces started to withdraw from Chad. Qadhafi's drive into Africa was thus halted at least for the time being, without the expected military clash between Libya and its neighbours in the Nile Valley, Egypt and the Sudan. However, the continued threat of Libyan territorial expansion has driven the occupants of the Nile Valley into an even closer alliance.

EGYPTIAN RELATIONS IN THE NILE VALLEY AND THE RED SEA

Sadat's special attitude to the Sudan was clearly demonstrated in July 1971, when Egyptian intervention helped Numayri to regain power, following his arrest by the abortive pro-Communist coup. But this special relationship began to flourish only after the October 1973 war when the two countries actually signed, in February 1974, an agreement for their political and economic integration. They started to coordinate their development projects as well as plan combined cultural and religious institutions. This development was part of a common regional and international outlook. Both Numayri and Sadat regarded Qadhafi as a dangerous threat to their regimes. They had similar feelings regarding the new pro-Soviet regime in Ethiopia and hence cooperation was a natural conclusion. In September 1975, Numayri was the only Arab leader who openly supported Sadat over the second Sinai disengagement agreement. But if one has to point to a single event which brought the two leaders even closer, it was the Egyptian intervention in the July 1976 coup which saved Numayri's regime once again. Moreover, it clearly proved that Qadhafi was openly involved in attempts to overthrow Numayri and in helping the Sudanese opposition parties, organized in the National Front. In July 1976, Egypt and the Sudan signed a joint defence agreement which provided for closer cooperation in all matters of security and defence than the cooperation that existed between Egypt and any other country. Matters of mutual concern, such as the security of the Red Sea, the prevention of Soviet penetration into adjacent regions, or Libyan plots against the Sudan or other African states, were hereafter dealt with by the joint defence council which was set up by the two countries.[20]

Sadat and Numayri also agreed with regard to the Soviet threat to Africa. In 1977 they cooperated in repelling the Angolan invasion into Zaïre, while in May 1977 the Sudan announced the termination of contracts of all Soviet experts who had been seconded to the Sudan Defence Force. Thus, by the end of 1977, there was complete agreement between Egypt and the Sudan and close cooperation between the two of them and Saudi Arabia, as the three countries shared a common concern for the Arabization of the Red Sea and the necessity to stop Soviet penetration into the region.

This trilateral harmony was disturbed by Sadat's visit to Jerusalem. While Numayri gave his immediate blessing to Sadat's initiative, the Saudis reacted negatively and thereby created a difficult situation for Numayri who was torn between his political loyalty to Sadat and his economic dependence on Saudi Arabia. But Numayri prevailed in his support of Egypt's peace initiative, despite Saudi and Libyan pressures and growing internal opposition, especially from the Ansar. The Sudan did not join the economic sanctions imposed against Egypt at the Baghdad summit in November 1978, nor did it sever diplomatic relations. Throughout the period, following the signing of the Camp David accords in September 1978, Numayri continually emphasized the Sudan's close relations with Egypt, based on their historic ties and common heritage. Hence, Numayri claimed that the Sudan had a better understanding of Egypt's circumstances and of the enormous sacrifices made by the Egyptians for the sake of the Palestinians. An attempt to boycott and isolate Egypt was therefore uncalled for.[21] The convening of the National Assemblies of Egypt and the Sudan in a joint session in January 1979 symbolised the Sudan's determination not to succumb to Arab pressures. But in March 1979, following the signing of the Egyptian-Israeli peace treaty, there were signs that Numayri was beginning to succumb to internal and external pressure. Criticism of Sadat's policy started to appear frequently in the Sudanese press and consequently the relationship between Sudan, Saudi Arabia and Libya improved. Saudi Arabia supplied all the Sudan's requirements, as far as oil was concerned, in order to save it from the consequences of an Iraqi imposed embargo. Libya filled its part of the bargain and closed the Ansar's training camp in Kufra and helped in furthering the reconciliation between Numayri and the opposition National Front.[22]

Numayri's participation in the Tunisia Summit in November 1979, and his subsequent signing of the resolution condemning the Egyptian-Israeli peace treaty, was regarded as a low ebb in Sudanese-Egyptian relations. The Sudan seemed to be returning to the Arab fold. The anti-Egyptian resolution, calling for the liberation of Palestine and the realization of the full rights of the Palestinians, was supported even by Oman and Somalia, who along with the Sudan had hitherto sided with Egypt.[23] One month later the Sudan announced that should the Israeli flag be raised in Cairo, its ambassador in Egypt would be recalled. Thus, while diplomatic relations between Egypt and the Sudan were not broken, the establishment of diplomatic relations between Egypt and Israel brought about a further decline in Egyptian-Sudanese relations.[24]

But even after this setback in the relationship, Sadat's attitude to the Sudan and to Numayri continued to be moderate. Egypt blamed Saudi Arabia for plotting against the Sudan and putting pressure on its leaders. Sadat declared that the Sudan was free to return its ambassador to Cairo whenever it desired to do so, while he stated that this privilege would not be granted to other Arab States.[25] However, throughout 1980 the Sudan continued to improve its relations with Saudi Arabia, the Gulf Emirates and even with Iraq. Only the Libyan intervention in Chad since December 1980 changed the course of Sudanese politics, and by March 1981 diplomatic relations with Egypt were once again at ambassadorial level. On March 18 Numayri announced that foreign elements were again plotting against his regime, mentioning the Syrian Ba'th as a possible suspect, and invited the United States to use Sudanese territory for its military facilities. On the same day, Egypt's Kamal Hasan 'Ali promised full Egyptian backing to the Sudan against its Libyan enemy.[26] In June 1981 Sudan expelled all Libyan diplomats from the Sudan and suspended all flights between Khartoum and Tripoli. The new deterioration was connected with the situation in Chad, where opposition to the Libyan presence was increasing.[27] The close relationship between Egypt and the Sudan, which had characterised most of the years since Sadat and Numayri came to power, was once again approaching its peak and the economic, cultural and political integration of Egypt and the Sudan was advancing smoothly.

If proof was needed regarding the depth of Numayri's solidarity, it came after Sadat's assassination. Numayri attended Sadat's funeral, while other Arab heads of state were either openly jubilant or suspiciously quiet. Furthermore, while in Cairo, Numayri declared his full and unflinching support for the late president's policy and even took part in the election of Husni Mubarak as Egypt's new president – surely an unheard of act of solidarity and close alliance.

Ethiopia and the Horn of Africa emerged as another region of concern for Egypt in the 1970s. This was by no means a new development since, as mentioned above, Egypt had attempted to conquer Ethiopia one hundred years earlier, while the threat of diverting the waters of the Blue Nile, at their source in Ethiopia, had arisen many times since the eleventh century. However, the developments of the 1970s were unique because there was a close connection between the Soviet threat, as perceived in Cairo and Khartoum, and internal developments in the Horn of Africa, both of which brought about increased Egyptian involvement in the Red Sea region.[28]

In a way Egypt and Ethiopia moved in opposite directions in the 1970s. Egypt moved from revolution to conservatism, from being a Soviet client to reliance on the U.S., while Ethiopia moved to a position which was pro-Soviet and revolutionary, becoming the most important Soviet base in the Red Sea. Egypt's policy towards Ethiopia and the Horn of Africa was therefore formulated in 1976–77 in order to counteract these trends. It seemed at that time that since the Soviets were entrenched in Ethiopia and Somalia, on the African side of the Horn, and in the People's Democratic Republic of Yemen on the Eastern shores of the Red Sea, they were in a position to hold Egypt to ransom. It was under these circumstances that Egypt, Saudi

Arabia and the Sudan formulated and coordinated their policy in 1976 to preserve the Arab predominance in the Red Sea. When, in 1977, Somalia and Ethiopia went to war over the Ogaden desert and the Soviets, having decided to back Ethiopia, were expelled from Somalia, the Arabization of the Red Sea appeared to be on its way toward realization. Further gains for Egypt and its allies were made in Eritrea where the various independence movements conquered most of that province, while newly independent Djibuti joined the Arab League as a junior ally of Egypt and Saudi Arabia.

However, since 1978 the Egyptian policy in the Red Sea and the Horn of Africa has suffered considerable set-backs. First, Ethiopia has all but succeeded in overcoming Somalia as well as the Eritrean separatists, owing primarily to their internal divisions. Second, Sadat's peace initiative has undermined the Cairo-Riad axis which was further weakened following the Islamic revolution in Iran and its repercussions in the Persian Gulf. Hence, the Egyptian initiative in the Horn of Africa rested primarily on its two African allies, the Sudan and Somali, while Oman was its sole solid supporter in the Arabian peninsula. Even the Sudan, following the influx of Eritrean refugees and the realization that Ethiopia has regained the initiative, has all but mended its fences with Mangistu and the Derg and closed its borders to the continuing flow of refugees. While the Sudan remained committed to the anti-Soviet policy centred in Cairo, it had stopped playing an active role against Ethiopia, the current centre of Soviet power in the Red Sea.

Egypt thus seemed to follow a policy which enjoyed little support in Africa. By aiding Somalia both politically and militarily, Egypt was undermining one of the most sacred principles of that continent, namely the permanence of the present borders. Somalia was claiming territories from both Kenya and Ethiopia, thereby undermining the very precarious balance in the region. In following this line Sadat seems to have alienated prospective African support for his regional policy. However, recent developments in Chad, the Sudan and Ethiopia suggest that Egypt may not be as isolated as it appeared.

THE EXPLOITATION OF ISLAM IN EGYPT'S REGIONAL RELATIONS

The decline of Arabism as a major ideological factor after the 1967 defeat had enhanced the position of Islam both internally, in fighting the anti-Sadat opposition in the early years, and externally, in rallying many supporters behind Sadat's new foreign policy. This, of course, was not a new venture. Islam had been exploited in Egypt's foreign relations in the nineteenth century and the 'Islamic Circle' had been an important feature in Nasser's *Philosophy of the Revolution*. However, under Nasser, the emphasis was definitely on the 'Arab Circle' while Islam never achieved similar prominence.[29] Sadat's foreign policy was, as stated above, concerned with two major considerations: first, how to combat Soviet-inspired intrigues in the region, and second, how to enable Egypt to detemine its own priorities vis-à-vis the Middle East conflict, without undue concern for possible Arab reactions. The role of Islam in legitimizing these policies both inside Egypt and within the Islamic world should not be overrated, but neither should it be ignored.

But while Sadat's emphasis on confronting the Soviet Union and communism continued to receive impressive support in the Muslim world, his peace initiative with Israel was, at least on the official level, rejected. Arab pressures, and in particular those of Saudi Arabia, had succeeded in swaying, at least temporarily, even those of Egypt's allies, like Morocco and Sudan, whose future depends to a very large extent on continued Egyptian support against their radical enemies. It was therefore of particular importance to Sadat to have the full support of al-Azhar and of as many Muslim 'ulama as possible for his peace initiative since its inception. Sadat's visit to Jerusalem in November 1977 received the blessings of the Islamic establishment. Those supporting this historic act included the rector of al-Azhar, the presidents of Egyptian student unions and the Muslim Youth Association. The latter conveyed its blessings through its chairman, Shaykh Ahmad Hasan al-Baquri. In thanking those who had come to bless him, Sadat stated that only faith in God had prompted his initiative, and stressed that the only way to build a better Egypt was to educate the young Egyptians to be faithful to their religious principles. Similar support was granted to the peace initiative and the Camp David accords by the Shaykh of al-Azhar and the Ministry of *Waqfs*.[30] When the Islamic Conference in Rabat denounced Sadat's initiative, the staff of al-Azhar and all its affiliated institutions, under the chairmanship of Shaykh Rajab al-'Ayidi, reaffirmed their full support of Sadat's policy and stated that the peace treaty between Egypt and Israel was 'a blessed Islamic step, founded on the principles of religion'.[31]

Egypt's Regional Policy

So despite the general trend among the Muslim rulers outside Egypt to denounce Sadat's peace initiative as a betrayal of Islam, the Islamic establishment of Egypt continued to stress its religious blessings. Indeed, there was a growing tendency to emphasize the unreliability and the treason prevailing among the Arab rulers, while praising Islam and its potential blessings for the future of the region. In a long interview published in *October* magazine on 30 September 1979, Sadat listed the crimes committed by the Arabs against the Palestinians and against each other, not sparing even his erstwhile allies such as Saudi Arabia and Morocco. In concluding the interview he stated: 'I regret to say that the Arabs have not changed, but have instead regressed. Egypt alone has changed. We were and still are more civilized and advanced. The Arabs have become small in our eyes because we have grown bigger'.[32] It was therefore hardly surprising that after the Arab League Summit, which was convened in Tunisia in November 1979, following the removal of its headquarters from Cairo, Sadat declared that 'the latest comedy in Arab solidarity had ended ... This new Arab League has ended, and it had to end. *There will be no Arab League, but there must be a wider and greater Islamic League*'.[33] A week later, Sadat's close friend, the editor of *October*, Anis Mansur, called on all Muslims to establish an 'Islamic Peoples' League to confront the enemies of Islam and to *rise from the abyss of Arab policy to the glory of Islam*'. Only the Muslim people could achieve this, as certain Muslim rulers, notably those of Saudi Arabia, Syria, Iran, and Afghanistan, were distorting Islam in order to serve their own interests.[34]

But this was the accusation levelled with ever-growing vehemence against Sadat himself. The spokesmen of the more radical populist Islamic movements in Egypt, including the very strong Muslim Brethren, denounced Sadat's peace treaty with Israel as an act of heresy, while his internal policies in Egypt fared no better. Sadat's attempt to crush this radical opposition shortly before his assassination, when he ordered the arrest of some fifteen hundred of its leaders in September 1981, was probably an admission that he had underestimated their growing popularity.

CONCLUSION

This brief survey of Egypt's regional policy over the last two centuries has shown that there are definite shifts in emphasis rather than permanent changes in Egypt's foreign relations. If we evaluate these changing relations and analyse them we will discover the following. First, that the Sudan and the Nile Valley played a constant and central role in Egypt's regional considerations for most of that period both in the nineteenth and twentieth centuries. Second, that shifts in emphasis between the Arab Middle East and the East African region were to a large degree based on Egypt's reaction to international power politics and their repercussions, as interpreted in Cairo. It was Muhammad 'Ali's reading of the 'Eastern Question' which dictated his handling – or mishandling – of the Syrian campaigns in the 1830s. Isma'il's appreciation of the difficulties faced by his grandfather in the Fertile Crescent and the potential offered by aligning Egypt with British interests in Africa was a major consideration when he planned and executed his African campaigns and conquests in the 1860s and 1870s. When Egypt, once again, turned to Syria, after the second world war, it did so because of its interpretation of the repercussions of the Anglo-French evacuation of the region, and the consequent dangers of the vacuum being filled by a hostile Hashemite bloc. Later, in the 1950s, Nasser's concept of Arabism was linked to his ability to exploit the advantages offered by the cold war. The exploitation of superpower antagonisms in a regional context, with the aid of so-called positive neutralism, enabled Egypt to play a leading role in that region for a period of some ten years. Nasser failed to realise in the early 1960s that the cold war was declining and hence positive neutralism no longer offered the same dividends. Egypt therefore found herself in a position of growing dependence on the Soviet Union. Her regional policy, leading to the June 1967 war, was based to a certain degree on Soviet desire to undermine western influence in the Middle East to a vanishing point. With the 1969 coups in Libya and the Sudan this policy seemed to be paying off, but in reality neither Nasser nor Soviet Middle Eastern interests ever recovered completely from the 1967 defeat.

Sadat's shift in regional politics was based on the following assumptions: first, that the Soviet connection no longer carried with it any advantages for Egypt but rather presented acute dangers; second, that in the Fertile Crescent, with its ever-growing entanglements, Egypt would be served best by certain aloofness. Sadat neither foresaw nor planned the breakdown in Egypt's relations with the Arab world which followed the Camp David accords. But his policy, even prior to 1977, clearly indicated his determination to formulate Egypt's priorities in foreign policy in Cairo according to Egyptian interests, regardless of the repercussions in Damascus, Baghdad, or even Riad. According to these considerations, Egypt's top priority, based on its strategic position, as interpreted by Sadat and his close associates, was to forge the kind of alliances which would enable it to withstand the ever-growing Soviet threat. This meant, in the first place, closer relations with the United States, who had to be convinced that an alliance with Egypt was at least as important for western interests as America's commitment to Israel or to Saudi Arabia. It further indicated the necessity of peace with Israel, both because of Egypt's economic problems and in order to enable the shift in American Middle East policy as indicated above. For Sadat realised quite clearly, and especially after his futile pro-American gestures in 1971–72, that only a major breakthrough in regional politics, ending the Arab-Israeli stalemate, would convince Washington that Egypt was serious in her desire to return to the western fold. The October 1973 war, leading to the Sinai disengagement agreements and from there to the November 1977 peace initiative, supplied the necessary proof.

The changing pattern of Egypt's regional relations was therefore the result of several accumulated factors, as mentioned above, rather than a carefully considered, consistent and well-planned policy. Had Saudi Arabia, Morocco, Jordan or even Syria and the P.L.O. fallen into line, Sadat's Egypt would probably have regarded it as a blessing. Since the reverse happened, Sadat, unlike Nasser, refused to change course and was willing to risk a confrontation with the Arabs. Sadat was convinced that Egypt's isolation among the Arabs was a passing phase and that her superior strength enabled her to ignore the objections of those whom he defined derogatively as 'dwarfs'.

But the Sudan, owing to its geo-political position, was in a different category. The Sudan is Egypt's hinterland and the danger of a hostile government in the upper Nile regions was always regarded in Cairo as a far greater threat than the cumulative threats made by Qadhafi, Assad or 'Arafat. Qadhafi could and did encourage the anti-Sadat opposition both in Egypt and in Tripoli, but he was never more than a nuisance and could, if it became necessary, be disposed of. Numayri's continued support for Egypt's regional and international policy continued to be an important feature of Sadat's foreign relations and has remained so under Egypt's new President, Husni Mubarak. Numayri's presence in Cairo throughout the crucial week following Sadat's assassination, and his outspoken support for the new president, were clear indications as to his intentions.

Sadat's disappearance from the Middle Eastern scene may yet present a further shift in Egypt's regional relations. On the one hand it may enable the more conservative Arab rulers to modify their anti-Egyptian stance, and on the other it may ease Egypt's re-entering the scene of inter-Arab relations, in order to weaken the extremist pro-Soviet front. Egypt's gradual return to the Arab fold should, however not be viewed as a major switch in her regional policy. For Sadat's assassination was not a verdict on his regional policy but rather the result of his underestimating the fundamentalist Muslim forces in Egypt and his short-sighted socio-economic policies. Sadat's plan to westernize Egypt and, through massive import of western technology and culture, turn her into an anti-Soviet outpost, drove the radical Muslim *jihad* movements to a militant anti-western offensive.

'I shot the pharaoh,' said one of Sadat's young assassins during the trial. Yet even as the words were being uttered another pharaoh was in place. He would, judging by his record so far, do things with greater caution. But he would stay on Sadat's course, for no other way out existed for Egypt. Thus Egypt would proceed to retrieve what Sadat had worked for and then go beyond him.[35]

President Mubarak's performance during his first year in office bears witness both to his caution and to his refusal to stray away from his predecessor's regional and international policy. His moderation during Israel's invasion of Lebanon and his declared support for the continuation of the peace process, despite what may be viewed as Israeli provocations, seems to indicate that at present Egypt is continuing on the path of the *Realpolitik* which had been formulated under Sadat after the October 1973 war.

In the words of Boutros Ghali, Egypt's minister of state for foreign affairs, this continuity is the natural consequence of geopolitical, historical and economic components:

From Gamal Abdel Nasser to Anwar el-Sadat, from Anwar el-Sadat to Hosni Mubarak, these same components have influenced and shaped the foreign policy of Egypt. Therefore, it is in the nature of things that this policy should have a character of continuity through the various periods, and, consequently, after the tragic death of President Sadat, that this continuity should prevail.[36]

But in defining this continuity Ghali tends to gloss over the major shifts which have occurred in Egypt's global and regional relations during the last three decades. The two main challenges confronting Egypt's foreign relations in these years were according to Ghali 'how to contain Israeli ambitions and how to solve the Palestinian problem'.

Sadat's peace initiative of November 1977 was therefore only a new methodology to reach the same aim.[37] If we accept this thesis, then Nasser's positive neutralism in the 1950s and 1960s or Sadat's preoccupation with the Soviet encroachment in the 1970s, must be explained as by-products of the Israeli-Palestinian problem, which would be both inaccurate and misleading. Egypt's international relations would have remained central in the formulation of her foreign policy regardless of Israel and the Palestinian problem. Furthermore, Egypt's special relationship with the Sudan and her keen interest in the African continent and especially the Nile basin are hardly affected by the Israeli-Palestinian conflict. And yet, as Ghali rightly observes, Egypt's commitment to African causes and especially to the security of the Sudan and the Nile Valley, are likely to remain central issues in her regional policy.

This trend has indeed been further strengthened as indicated by the 'Integration Charter' (*mithaq al-takamul*) which was signed by President Mubarak and President Numayri on 12 October 1982 and approved by the Egyptian and Sudanese Parliaments a week later. While there had been previous moves in this direction, especially since 1974, this was the most comprehensive and far-reaching charter signed between these two countries. It set definite goals for integration in the fields of foreign relations, security, economic and social welfare, and specified the timetable allotted to achieving these goals which would not exceed ten years. But what was probably even more significant was the fact that the new charter set up a special 'Integration Fund', with its own budget, and thus enabled the Higher Council for Integration to start its activities without further delay. The inaugural session of this new Council took place in Khartoum on 22 February 1983 and approved the first eight 'integration laws' which would gradually bring about the free passage of both people and goods across the common borders of Egypt and the Sudan. For this purpose work has already been started on building a new port in Wadi Halfa, while the road from Aswan to Wadi Halfa and from there through Dongola to Khartoum was being completed, the first ever such overland link between the two countries. The agricultural integration plan included joint cultivation of some 250,000 *feddan* and enabled the two countries to undertake common activities in the production and the marketing of their main agricultural products, including cotton, tea and fish from the Nubian lake.

Would this new 'Integration Charter' lead to the long cherished

'Unity of the Nile Valley'? While political unity was not specified as an immediate aim of the Integration programme, the preamble of the Charter emphasized the historical and cultural unity of the Egyptian and Sudanese people. This unity, brought about by the Nile, made the two countries and their people into an inseparable entity.[38] But while formal unity seems at present to be a far-away dream, there can be no doubt that the people of Egypt and the Sudan, as well as their respective rulers, regard the ultimate integration of their two countries as far more feasible and desirable than the ideas of Arab unity which were rampant in Egypt in the 1950s and 1960s.

NOTES

1. For details on Muhammad 'Ali's and Isma'il's foreign policy see: Henry Dodwell, *The Founder of Modern Egypt*, Cambridge 1931, pp. 39-67, 125-191; L.A. Fabunmi, *The Sudan in Anglo-Egyptian Relations*, London 1964, pp. 22-51; J.C. Hurewitz, *The Middle East and North Africa, A Documentary Record*, Vol. 1, New Haven & London 1975, pp. 271-278; Lord Cromer, *Modern Egypt*, Vol. 1 London 1908, pp. 371-395; Rifaat Bey, *The Awakening of Modern Egypt*, Lahore 1964, pp. 140-151; M.S. Anderson, *The Eastern Question*, New York 1966, pp. 88-109.
2. Fabumni, pp. 62-112, 114-202; G. Warburg, *The Sudan Under Wingate*, London 1971, pp. 13-45; G. Warburg, *Islam, Nationalism and Communism in a Traditional Society*, London 1978, pp. 67-89; Lord Lloyd, *Egypt Since Cromer*, Vol. 2, New York 1970, pp. 123-139, 285-302, 395-399.
3. On Britain's Middle Eastern policy see E. Monroe, *Britain's Moment in the Middle East*, London 1963, pp. 131-177; E. Kedourie, *The Chatham House Version and Other Middle Eastern Studies*, London 1970, pp. 213-235, 351-394; P.J. Vatikiotis, *Nasser and His Generation*, London 1978, pp. 85-96; Y. Gershuni, *Egypt Between Distinctiveness and Unity: The Search for National Identity 1919–1948*, Tel Aviv 1980, pp. 200-282 (in Hebrew).
4. Vatikiotis, pp. 225-261; S. Shamire (ed.) *The Decline of Nasserism, 1965–1970*, Tel Aviv 1978, (in Hebrew), pp. 1-38, 208-309; M. Kerr, *The Arab Cold War 1958–1967*, London, New York, Toronto, 1967; O.M. Smolansky, *The Soviet Union and the Arab East under Kruschchev*, Lewisburg 1974.
5. For details see: G.G. Gilbar, 'Egypt's Economy: the Challenge of Peace', *The Opening of the Peace Process*, A Study Day of the Levi Eshkol Institute, Jerusalem 1981, pp. v-xxii; see also E. Kanovsky, 'Major Trends in the Middle East Economic Developments', in C. Legum (ed.) *Middle East Contemporary Survey*, Vol. 1, 1976–1977, New York & London 1978, pp. 227-234 (hereafter *MECS*); *MECS 1977–1978*, pp. 398-406.
6. A.Z. Rubinstein, *Red Star on the Nile*, Princeton 1977, especially pp. 129-345; Anwar el-Sadat, *In Search of Identity*, New York & London 1978, pp. 210-313; see also *MECS 1976–1977*, pp. 35-6, 305-310; *MECS 1977–1978*, pp. 19-39, 387-390; *MECS 1978–1979*, pp. 409-412.
7. Sadat, pp. 204-231; A.I. Dawisha, *Egypt in the Arab World*, London 1976, pp. 197-198.

Egypt's Regional Policy

8. F. Ajami, 'The end of Pan Arabism', *Foreign Affairs* (winter 1979).
9. R.M. Burrell, A.R. Kelidar, *Egypt: The Dilemmas of a Nation 1970–1977* Washington Papers Vol. V No. 48, Beverly Hills & London 1977, pp. 59, 69.
10. M.H. Heikal, 'Egyptian Foreign Policy', *Foreign Affairs* (summer 1978).
11. For details see article in *al-sharq al-awsat*, 17.9.1979; quoted in FBIS-MEA, 19.9.1979; Iraq was also aiding the anti-Sadat opposition; see also *MECS 1976–1977*, pp. 314-316 and *MECS 1977–1978*, p. 391.
12. *al-Dustur*, Jordan, 2.3.1979; the treaty was in effect signed in the summer of 1981 and included South Yemen too.
13. *N.Y. Times*, 29.3.1979.
14. *Afro-Asian Affairs*, London, June 1979.
15. *N.Y. Times*, 17.6.1980.
16. Quoted from Tripoli Radio 5-6 Nov. 1980; by BBC-ME, 7-8 Nov. 1980.
17. Benjamin Neuberger, *Involvement Invasion and Withdrawal: Qaddafi's Libya and Chad 1969–1981*, Shiloah Center Occasional Papers, Tel Aviv 1982, pp. 51-53.
18. Tripoli Radio, 17.12.1980, BBC-ME, 19.12.1980.
19. C. Legum, 'The Syrian connection in Africa', *Jerusalem Post*, 1.3.1981.
20. *MECS 1976–1977*, pp. 316-317, 595-598; *MECS 1977–1978*, pp. 213-243, 390-395; *MECS 1978–1979*, pp. 75-78, 416-417.
21. Y. Ronen, 'Sudan's Position towards the Egyptian Peace Policy', Occasional paper No. 72, The Shiloah Center, Tel Aviv 1980, [in Hebrew].
22. G.R. Warburg, 'Islam in Sudanese Politics', *The Jerusalem Quarterly*, Vol. 13 (Fall 1979), pp. 47-61; for details see also Chapter 6, below.
23. *FBIS-MEA*, 23.11.1979 quoting QNA 22.11.1979.
24. *Herald Tribune*, 20.12.1979; *October*, 31.12.1979.
25. *al-sharq al-awsat*, 11.6.1980.
26. BBC, 18.3.1981; quoting MENA, 16.3.1981; and SUNA, 16.3.1981.
27. U.P.A. quoted by *Davar*, 26 June 1981.
28. The following is based on *MECS 1976–1977*, pp. 58-73; *MECS 1977–1978*, pp. 56-60, 237-242; I am also grateful to Dr. H. Erlich of Tel Aviv University for letting me use his notes of a lecture on this topic, delivered to the Israel Oriental Society in March 1981.
29. P.J. Vatikiotis, 'Islam and the Foreign Policy of Egypt', in J.H. Proctor (ed.), *Islam and International Relations*, London 1965, pp. 120-157.
30. I. Altman, 'Recent Radical Trends in the Positions of the Moslem Brothers', Shiloah Center Occasional Papers, Tel Aviv 1979, [in Hebrew], p. 9; quoting from *Ruz al-Yusuf*, 12 December 1977; *al-Ahram*, 28 September 1978; *FBIS-MEA*, V. 231, 1 December 1977, quoting R. Cairo, 30 November 1977.
31. *FBIS-MEA*, V. 98, 18 May 1979, quoting MENA.
32. Quoted from *FBIS-MEA*, V. 192, 2 October 1979.
33. Quoted from *October*, 30 December 1979, by *FBIS-MEA*, V. 252 31 December 1979, [italics mine].
34. *FBIS-MEA*, V. 5, 8 January 1980, [Italics mine]; for details see below Ch. 6.
35. Fouad Ajami, 'The Arab World', *Foreign Policy* 47 (summer 1982): 7.
36. Boutros Boutros-Ghali, 'The Foreign Policy of Egypt in the Post-Sadat Era', *Foreign Affairs*, 60/4 (spring 1982): 769.
37. Ibid., pp. 769, 771.
38. For the full text of the Integration Charter see *al-Ahram*, 10 October 1982; see also interview with Dr. Fu'ad Muhi al-Din, Egypt's Prime Minister, on integration and unity, as quoted from MENA, in *FBIS-MEA*, V. 196, 8 October 1982; On the first meeting of the Higher Council of Integration in Khartoum, see *al-Ahram*, 23 February 1983.

6

ISLAM AND POLITICS IN EGYPT AND THE SUDAN UNDER THE MILITARY

The 'resurgence of Islam' has become one of the most popular topics for contemporary research on the Muslim world. Since the Islamic revolution in Iran and the assassination of President Sadat by a neo-Mahdist militant Muslim organization, these militant Muslim movements have inadvertently contributed to the production of an ever-growing volume of both popular and academic literature on this topic. The following study is not concerned with this so-called 'resurgence'. In previous studies analyzing the role of popular Islam in Sudanese society and politics,[1] I have attempted to show the predominant role which these movements have played in Sudanese society and politics during the first half of the twentieth century, long before this so-called resurgence ever started. In Egypt developments took a different course, since the political role of both the Muslim establishment and of its more popular oriented counterparts was largely overshadowed by the emerging secular nationalist movement at least until the 1930s. However, in both regions Islam maintained its predominant role in the daily life of the mass of the inhabitants and the term 'resurgence' is therefore not appropriate.

My aim in this study is to examine only one aspect of this multi-faceted problem, namely, the exploitation of Islam by the military rulers of Egypt and the Sudan, in order to legitimize their rule and to enhance their political standing both within their own countries and in the surrounding Muslim world. This study is limited to the period of the Free Officers in Egypt and of Numayri's rule in the Sudan and is thus primarily concerned with the role of Islam under a particular form of military rule in the Nile Valley.

Both Egypt and the Sudan have significant non-Muslim minorities.

Islam and Politics in Egypt and the Sudan

However, since the topic of this study is politicized Islam, the non-Muslim minorities will feature in it only insofar as they had an impact on the role of Islam in their respective countries' political systems.

A second clarification is called for in order to define the distinction between two major Islamic centres of influence. The first may be called, for lack of a better term, the Islamic establishment. The second is not really a centre, as it is much more diffused than the first. It may be defined as popular Islam mainly because it generally represents popular (or populist) Muslim movements which at times have collaborated with central power but in many instances have fought against the *status quo*. In the case of Egypt, al-Azhar and its hierarchy, as well as the various ministries dealing with religious institutions, such as waqfs, mosques, or *sufi* orders, are part of the establishment, while the Muslim Brethren and various neo-Mahdist groups are within the so-called popular-Islamic orbit. In the Sudan, the Islamic establishment has never enjoyed the aura of the al-Azhar-dominated Muslim leadership of its northern neighbour. Despite continuous attempts to enhance its standing, whether by importing 'ulama educated in al-Azhar from Egypt, or by sending young Sudanese to study there, thereby attempting to elevate the standing of the Omdurman Center of Islamic Studies, the top echelon of Sudanese 'ulama has so far not achieved a prominent position. However, the regime was able to harness several of the leading *sufi* orders to support it. Popular Islam, on the other hand, was much more predominant in Sudanese politics than it was in Egypt. This was true even before the Mahdist revolt in the 1880s which brought such a radical militant movement to the helm of government. It remained so throughout the Sudan's domination by England, in the years 1899–1955, and continued to be a central factor in Sudanese society and politics since independence.

Lastly, while this Chapter examines the role of Islam in Egyptian and Sudanese politics and its exploitation by their respective rulers, this in no way implies that other factors are of inferior status in determining these policies. In fact, we are basically concerned with regimes who owe their coming to power to military intervention. Hence, though we have no reason to question the piety of the respective rulers, we have even less reason to assume their willingness to share their power with others, be they of a secular or a devout Muslim outlook.

THE HISTORICAL BACKGROUND

I

In 1879 Jamal al-Din al-Afghani, the first propagator of political pan-Islam in modern times, was expelled from Egypt. During the eight years of his sojourn in Cairo, Afghani had left his mark on the Egyptian religious and political elite which was soon to be embroiled in the first proto-nationalist uprising in the Middle East. Indeed a list of Afghani's disciples and their followers reads like a *Who's Who* of Egyptian religious and political leadership. Some of his disciples, like Muhammad 'Abduh, joined the Urabist movement in 1881–82, helped in formulating its ideology and later led Islamic reformism in Egypt with Lord Cromer's blessings. Others, like Sa'd Zaghlul and Ahmad Lutfi al-Sayyid, became the political and intellectual leaders in Egyptian nationalism after the turn of the century. But while political pan-Islam continued to play a significant role in the Ottoman Empire's policy under Sultan 'Abdul Hamid II, its impact on Egypt was rather more limited. It remained a political, anti-British tool in the hands of Mustafa Kamil's Nationalist party, directed against the occupation of Egypt and the Sudan by British infidels. But following the young Turks' revolution in 1908, Egyptian politics turned inwards and the propagation of pan-Islamic themes was left primarily to Syrian Muslim emigrés, such as Muhammad Rashid Rida, who continued to preach Afghani's and 'Abduh's messages, in what seemed to be growing isolation. Indeed, while the mainstream of Egyptian political thinking was seemingly moving towards secular nationalism in the 1920s and 1930s, Rida and his few adherents were becoming ever more conservative in their outlook and propagated Islamic puritanism of the Wahhabi brand through the medium of his prestigious *al-Manar*. With the rise of Egyptian nationalism under the Wafd's leadership, after World War I, and following the promulgation of a Western type constitution in 1923, al-Azhar and its leadership were to an ever growing extent left out of touch with political and cultural realities. Al-Azhar's hostile attitude to both the British occupation and to the seemingly secular nationalist leadership, made it into a royalist bastion, giving tacit support to King Fu'ad and King Faruq in their anti-Wafdist endeavours and helping them and their camp-followers to further their dreams of pan-Islamic leadership.

The Islamic establishment had thus been relegated to the back benches of Egyptian politics — or so at least it must have seemed to the very few disciples of Rashid Rida who came to his funeral service in 1935. However, in 1935 the Muslim Brethren, though still a fledgling movement, had already made their mark in Ismailiyya, where the movement was founded in 1928 by Hasan al-Banna. Indeed, such an eminent so-called secular nationalist as Muhammad Husayn Haykal, one of the most prominent leaders of the Liberal Constitutionalist Party, published his book on the life of the Prophet Muhammad in 1935, to be followed by many volumes on Islamic themes written both by Haykal himself and by other eminent liberal nationalists. Thus, according to Nadav Safran, they ushered in a reactionary phase in Egyptian political thinking,[2] a phase which, as the result of the failure of European imported ideologies and constitutions, brought Islam forward once again as a possible alternative. It is unimportant for our study whether Egypt in the 1930s witnessed a genuine revival of Muslim thinking or whether it was merely a pragmatic shift to Islamic values, with the intention of placating the religious and political opposition of the time, as exemplified in the resurgence of Islam and the emergence of such popular movements as the Muslim Brethren.[3] What matters is that in the 1930s and 1940s it was once again quite clear that western imported constitutions or secular nationalist ideologies had very little attraction for the Egyptian masses. Islam, which had co-existed with so-called secular ideologies in the 1920s, became predominant. It was the Muslim Brethren alone who succeeded in attaining grass-roots support among the lower classes of the urban population, despite the fact that they did not use power in order to gain their support, as the Wafd and the other political parties had done. It was largely the discontent of the Egyptian farmers and their relatives who had emigrated to the urban centres during the second world war, which swelled the membership of the Muslim Brethren immediately after the war. This impressive popularity had an effect on Jamal 'Abd al-Nasir (Nasser), Muhammad Anwar al-Sadat, and their fellow Free Officers, when they made their plans to overthrow the constitutional monarchy in the wake of the 1948 war against Israel. To them it had become quite clear that unless the Muslim Brethren could be forced to submit and to cooperate with the new military leadership, they would have to be suppressed so as to neutralize their impact on the Egyptian population.

II

In June 1881, some two years after Afghani's expulsion from Egypt, Muhammad Ahmad b. 'Abdallah declared himself Mahdi on Aba Island on the White Nile. The thirteenth century of Islam was drawing to its end and the Muslims in the Sudan, as in many other regions, were expecting the saviour to lead them on the righteous path against their Turco-Egyptian and European oppressors, and to enforce Islam, the only true religion which would bring justice to the world.[4] With hardly any modern weapons at their disposal, the Mahdi and his *ansar* (supporters) succeeded in less than four years in defeating the Egyptian army in several major battles. In January 1885 they conquered Khartoum and assassinated its British imported governor-general, General Charles (Chinese) Gordon Pasha, thus eliminating the final traces of Turco-Egyptian sovereignty from the Sudan after some sixty-four years of foreign rule.

The historical significance of these events lies in the fact that a fanatical Muslim puritan movement succeeded in uniting most of the Muslims of the Sudan, split as they were into tribes, *sufi* orders and a wide variety of ethnic groups, and in overcoming a modern well-equipped army, commanded at times by British officers. A number of factors combined to bring about this victory even if we limit ourselves to those in the Nile valley. It is clear that the defeat of the Urabist rebellion in Egypt in 1882, resulting in the British conquest and the weakening of the Egyptian army, was of major significance. However, there can be no doubt that only a popular Muslim rebellion, led by a generally accepted leader (the Mahdi), could have succeeded in uniting the Sudanese Muslims in the *jihad* (holy war) against the Egyptian unbelievers. For the Mahdi and his followers had no doubt that the Khedive Tawfiq, Sultan Abdul Hamid II, Queen Victoria and General Charles Gordon, were all infidels whom a true believer was obliged to fight for the sake of Islam, the only true religion.

The Mahdist state was the first expression of Sudanese independence and Mahdism is regarded by many Sudanese and other scholars as the first expression of Sudanese nationalism. Its importance was by no means limited to the seventeen years that the Mahdiyya reigned supreme in the Sudan until it was crushed by superior Anglo-Egyptian forces in 1898. The vitality of the Ansar under the able leadership of the Mahdi's son, Sayyid 'Abd al-Rahman al-Mahdi, was such that it dominated Sudanese society and politics in the first half of the

Islam and Politics in Egypt and the Sudan

twentieth century.[5] But what is even more significant is that despite British attempts to suppress the Mahdists as a political force, especially after 1924, they emerged again and again as a major contender for power. Britain naturally regarded a Westminster-type government as its ideal for the Sudan and hence sought to separate Islam from politics. And yet, in the reality of the Sudan, Britain was faced with an Islamic political movement, the Ansar, evolving into a political party, the Umma, which embodied within itself both religion and politics. When independence came, in 1956, it was popular Islam which dominated the political scene and made constitutional government an abysmal failure. As in the case of Egypt, military intervention followed. First, there emerged a conservative military regime, headed by General Ibrahim 'Abbud, which, having been brought to power with the blessings of the religious-sectarian leadership, did its utmost in the years 1958–1964 to suppress popular Islam. Following a second brief and unsuccessful experiment in parliamentary government, in which sectarian politics once again reigned supreme, a Free Officers' coup, based on the Egyptian pattern, led to a seizure of power in May 1969. Under the leadership of Ja'far Muhammad al-Numayri, the new military regime had three initial goals when it came to power. First, to put an end to the civil war between the Muslim north and the non-Muslim Southern Sudan; second, to neutralize the communists, who had become too influential since the 1964 civilian coup; and third to overcome once and for all the curse of sectarianism which had harassed Sudanese politics since independence. Not unlike the Free Officers in Egypt, who had to overcome the challenge of the Muslim Brethren in order to survive, Numayri and his colleagues knew that the Ansar presented a major threat to their political success. Thus, in the early days of military rule in the Nile valley, it was popular Islam which presented the major challenge to the regimes of both Egypt and the Sudan.

III

In the 1950s and 1960s many observers of the Middle East scene regarded secular nationalism as the predominant force in politics, while Islam, so they claimed, was on its way out. To cite one example of many, Hisham Sharabi, in an article published in 1966 under the title: 'Islam and Modernization in the Arab World',[6] stated that 'in the contemporary Arab World Islam has simply been bypassed'.

Furthermore, he argued that 'the decline of Islam in the twentieth century as an organized institutional force capable of exerting direct influence on society and the state cannot be explained or accounted for by a simple or unitary diagnosis'.[7] Following a diagnosis of the disintegration of the social and economic system, Sharabi argued that Islamic revivalism as examplified by the Wahhabiyya in Saudi Arabia, or the Muslim Brethren in Egypt 'came too late to stem the tide of secularism, and its fate was sealed with the triumph of Abdul Nasser's secular revolution. The Muslim Brothers may well be the last serious effort of traditional Islam to regain its position in Arab society'.[8] However, taking stock of the situation in 1979, following not only Khomeini's Islamic revolution in Iran but what seems at present to indicate a widespread Islamic resurgence, Sharabi acknowledged that 'Islamic conservatism is at present the dominant ideological force in Arab society'.[9] Moreover, he argued that this dominance is going to prevail until 'the social and economic conditions that now sustain it are radically changed'. In order to understand how Islam, after more than thirty years of western imported constitutional government, followed by a quarter of a century of Arab nationalism and Arab socialism, has once again come to the fore, we should concentrate on the recent past and the contemporary scene in the Nile valley. Surely, to state that western imported ideologies have failed in Muslim society and were therefore rejected cannot be regarded as a sufficient answer, because such a statement ignores the main issue, namely, the ability of Islam to withstand the western ideological onslaught now well into its second century. The Ayatullah Khomeini, in an interview with Oriana Fallaci, gave only a partial answer when he stated: 'We are afraid of your ideas and of your customs. Which means that we fear you politically and socially.'[10] We are given a statement regarding the dangers of western ideologies, as seen by a devout Muslim *faqih*, but we are left at a loss as to how Islam succeeded in its resistance. However, views continue to be divided regarding Islam's ability to withstand these western ideologies. Many Muslims regard the Islamic revival as an essentially defensive movement, 'a sort of holding operation against modernity', and argue that if present conditions prevail, Islam is indeed fighting a losing battle.[11]

Just as views regarding the present and future differ, so do the attempts to explain the causes of this Islamic revival, regardless of whether or not it is indeed a losing battle. Let us first indicate the more obvious causes of the failure of the so-called western ideologies. In the 1930s when the unsuccessful attempts at democratic government in several Middle Eastern states were in full swing, fascism, nazism and communism were already questioning the viability of democracy in Europe itself. Moreover, in countries like Egypt or the Sudan only a small intellectual elite was able to comprehend western ideologies; to the mass of the population they had next to no significance. To teach primary or high-school pupils, who, anyway, were only a small minority, to recite the 1923 Egyptian Constitution or later on the 1962 National Charter, could hardly be regarded as a sound ideological education in democracy or socialism. Finally, if, as the 'ulama claimed, the ideological basis for democracy or socialism was to be sought in the Qur'an itself, we are indeed back at square one, for there seems little logic in importing democracy or other so-called western ideologies if the Islamic principles of the *shura* incorporate all that western democracy has to offer, just as the principles of socialism are to be found in the Qur'an.[12]

In his article 'Basic Factors Affecting Social Structure, Tensions, and Change in Modern Egyptian Society',[13] Gabriel Baer argued that the strength and relative efficiency of central government in Egyptian society and politics prevented the emergence of alternative social agencies on the local level. Hence, the settlement of the nomad bedouins, the dissolution of the village community, and the disintegration of the Egyptian guilds, did not result in the emergence of strong trade unions, village cooperatives or other genuine modern associations. What was left was therefore the remote but strong central government on the one hand, and, on the more intimate level, kinship and religious ties. Baer argued that even after the Nasserist land reforms and the institutionalization of Arab socialism and village cooperatives the community of believers remained the only meaningful unit in Egyptian villages. The situation among the lower classes in the towns, and even more so among those without permanent employment or means of livelihood, was no different. Theoretically, this gap should have been filled by the 'ulama. However, under Nasser and Sadat, the religious establishment had lost the remains of its economic independence while its credibility had been further undermined. Thus it became a servile part of the feared, but remote, centre. Those who stepped in to fill this gap were Muslim Brethren who, both before the Free Officers came to power and after, were the only major movement which addressed itself to the true beliefs and socio-economic needs of the Egyptian masses. Sadat's attempt at attracting mass participation in the political system through the creation of his three platforms (after 1977 political parties), a so-called attempt at liberalization and democracy, seems to have had no more chance of success than previous similar attempts. Indeed, Baer was probably right in his rather pessimistic views regarding the future. Though written in 1970, his conclusion that as long as the overwhelming preponderance of the centre in the social structure and its detrimental effect on social change continues, there is little hope for the emergence of genuine participation in political and social associations. The gap between rulers and ruled is therefore liable to grow, not only economically but also socially and ideologically, with religious and ethnic homogeneity mitigating the disintegration but unable to overcome it.

Neither Nasser nor Sadat, though probably aware of the problem, have ever really addressed themselves seriously to the challenge of popular Islam. They harnessed the Muslim hierarchy, through financial dependence and political favouritism, and made it a submissive tool of the centre. But despite their own piety, their attitude to the challenges of popular Islam to present-day society and politcs, especially among the lower classes, can only be defined as superficial. This is especially surprising if we take into account that both Nasser and Sadat continuously stressed their rural roots in order to maintain their claim for mass support from the Egyptian villages. Indeed, according to Binder 'the Nasserist regime attempted, rather, to transfer the spirit of Village Egypt to the seat of power in Cairo'.[14] But, while the interests of the peasants were continually put forward as the regime's main concern, their Islamic roots were hardly taken into account when Nasser formulated his pan-Arab or Arab-socialist policies. Sadat's attachment to his own village Mit Abu al-Kawm, and to the values of village life, including Islam, were central themes in his *In Search of Identity*.[15] 'This land on which I walked, the running water of the Canal, indeed everything around me, was made by an overseeing God — a vast mighty being that watches and takes care of all, including me ... We all came out of the land and could never exist without it.'[16] The adoption of the values of the Egyptian village and the advocacy of Islamic ideals was a recurrent theme in Sadat's autobiography and he ended his book thanking God that he had remained loyal to his origins in all his actions 'for with every action we take to realize ourselves, we fulfil the will of God, and his will is everlasting'.[17] Yet, even Sadat failed to realize that the advocation of Islamic ideals would lead to political consequences.

Islam and Politics in Egypt and the Sudan

If we move to observe the Sudanese scene, many differences come to mind. First, in the Sudan, unlike in Egypt, the so-called return of Islam was not primarily a reaction against western imported ideologies. Popular Islam, dominated by holy families, was dominant in Sudanese tribal society long before the Egyptian conquest in 1820. Despite Egyptian attempts to undermine its strength through the importation of an Egyptian Azhar-educated Muslim leadership, popular Islam survived and proved its vitality in the Mahdist uprising. The historical reasons for this phenomenon need not be dealt with here.[18] What is important for an understanding of the present situation is the fact that the Mahdiyya, a popular Islamic movement, gave the Sudan its first independent theocratic government. Indeed, many regarded the Mahdi as the founder of modern Sudanese nationalism and the Ansar, the neo-Mahdist movement of the twentieth century, thus became a prime contender for power in the new independent Sudan. The reasons for this predominance, which is far more central in the Sudan than in Egypt, are to be sought in several directions. First, it was not the strength of central government but rather its weakness which enabled popular Islamic leaders to step in and contend for power. Those who stood in their way were not the 'ulama of the establishment but rather tribal leaders who, until the Mahdiyya established central autocratic government, were extremely powerful. It was the vacuum left in the vast rural areas of the Northern Muslim Sudan, following the disintegration of tribal leadership, which enabled the Ansar to rise to prominence once more, despite British and later Sudanese attempts to curtail them. The rural population of the Sudan, like their brethren in Egypt, had little use for Westminster style democracy, Sudanese socialism, or other imported ideologies. Herein lies the strength of popular Islam in the Sudan: its ability to address itself to the belief system and the needs of the mass of the Sudanese people.[19]

THE ISLAMIC ESTABLISHMENT IN EGYPT

In observing the 'politicization' of Islam in the Nile valley, one has to distinguish between the exploitation of Islam for external use, especially in foreign relations, and its place within the states' policies as they apply to their own people. In both these spheres al-Azhar, as the most prestigious Muslim institution in Egypt, as well as the 'ulama in general, had to play a central role. First, they were expected to grant the Free Officers the backing they required in their internal quest for legitimacy; and second, the 'ulama of al-Azhar, by exploiting their prestige throughout the Muslim world, were called upon to bless Nasser's Arabism, in the name of Islam, thus helping the new creed to gain respectability and become acceptable, in other Muslim, and especially Arab states. Under Sadat, the role of the Islamic establishment was enhanced at least partly because of his emphasis on his own religious faith. But more significant were the new roles which Islam was called upon to perform, both internally, in helping overcome the leftist and Nasserist oppositions, and externally, in providing Muslim blessings for Sadat's controversial peace initiative, in the face of growing Muslim opposition.

I

Al-Azhar gained in importance especially after the clash with the Muslim Brethren, in October 1954. In crushing the 1,700 cells which the Brethren claimed to have had in the Egyptian countryside, Nasser and his colleagues needed the blessings of the 'ulama and their cooperation both at the centre of government and in helping to mobilize the local *imams* and *kuttab* teachers to the support of their regime. Indeed the Free Officers soon learned, with Azharite help, to copy the techniques so successfully used by the Brethren, of having their Friday sermons preached in the village mosque throughout Egypt.[20] The importance of the Azharite establishment was also demonstrated in the frequent visits of members of the Revolutionary Command Council (R.C.C.), including Nasser, to the shaykhs of al-Azhar, and their not less frequent attendance at the al-Azhar Friday prayers.[21] The result of this dependence was a delay in reforms aimed at curtailing the independent status of the 'ulama. A brief look at some of these reforms indicates that the gradual undermining of the 'ulama's independence started with the abolition of the family waqfs, as early as 1952. But the next blow came only in January 1956, when the officers felt secure enough to abolish the Shar'ia courts, and in 1957 to nationalize the waqf khayri (public endowments), thus undermining the economic basis of the Islamic establishment, and hence curtailing its influence even further. The abolishing of the Shar'ia courts was, according to *al-Ahram*, blessed by Shaykh 'Abd al-Rahman Taj of al-Azhar, as a liberating step. Even more humiliating, as far as the Islamic establishment was concerned, was the reform of

Islam and Politics in Egypt and the Sudan

al-Azhar itself, in 1961, turning it into a government controlled state university. This act, bitterly opposed by many of the helpless 'ulama, received the official blessings of Shaykh al-Azhar himself, Mahmud Shaltut, who denounced the opposition for using Islam as a profession while 'the new law includes a solution for every field ... It wants Islam to be revived. 'ulama to be of strong faith, living for the sake and not by means of it'.[22] In placing al-Azhar under the overall supervision of the President's office, one of its prime roles was both enhanced and facilitated. It enforced al-Azhar's role as a major channel of communication between Egypt and the Arab and Muslim world and as the leading Muslim interpreter of Nasser's revolution. Meanwhile, through the close supervision of al-Azhar's affairs, the president's office could rely on the Azharite hierarchy to preach the gospel of Arabism and socialism as synonymous with the aims and principles of the Islamic revolution. Conservative Muslim scholars such as Muhammad al-Bahi, one time chancellor of al-Azhar, came out in support of Nasser's Arab Socialism, stating that it was a reiteration of Islamic values. Others like Ahmad Hasan al-Zayyat, editor of *Majallat al-Azhar*, claimed that Nasser, like the Mahdi, had come to stamp out corruption and tyranny and to establish social justice based on Islam. Here we have a clear indication of Nasser's success in harnessing this important body of opinion in the service of his revolution.[23]

The subordination of the 'ulama was, in the first few years, entrusted to the ministry of waqfs under a leading Muslim Brother, Shaykh Ahmad Hasan al-Baquri, who had jumped on the Free Officers' band wagon when the rupture with the Brethren occurred in 1953–1954. Later, while Nasser was still in power, even this symbolic political position was entrusted to a retired army officer. The ministry of waqfs supervised most of the religious institutions, including all mosques, both public and private, which since the abolition of the waqfs relied on a government subsidy for their upkeep. One might have assumed that under a revolutionary regime which later declared Arab Socialism as its ideology, the mosques would at best have maintained their pre-revolutionary standing. Surprisingly enough the number of mosques and their personnel increased considerably in the first ten years after the revolution. In the years 1954–1963 the total number of employees and officials in all government mosques increased from 6,919 to 12,357.[24] This is of special significance if we take into account that the biggest increase was in the number of *imams* (preachers) whose task was to spread the messianic gospel of Nasserism throughout Egypt. But here was the inherent weakness, since al-Azhar could not cope with the training of new *imams* and thus by 1982 the number of private mosques increased to 40,000, while the government could not even find trained *imams* for its own mosques.

II

The interest of the Nasserist regime in *sufi* orders started in March 1955 when 'Abd al-Hakim 'Amir was entrusted with their supervision. This sudden interest was probably the result of the realization by Nasser and his colleagues that the administrative organization of the *sufi* orders could be exploited in order to combat the opposition of the Muslim Brothers who had just been outlawed.[25] The revival of Sufism, as a government tool, brought about the appearance of an official *sufi* periodical: *al-Islam wa'l-Tasawwuf*; official recognition of several *sufi* orders; an increase in their membership; and an increase in the number of *mawalid* (Saints' birthdays) which were celebrated throughout Egypt. Since 1961, the Arab Socialist Union (ASU) was involved in organizing the *mawalid*, which offered an ideal platform for transmitting government propaganda to mass captive audiences. Not less significant was the fact that the Supreme Sufi Council was increasingly used by the ASU to distribute its ideological propaganda throughout Egypt. Thus several orders and their respective *mashayikh* owed their increasing popularity and the growth in the number of their adherents to their close association with the authorities. First among those was the Shaykh of the Khalwatiyya order, Muhammad Mahmud 'Ilwan, who as 'Abd al-Hakim Amir's intimate friend became in 1957 the supreme shaykh of all *sufi* orders. The Supreme Sufi Council over which he presided had some sixty-four active *sufi* orders under its supervision. However, *sufi* orders remained one of the few areas, in a centralized authoritarian police state, where trust and intimacy remained feasible despite association with the government. The ASU therefore sought to have the *sufi* establishment's blessings for government policies, alongside those of the Azharite 'ulama. The Guide to Sufism, published in 1958 by the Supreme Sufi Council, therefore gave its full approval to the 1952 revolution and claimed that Sufism continued to flourish in Egypt due to 'God's blessing and support and to the encouragement and help of the Revolution and its great leader'.[26]

A clear indication, if indeed one was needed, of the total submissiveness of the Islamic hierarchy under Nasser, was their acquiescence in the National Charter of 1962. While Islam, as in the 1956 constitution, continued to be decreed the religion of the state, its general treatment in the Charter was rather ambivalent. Thus the Ottoman Caliphate was defined as colonialist and reactionary, clearly no compliment for the last universal Muslim Empire. The humiliation of Islam was even further emphasized when in the chapter dealing with foreign relations, Islam and the United Nations received equal status – once again hardly a compliment.[27] The National Charter may therefore be regarded as a turning point in the relationship between Nasser and the Islamic establishment. With Arab socialism, quasi-Marxist ideologies and mystical nationalism all seeking to replace orthodox Islam, the growing gap became even more difficult to bridge.[28] This did not stop Muslim scholars, such as Mahmud Shalabi or Mustafa al-Siba'i, from attempting to demonstrate the Islamic origins of Arab Socialism. Shalabi systematically collected all sayings attributed to the Prophet and to the four just Caliphs, to which the idea of a socialist outlook could be attributed.[29] Al-Siba'i, in his book *Ishtirakiyyat al-Islam* ('The Socialism of Islam'), summed up the aims of socialism as an end to exploitation and the achievement of social equality, both of which, he stated, were clearly the aims of Islam too.[30]

So it would seem that the leaders of the Islamic establishment, having already endorsed the regime's policies curtailing their own status, were in the 1960s giving Islamic sanction to the secularization of Egyptian society. Such Muslim leaders as Shaykh Mahmud Shaltut provided in effect the Islamic legitimization for every Nasserist policy. However, while it was easy enough to force the Cairo centred religious leadership to cooperate with the government, the same did not apply to the thousands of the rank and file rural religious functionaries. These lived too close to the people and hence were not willing to change their traditional attitudes or belief system, which in many cases clashed with government policies. Family planning, as ordained by the government and sanctioned by al-Azhar, was a case in point. The Cairo-based shaykhs and muftis declared, as expected, their full endorsement of this policy and stated that Islam was not opposed to birth control, while the local – especially the rural–*imams*, who as mentioned above were mostly not government employees, maintained their resistance.[31] Needless to say, family planning and birth control were a complete failure, as they clashed with social norms and family traditions, which remained stronger than government sanctions.

III

After Sadat came to power, the status of the Islamic establishment was considerably enhanced. This was primarily due to Sadat's need for the 'ulama's support in several of his political steps aimed specifically at curtailing the power of his Nasserist and communist opposition. Indeed, it was claimed that 'the Egyptian 'ulama are again endeavoring to take a more active role in keeping the country on "the right path".'[32] The occasion already presented itself in 1971 when Egypt's new constitution was promulgated. The Rector of al-Azhar, speaking on behalf of all the 'ulama and personnel of the institution, demanded a clear statement in the constitution to the effect that Islam was the state's religion. This demand was reiterated by many others, not necessarily 'ulama, and even received the full backing of the Coptic clergy.[33] Indeed of the nearly seven thousand proposals from the public regarding the new constitution, which poured into the headquarters of the preparatory committee, a substantial portion dealt with Islam in the new constitution. The place of the Shari'a in legislation became the topic of a major debate both in the daily press and in the National Assembly, with the extremists demanding that the Shari'a become the sole source of legislation and the moderates suggesting a less binding formula. The text, as approved by referendum and published on 6 September 1971, was a victory for the so-called moderates, but a far cry indeed from the hey-day of Nasserism when Islam had been relegated to an inferior position in the National Charter of 1962. Part I, Article 2 of the Constitution read: 'Islam is the religion of the State, Arabic is its official language and the principles of the Islamic Shari'a are *a* major source of legislation.'[34]

The compromise offered by the new constitution was unacceptable to the more orthodox Muslim 'ulama as well as to the Muslim Brothers and the more extreme Jama'at al-Islamiyya. This opposition moved its campaign to the People's Assembly and the mass media. In the Assembly the Brethren proposed a number of legislative amendments such as the immediate imposition of the penalties prescribed by the Shari'a for theft and embezzlement; mandatory memorization of the Qur'an in all government institutions; the imposition of a dressing code for women; and the prohibition of alcoholic beverages. But generally speaking the government succeeded in withstanding opposition initiatives in this respect and passed its own legislative reforms in the People's Assembly, applying its own concept of the Shari'a which differed substantially from that of the fundamentalists.

But the battle over the application of the Shari'a (*tatbiq al-shari'a*) was no longer limited to the fundamentalists, it embraced the Muslim orthodoxy as well as the political platforms. To appease this opposition the government introduced its own amendment to article 2 of the 1971 constitution which now read: 'The principles of the Islamic Shari'a are *the* principal source of legislation'. The speaker of the People's Assembly, Sufi Abu Talib, who had previously opposed such a change, now claimed that it changed nothing since it only emphasized the government's commitment to the application of the Shari'a.[35] Nonetheless, this amendment, which was approved by referendum in May 1980, was regarded by many non-Muslims as a major set-back in their struggle against radical fundamentalism.

Whereas the implementation of the Shari'a was a cause for certain tensions between Sadat and the Islamic establishment, he continued to receive all the backing he required in his battle against the left. During the October 1976 elections muftis and 'ulama openly supported Sadat's centrist platform and denounced Khaled Muhyi al-Din's Socialist platform as irreligious.[36] But even more significant was the involvement of the Muslim shaykhs following the January 1977 so-called food riots. The riots started on January 18, following an announcement made in the National Assembly, that the government had decided to cut down drastically on the subsidies, thus causing a considerable rise in the price of staple foods such as sugar, rice and oil. While the demonstrations seemed to enjoy wide popular support, even before they turned into riots, the weak clandestine communist group, as well as the official leftist platform under Muhyi al-Din, were accused of attempting to overthrow the regime and instal a communist one instead.[37] The Rector of al-Azhar, Dr. 'Abd al-Halim Mahmud, appealed on Radio Cairo to all Muslims, denouncing the riots as 'the lowest that humanity could stoop to' and declaring that they were organized by 'The enemy lying in wait to destroy all our aspirations'.[38]

However, the reliance on religion, on the religious hierarchy and on the various Muslim groups, in the battle against the leftists and the Nasserists, was not without price. Once religion had become a legitimate political force in service of the regime it was not long before these same groups exploited religion in order to criticize and even attack Sadat's own policies. This was especially true in the universities where the Islamic student groups (al-jama'at al-Islamiyya), Sadat's erstwhile allies, became his most vocal opponents. Their opposition was in no way limited to internal policies only, nor were these opponents a united front. Indeed, as the 1970s came to an end even the docile Azharite establishment started to criticize some of Sadat's policies and to demand a greater measure of independence for their venerated institution. An attempt to renew the Sadat-Azharite alliance seems to have been undertaken with the founding, in November 1979, of the 'Supreme Muslim Council'. The Council, under the chairmanship of Shaykh al-Azhar, Dr. Abd al-Rahman Bissar, was to be composed of fifty members, representing 'ulama, *sufi* shaykhs, leaders of Islamic associations, and government representatives. The Council, fully financed by the State, was entrusted with the supervision of all Muslim associations and institutions and with the integration of their activities. Furthermore, the Council was to promote Islamic teaching throughout Egypt, printing the necessary books and providing guidance to all schools and universities. In stating the Council's goals, the government made it quite clear that one of the dangers the 'Supreme Muslim Council' was expected to overcome was that of the growing opposition to Sadat which had begun to raise its head among the Muslim Brethren and other 'extremist, religious and subversive' groups.[39] However, criticism of Sadat's policy had already penetrated the high echelons of al-Azhar, who, under the leadership of Shaykh 'Abd al-Halim Mahmud, called for an independent al-Azhar and gave tacit support to the more moderate wing of the Muslim Brothers, demanding the implementation of the Shari'a.

IV

In his *Philosophy of the Revolution* Nasser clearly saw a new and more active role for Islam in contemporary Egyptian foreign relations. He envisioned an 'Islamic Circle' encompassing hundreds of millions of Muslims, from China to Morocco, all welded into a homogeneous whole by the same faith. Moreover, he foresaw the tremendous impact that the pilgrimage to Mecca could play in Muslim world politics. If instead of an 'admission card to paradise', the pilgrimage was to become an annual world and conference of all Muslim heads of state, leaders of opinion, scientists, and so on, a new international centre of power could be created. However, in Nasser's order of priorities the 'Arab Circle' came first and was defined by him as 'the most important and the most clearly connected with us'.[40] Even the 'African Circle' came before Islam, most probably because of the importance of the Nile valley and of Nasser's hopes, in the 1950s and 1960s, to become the major spokesman of an independent Africa, having already assumed a similar role in the Arab world since 1955.

In the Muslim world such a central role was clearly beyond Nasser's capabilities: first, because of the great prestige of the Sa'udi dynasty, the guardians of the most holy shrines of Islam; second, because his policies, especially his growing reliance on the Soviets, and his so-called Arab-Socialist ideology, made him and his regime anathema to the majority of conservative Muslim rulers, who reigned supreme in many of the Arab and other Muslim countries. Lastly, it would have made little sense to many of his most ardent supporters if his secular policies at home and his suppression of such movements as the Muslim Brethren were to have been wedded to an aggressive pan-Islamic stance in his foreign relations.

It is of little use to attempt an analysis of the Islamic contents of Nasser's statements on Egypt's foreign relations. As Vatikiotis showed as early as 1964, the ambivalence and contradictions which prevailed in Nasser's declarations in this field indicate that it is impossible to elicit any clear role for Islam in Egypt's foreign relations during the first ten years of the Free Officers' regime. Indeed, Nasser could state explicitly that religion and politics should not be mixed, while claiming at the same time that Islamic bonds of brotherhood united Egypt and other Muslim states thus making a common link between them both feasible and desirable. There was, according to Vatikiotis, a clear distinction in Nasser's pronouncements between true Islam, the religion of justice and equality, and deviationist Islam, the religion of corruption, reaction and tyranny.[41] What Nasser attempted was to gain the support of the leaders of the religious establishment, who, in turn, presented Nasser's Egypt to the rest of the Arab world as 'the model of regenerated Islam and the harbinger of another Islamic Age'. According to Ahmad Hasan al-Zayyat, editor of *Majallat al-Azhar*, Nasser's was the fourth 'Golden Age' of Islam, while his National Charter, proclaimed in 1962, was the ultimate godly truth as stated in the Shari'a, a truth which would soon reach every person and every land.[42]

To achieve this end Nasser created, as early as 1955, the so-called

Islamic Congress. Sadat who served as the first secretary-general of the new congress related that his task was 'to work for closer links between Arab and Muslim countries as well as for certain objectives of our [Egypt's] national cause'. One of these causes, according to Sadat, was his role in frustrating the Baghdad pact.[43] Other Islamic organizations were later founded to serve additional Egyptian objectives. The Supreme Council for Islamic Affairs, created within the ministry of wafqs in 1960 was adjusted, in the words of a leading member of Nasser's entourage, to serve the 'new needs of the Islamic community in the modern world'.[44] The Council's aim was 'to extend its [Islam's] brilliant rays of light from the United Arab Republic to all quarters of the world, East and West equally, regardless of race and color'.[45] In carrying out this aim the Council published numerous books and pamphlets on Islamic themes, which were distributed throughout the Muslim and Arab world. It also promoted visits of prominent Muslims from abroad to see the achievements of Islamic-Socialist Egypt with their own eyes. On a somewhat more theological basis, though with clear political aims, was the Academy of Islamic Research which was first convened in 1964, at the height of the war in Yemen, in order to combat the Saudi sponsored World Muslim League which aimed at isolating Nasser and was thus regarded by him as a reactionary imperialist tool. The new Academy, which was under the auspices of al-Azhar, provided Nasser with Islamic studies on the religious basis of his Arab Socialism, as well as denunciations of the Muslim Brethren, who were labelled terrorists and bribe takers.[46] All these institutions were also active in supplying the religious legitimization of Nasser's anti-Israeli policy, especially of course at times of war when the supreme Muslim authorities in Egypt declared *jihad* against Israel and sought the solidarity and cooperation of all Muslims.[47]

However, after June 1967, largely as a result of Egypt's catastrophic defeat in the six-day war, Nasser's messianic aura, or the remnants of it, was even further tarnished. His evacuations of Yemen, where Egypt had for five years fought a losing and expensive battle, without any benefits and with lots of bloodshed, in a way symbolized Nasser's end as the first and most dominant Arab-Muslim leader of the twentieth century. Hence the first Islamic Summit Conference, in September 1969, was convened in Rabat and not in Cairo, and its headquarters were in Jedda, under the auspices of the hated reactionary Sa'udis. Nasser had opposed the convening of such a conference in

1966, labelling it an imperialist plot. But in 1969 Nasser was no longer in a position to call the tune. The Islamic Summit's advocacy of a return to the pure values of Islam, as the only way of saving the Arabs from further humiliation, clearly implied a condemnation and a challenge to Nasser's Arabism and socialism.[48]

V

As noted above, Sadat's internal politics dictated a greater emphasis on Islam, owing to his struggles against the Nasserist and leftist oppositions. This shift manifested itself also in his foreign relations. Egypt's regional priorities were defined in accordance with Egyptian national interests, as conceived by Sadat, and not subjected to considerations of Egypt's leadership role in the Arab world. It was this shift which helped to formulate such diverse policy decisions as the expulsion of the Soviets from Egypt in July 1972, the October 1973 War against Israel, the close alliance with the anti-Soviet regimes both in the Arabian Peninsula and East Africa, especially with the Sudan, as well as the peace initiative with Israel initiated in November 1977. Egypt first, as conceived by Sadat, meant close cooperation with the United States as the only power which could help Egypt achieve both its regional and internal goals without losing its independence.

According to Muhammad Hasanayn Heikal, one the more outspoken of Sadat's many critics, Sadat lost as a result of this policy 'his real constituency and with it his regional and international standing' as he had forsaken the Arab world which Heikal regarded as the only real constituency of any Egyptian leader.[49] However, while Heikal has been consistent in these views since the 1960s, it is rather questionable whether even Nasser had ever fully enjoyed the support of this so-called Arab constituency. After the break-up of the United Arab Republic in 1961, and the Egyptian involvement in the Yemen, one may at best define Nasser's image amongst most of the Arab rulers in terms of fear combined with resentment of his manipulation of local opposition groups. But how deep were the roots of Egypt's newly discovered Arab identity within Egypt itself? One should first of all remember that the link to Arabism, while not central in the pre-Nasserist period, had nonetheless already gained considerable support within Egypt's political leadership in the 1930s. In its foreign relations this was best illustrated by the Wafd's shift from Egyptian nationalism, as conceived by Sa'd Zaghlul and Ahmad Lutfi al-Sayyid, to the leadership role in the Arab league as preached by such Wafdists as Makram 'Ubayd and Mustafa Nahhas. Some Egyptian student groups and non-Wafdist political leaders had already started propagating this shift in the 1930s. But, as Anwar Abdel Malek has indicated: 'The Egyptian people wanted to be Arab, but for all that it was not going to renounce its seventy-century old individuality.' Nasser, therefore, had to draw on non-Egyptian Arab intellectuals when he sought to strengthen the theoretical basis of Egypt's Arabism. The task was entrusted to several young Egyptian writers, who drew on the nationalist writings of Syrian, Lebanese and Palestinian theoreticians and, since 1956, relied to a growing extent on the philosophy of the Ba'th as expressed by its founder Michel Aflaq.[50] In Egyptian schools and universities special compulsory courses on Arab society were introduced in order to strengthen the Arab roots of the young intelligentsia. However, even while Arabism was at its height, its ideological impact remained, on the whole, marginal. Islam, according to Abdel Malek, was by far the more deeply rooted, and he claims that approximately one third of all books published in Egypt between 1958 and 1962, the years when Nasser's Arabism was at its peak, were on Islamic themes, including many works of the outlawed Muslim Brethren's theoreticians. Indeed, in order to enhance Arabism, Islam had to be brought into service, as stated by Shaykh Hasan al-Baquri: 'If we say that the Arabs are the best nation offered to mankind, it is because that is a truth revealed by the Koran and a reality expressed in its verses.'[51] One is tempted to compare this phenomenon with the similar movement in the 1930s, when the then leaders of so-called secular nationalism realized that they had to use Islamic themes in order to be effective in propagating their modernist reforms while thirty years later Islam was once again called upon, this time by a so-called revolutionary Arab-Socialist leadership, to propagate its brand of secular politics.

It is against this background of the inherent weakness of Arabism among the masses of Egyptian society, combined with its political failure and the enormous price the Egyptians were forced to pay for it, that we should examine Sadat's foreign policy. In July 1971 Sadat helped Numayri against an attempted communist coup; a year later he expelled the Soviets from Egypt and from then on the Soviet threat, especially in the Horn of Africa, Ethiopia and South Yemen, became Sadat's major concern. To deal with this threat, two problems had to be overcome. First, Israeli occupation of Arab and especially

Egyptian territories had to be terminated. Second, United States support was crucial both for exerting the necessary pressure on Israel and for stopping Soviet penetration into the Middle East and East Africa. How could Islam be of service in realizing these policies?

It was fairly easy to receive full backing from both the Islamic establishment and its populist counterpart in the fight against communism, both inside Egypt and in its external relations. Islam was employed against the Soviet-backed Ethiopians, denouncing their fighting in Erithrea and the Ogaden desert. Indeed, even after Sadat had been branded as traitor by the bulk of the Arab governments, anti-communism continued to serve as a common denominator with Muslim states. The ban on all communist movements, which was adopted by the League of Islamic World in its twentieth session held in August 1979 in Mecca, illustrates the affinity in views in this respect. Moreover, the declaration of Shaykh Muhammad 'Ali al-Harakan, the League's General Secretary, that 'there is no place in our Islamic World for the emergence of any ideology other than Islam',[52] is a clear indication that Sadat's policy in this respect has continued to be supported by most Muslim governments. But when Sadat attempted, several months earlier, to receive Muslim support for his plan for the liberation of Arab Jerusalem, he was of course rebuffed. Indeed, Egypt's declaration that it would not attend the Rabat meeting of Muslim foreign ministers in May 1979, unless an Islamic Summit were convened to discuss Jerusalem,[53] was probably a face-saving device. However, when the Islamic meeting decided to consider Egypt's suspension from membership, Hasan al-Tuhami, Egypt's deputy prime minister, denounced it as illegal, claiming that Egypt was not only one of the most important pillars of Islam but had also 'contributed most to the preservation of Islamic heritage'.[54] Sadat himself reacted almost immediately and declared that the Grand Imam of al-Azhar, backed by the 'ulama and the Islamic Research Council, had already condemned this decision as illegal. They stated, according to Sadat, that for the last one thousand years al-Azhar had defended Islam 'and has protected it from those who are now exploiting it'. Hence 'neither the Arab nor the Islamic mission will proceed without Egypt and without Egypt's al-Azhar'. Sadat complimented the six African states, who did not support Egypt's suspension, saying 'the Africans know the truth about our cousins, the Arabs'.[55]

So while Sadat's emphasis on confronting the Soviet Union and communism continued to receive impressive support in the Muslim world, his peace initiative with Israel was, at least on the official level, rejected. Arab pressures, and in particular those of Saudi Arabia, have succeeded in swaying even Egypt's allies, like Morocco and Sudan, whose future depends to a very large extent on continued Egyptian support against their radical enemies. It was therefore of particular importance to Sadat to have the full support of al-Azhar and of as many Muslim 'ulama as possible for his peace initiative. Sadat's visit to Jerusalem in November 1977 received the blessings of the Islamic establishment. Those supporting this historic act included the Rector of al-Azhar, the presidents of Egyptian student unions and the Muslim Youth Association. The latter conveyed its blessings through its chairman, Shaykh Ahmad Hasan al-Baquri. In thanking those who had come to bless him Sadat stated that only faith in God had prompted his initiative and stressed that the only way to build a better Egypt was to educate the young Egyptians to be faithful to their religious principles.[56] Similar support was granted to the peace initiative and the Camp David accords by the Shaykh of al-Azhar and the minister of waqfs.[57] When the Islamic Conference in Rabat denounced Sadat's initiative, the staff of al-Azhar and all its affiliated institutions, under the chairmanship of Shaykh Rajab al-'Ayidi, reaffirmed their full support of Sadat's policy and stated that 'the peace treaty between Egypt and Israel is a blessed Islamic step, founded on the principles of religion'.[58] Sadat himself continuously emphasized the religious aspects of his peace mission ever since his address to the *Knesset* in Jerusalem in November 1977. He stressed the historic ties between Islam and Judaism when he opened his speech at the Ben Gurion University in Beersheba, in May 1979, stating that it was the Prophet Muhammad who had ordered the people of Yathrab — Jews and Muslims — to form one nation and to practise their respective religions in peace and harmony. Following the return of the Santa Catarina Monastery to Egyptian rule, Sadat emphasized his desire to build a house of prayer for Christians, Jews and Muslims on that mountain, and ordered a study of the feasibility of a canal from the Nile to Jerusalem. On the latter, one of the most controversial projects, he said the following:

In the name of Egypt and its great Al-Azhar and in the name of defending peace, the Nile water will become the new 'Zamzam well' for believers in the three monotheistic religions ... The water will serve all pilgrims visiting the holy shrines in Jerusalem.[59]

So despite the general trend among the Muslim rulers outside Egypt to denounce Sadat's peace initiative as a betrayal of Islam, the Islamic establishment in Egypt, and of course Sadat himself, continued to stress its religious aspects. Indeed, there seemed to be a growing tendency to stress the unreliability and treason prevailing among Arab rulers, while praising Islam and its potential blessings for the future of the region. In a long interview published in *October* magazine on 30 September 1979, Sadat listed the crimes committed by the Arabs against the Palestinians and against each other, not sparing even his erstwhile allies such as Saudi Arabia and Morocco. In concluding the interview he stated 'I regret to say that the Arabs have not changed, but have instead regressed. Egypt alone has changed. We were and still are more civilized and advanced. The Arabs have become small in our eyes because we have grown bigger'.[60] It is therefore hardly surprising that after the Arab League Summit, which was convened in Tunisia in November 1979, Sadat declared that 'the latest comedy in Arab solidarity has ended ... This new Arab League has ended, and it had to end. There will be no Arab League, but there must be a wider and greater Islamic League'.[61] A week later, the editor of *October*, Anis Mansur, called on all Muslims to establish an 'Islamic Peoples' League to confront the enemies of Islam and rise from the abyss of Arab policy to the glory of Islam'. Only the Muslim people could achieve this, as certain Muslim rulers, notably those of Saudi Arabia, Syria, Iran and Afghanistan, were distorting Islam in order to serve their own interests.[62] The different attitude towards Islam and Arabism was clearly indicated when Sadat was interviewed on his birthday, which he as always celebrated in his village Mit abu al-Kawm:

Sad as I am for the Arabs, I am just as sad for Iran because it is regrettable that Khomeini is exploiting Islam ... But when one like Khomeini, in the name of Islam, misleads the Muslims, my sorrow is not for the Arabs, because I have stopped feeling sad for them because of their grudges; I am now sad for the Islamic nation ... Nothing the Arabs will do will either stop or change the course of history or make history turn back, never. Everything they do is an abuse. Egypt will permit no insolence from weakling dwarfs.[63]

Sadat's priorities therefore seem to have been clearly defined as Egypt entered the 1980s. Declarations such as those of the then prime minister Mustafa Khalil that 'Egypt will remain loyal to its pan-Arab commitments which stem from its faith in the unity of aim and destiny with the other people of our glorious nation'[64] hardly expressed the currently prevailing trend, but rather may be regarded as an attempt to keep the doors open for any eventualities.

POPULIST ISLAMIC MOVEMENTS IN EGYPT

I

With the title 'The Short Honeymoon', Richard P. Mitchell described the relationship between the Muslim Brethren and the Free Officers on the morrow of the July 1952 revolution.[65] The leadership of the Brethren embraced the 'blessed movement' calling upon its adherents to fight for the revolution's success. Yet, while several senior members of the Free Officers, including Najib, Nasser and especially Sadat, had close relations with the Muslim Brethren in the pre-revoltuion period, none of the officers within the Revolutionary Command Council (R.C.C.) were members of the Brethren, nor did they intend to submit to political pressures which started coming from the movement's headquarters soon after the first post-revolutionary euphoria was over. Even before the so-called honeymoon came to its untimely end in October 1954, there were several serious clashes between the leadership of the Brethren and the R.C.C. The first clash centred on the demand that the Brethren be allowed to select their own representatives in the revolutionary government. This was refused by the R.C.C., and hence the only Muslim Brother in the Cabinet, Shaykh Ahmad Hasan al-Baquri, the minister of waqfs, was asked by his colleagues to resign. Instead he remained minister and resigned from the Brethrens' leadership. The second clash centred on the Brethrens' demand, presented to President Najib, that the new Egyptian constitution be based solely on Islamic principles. When this was rejected the Brethren demanded that all new laws be submitted to them for approval. But the R.C.C. had no intention of granting to the Brethren or anyone else a power to veto its decisions. The Muslim Brethrens' next move was to present to the Egyptian people their own programmes for the future of Egypt, including sweeping social econ omic and agrarian reforms, with the clear intention of undermining the young revolution's popularity. If one compares the Brethren's programme with the reforms undertaken in later years by Nasser's regime, one is indeed struck by the similarities.[66]

The first serious challenges to the government's authority came on

Islam and Politics in Egypt and the Sudan

12 January 1954, when the Brethren gathered at the University of Cairo to commemorate their martyrs. While the rally was gathering force they openly denounced the Free Officers' regime. The active participation of the leader of *Fidaiyan-i Islam*, the Iranian radical Islamic organization which had been involved in the assassination of General Ramzara, helped to convince the R.C.C. that it was time to act. On the same day the Muslim Brethren were declared illegal and their leadership was put in prison.[67]

The next crisis started on 23 February, when the R.C.C. was split between those who tended to accept Najib's so-called resignation and those who opposed it. While Nasser and his colleagues were deliberating future steps, thousands of Muslim Brothers, Wafdists and socialists were demonstrating in front of 'Abdin palace calling for the arrest of Nasser and Salah Salim and the immediate restoration of democracy with Muhammad Najib as President. This was the first time ever that the Muslim Brothers had demonstrated in order to restore 'democracy'. They had allied themselves previously, first with King Faruq and later with the Free Officers, since they regarded democracy, secular constitutions, liberal political parties and communism as anathema to Islam. The Brothers' leadership was thus, according to Ramadan, not really fighting to restore democracy but rather attempting to curb the R.C.C.'s exaggerated powers. This may be compared to Nasser's ambivalent attitude to the Brothers, following the R.C.C.'s 14 January decision to dissolve them. What he really wanted was to remove the old leadership, headed by Hudaybi, and to dissolve the Brothers' 'secret organization'. Nasser openly demonstrated his support for the Brothers when he visited Hasan al-Banna's grave, on the anniversary of his assassination, on 12 February 1954, and announced his full support for the Muslim Brothers's principles. Moreover, in his negotiations with 'Abd al-Qadir Awda, the Brothers' new leader (al-Hudaybi was arrested in the January confrontation), Nasser agreed to allow the organization to renew its legal activities provided it refrained from political activities, stopped its interference in the army and the police and dissolved its 'secret organization'.[68]

According to 'Abd al-Qadir Awda neither he nor his colleagues in the Brothers' executive leadership were involved in the 'Abdin demonstration on 27 February, since they had nearly reached an agreement with Nasser and his associates. However, since this agreement included the dissolution of the 'secret organization', those of its leaders who were not in prison were actively involved in the pro-Najib demonstrations and thus, paradoxically, demonstrated for a return to democratic rule.[69] That this was but a single episode, dictated by opportunism, became clear when Nasser and Hudaybi came to an agreement whereby the Brothers' leaders were released from prison and allowed to resume their activities. In return Hudaybi supported Nasser's dictatorial measures and the Brothers subsequently opposed Neguib's quest for the resumption of democratic rule.

As of March 1954 the Muslim Brothers thus remained the only legal political organization. During the following months the growing weakness of the Brothers' political leadership, which was paralyzed due to internal splits, brought the 'secret organization' to the fore and became the predominant factor in the Brothers's militant political struggle. The clash with Nasser and the R.C.C. was thus unavoidable. The armed struggle, which was to bring about the assassination of those members of the R.C.C. who opposed Najib, was planned by 'Abd al-Mun'im 'Abd al-Ra'uf, a one time member of the 'Free Officer' leadership, in collaboration with Yusuf Tal'at and other leaders of the 'secret organization'. Hudaybi and his associates, however, continued to oppose violence as a means to achieve political ends, and it therefore appears that the initiative which led the Brothers to their final clash with Nasser was solely in the hands of the militant 'secret organization'. On 26 October, 1954, Mahumud 'Abd al-Latif, one of the *fidaiyun* of the 'secret organization', attempted to assassinate Nasser while he was addressing some 10,000 workers in Alexandria. 'It was then,' wrote Sadat, 'that the Muslim Brotherhood openly declared war on us with the obvious aim of overthrowing us and taking over the rule of Egypt.'[70] However, Nasser and his colleagues, exploiting to the fullest extent their intimate knowledge of the Muslim Brethren's 'secret organization', acted swiftly and efficiently. Over one thousand Brethren were tried by a special peoples' court, consisting of three R.C.C. members, including Sadat. Many of them were sentenced to long terms in prison while six, who were found to have been implicated in the attempted assassination, were later executed.[71] To avoid popular support, the council of 'ulama of al-Azhar denounced the Brethren for 'deviating from the teachings of Islam' and declared that any Muslim plotting against the legitimate rulers of the Egyptian people, namely the Free Officers, were guilty of heresy.[72]

Thus ended the Muslim Brethren's first and most daring challenge to Nasser's regime. Indeed, following the emergence of Nasser as the most venerated Arab leader after 1955, many of the Brethren who were not imprisoned reconciled themselves to Nasserist ideology and refrained from militant opposition.[73] But the decline in Nasser's fortunes following first the breakup of the Egyptian-Syrian unity in 1961, and then the hopeless war in Yemen, begun in 1962, which brought Nasser into direct conflict with his conservative Muslim neighbours in Saudi Arabia, coincided with the release of the Muslim Brothers' leaders from prison. One of those was Sayyid Qutb, the leading ideologue of the Muslim Brethren, who openly attacked some of the most basic notions of Nasser's regime and the very foundations of its ideology, which he classified as *jahiliyya*. This *jahiliyya* (a term used as a derogatory description of the ignorance and paganism of pre-Islamic society) included, according to Qutb, both Arab Socialism and any solidarity based on clan, tribe, nation, race, colour and land, which the Prophet had described as 'rotten'.[74] Qutb and other leaders had neither forgotten nor forgiven the 1954 events, and were bent on revenge.

This, then, provided the background for the second major clash between Nasser's regime and the Muslim Brethren, in August 1965. Official reports at the time accused the Brethren of once again plotting to assassinate Nasser and overthrow the regime. More recent reports put the number of those arrested at 27,000, a remarkably high figure if one takes into consideration the fact that the Brethren had been disbanded in 1954. Furthermore, of the hundreds who were tried and sentenced by a special court, twenty-six were tortured to death and three, including Sayyid Qutb, were executed in 1966.[75] Sadat, who, as noted above, was himself involved in the trials of the Brethren in 1954, was less convinced with regard to the 1965 plot. He defined this so-called plot as purely imaginary and accused the authorities and especially 'Abd al-Hakim 'Amir, Nasser's protégé, of inventing it, in order 'to achieve certain objectives of their own'.[76] Whether the plot was indeed imaginary or, as others claimed, had been greatly exaggerated by the authorities, it succeeded in serving a double purpose. It enabled the regime to clamp down on the Brethren who were once again becoming too strong and too popular. It also served the Arab Socialist Union (A.S.U.) in its attempt to mobilize waning public support for Nasser's Arab Socialism. These attempts, under the new secretary general of the A.S.U., 'Ali Sabri, soon enabled the regime to build up the cadres of the organization and to mount a crusade against the Muslim and conservative oppositions to Nasser's policies. If we take into account that in 1965 the communist movement in Egypt declared its voluntary dissolution, in order to infiltrate into the political institutions of the regime, and especially the A.S.U., it will be easier to appreciate the Brethren's predicament.[77] Not only did they face an additional extremely anti-religious enemy, but they were soon once again to fill the prisons and concentration camps, which had just been vacated by the communists.

II

When Sadat came to power in October 1970, many of the Brethren arrested in 1965 were still lingering in detention camps, from which he released them in May 1971 after he had purged 'Nasser's major power blocs'.[78] Indeed, with his bitter fight against the leftists and the Nasserist elite, which was part of what he later called the 'corrective revolution', Sadat was in need of allies. He had the army behind him, as proven in May 1971, but the Brethren with their bitter memories of Nasser and his clique were ideal partners in Sadat's search for mass support in universities, industry and the overpopulated urban areas. Sadat, though aware of the political ambitions of the Muslim Brethren since his early meetings with their founder Shaykh Hasan al-Banna in the 1940s,[79] was willing to accept their collaboration as long as it did not challenge his authority and policies. Furthermore, since Sadat's regional policy brought him into close collaboration with Saudi Arabia, this in turn enhanced the political stature of the Muslim Brothers. The period of voluntary cooperation lasted until 1976–77 but deteriorated after the Camp David accords of September 1978. However, even while cooperation lasted, the Brethren openly challenged several of Sadat's policies. Similarly, it would be mistaken to describe the post 1978 period as one of open or total opposition to Sadat. However, although in the pre-1976 period the Muslim Brethren could be counted on as a useful partner against both the leftist and the militant neo-*mahdist* movements, this was no longer true in Sadat's last few years when the Brethren often presented a threat to established order and hence had to be neutralized. What Sadat probably failed to take fully into account was that the Brethren, though useful collaborators, would only support him as long as it served their own purpose and did not compromise their ideology. Furthermore, Sadat could not have foreseen in the early 1970s that the

Islam and Politics in Egypt and the Sudan 217

upsurge of fundamentalist Islam, culminating in the Islamic revolution in Iran, would help the Muslim Brethren in Egypt to achieve much greater prominence than had seemed likely when he sought their alliance in the years 1970–1976.

The growing power of the Brethren manifested itself especially in the universities where they have been instrumental in helping the regime to suppress the once powerful Nasserists and leftists. In his study on 'The Students Under Sadat: 1970–1977',[80] Hagai Erlich ascribed the victory of the Muslim Brethren in the December 1977 students' elections in most Egyptian universities to the following reasons. The first was the students' alienation, brought about by the enormous increase in their numbers, from some 100,000 in 1962–63 to about 400,000 in 1976, as compared to the inadequate increase in the numbers of faculty (in 1977 the ratio of faculty per student was 1 x 666), and poor teaching facilities. The second reason was the students' realization that their future prospects were rather gloomy. Hence their alienation and their willingness to 'march' against the regime whenever a 'right' cause appeared, as they did both in January 1972 and in January 1977, despite grave repercussions. Another reason, as mentioned above, was the suppression of communists, Marxists, and Nasserists on the campuses after the January 1977 riots. Hence when the elections were held the students had only two alternatives: to vote for the government sponsored *Misr* party or for the *jama'at al-Islamiyya*, supported by the Muslim Brethren, with the latter having a clear advantage. Two years later, in December 1979, the Brethren complained bitterly about the government's rigging of the student elections. In some universities they even went further and boycotted the elections, seeing that they had no chance of winning.[81] The reason for this change of heart was the growing extremism of the Muslim Brethren which, though a gradual process, had developed from mere criticism to an outright attack on the establishment, and the fact that the *jama'at* had become a threat to Sadat's regime.

In describing the Muslim Brethren in Egypt one has to take into account that during the 1970s a number of groups have assumed this name though their views differ on many major issues, including even the means to be pursued for the re-introduction of the Shari'a and the establishment of an 'Islamic order'. As none of the groups claiming to represent the Brethren had so far been allowed to form their own political platform or party, their views were propagated through their respective journals. The most important of these groups and the one enjoying substantial support is the one whose views were expressed by the prestigious *al-Da'wa*. *Al-Da'wa* under its editors, Salih 'Ashmawi and Umar al-Tilmisani, was allowed to renew publication in June 1976 after 22 years of suppression. It became an unofficial propagator of the views of the moderate wing of the Brethren, and challenged many of the regime's internal and external policies. It would therefore seem justified to reply primarily on *al-Da'wa* in attempting to assess the political and ideological orientations of the Muslim Brethren as they emerged throughout the 1970s.[82]

After 1972, the Muslim Brethren put continuous pressures on the government in order to achieve more prominence for Islamic principles both in the constitution and the legislative process. In line with Saudi Arabian practices, the Brethren demanded the implementation of the penalties (*hudud*) prescribed by Islamic law for offences such as assault, theft, consumption of alcoholic beverages, adultery, slander and apostasy. They believed that a prompt and strict implementation of these penalties on all Egyptians, regardless of religion, would have an immediate positive impact and would reverse the social and moral degradation from which Egypt had been suffering as a result of the western-Christian invasion. Already in June 1977 *al-Da'wa* called upon Sadat to adopt an Islamic policy, coordinated with Saudi Arabia, in order to combat communist-leftist atheism, which was being broadcast, so the Brethren claimed, over the mass media and undermining Islam.[83] Indeed, from the time of its reappearance in 1976, *al-Da'wa* has openly stated its criticism of many of the government's shortcomings. It attacked Arab pop-music and criticized the authorities for encouraging indecent and vulgar programmes to take up most of television and radio time, instead of utilizing it for valuable Islamic topics. Indeed the few religious programmes which were being broadcast were, according to the Brethren, of little moral value as they were limited to ritualistic Muslim practices such as prayers, fasting or the pilgrimage. The whole educational sustem in Egypt also came under bitter attack, as Islam had again been relegated to the margins. But even more far-reaching was the claim that Egyptian schools and university graduates, including those of al-Azhar itself, were not properly taught classical Arabic and hence were in effect cut off from their Islamic heritage.[84] The Brethren also criticized Sadat's so-called economic open-door policy. While maintaining their denunciation of Nasser's Arab Socialism, and their support for private initiative and ownership, the Muslim Brethren denounced Sadat's policy for raising false expectations among the masses and creating consumerist attitudes which could not be satisfied. An open door policy would benefit the foreigners and the upper classes only, while the bulk of the population would become even poorer. The solution, according to the Brethren, was to adopt an economic system based on Islam, as the only way to increase productivity. The Brethren claimed that only Islam would turn labour from a chore into a religious activity.[85]

But one of the Brethren's most bitter grievances against Sadat was the fact that despite his so-called liberalization, the Muslim Brethren had not been allowed to form their own Islamic party in a free democratic system especially since other parties had been allowed to function since 1977–78. Sadat had continuously warned against introducing religion into Egyptian politics, as this, he claimed, would antagonize religious minorities such as the Copts, and hence might harm national unity. The Brethren argued that since in Islam state and religion formed one united system, Sadat's argument was without foundation. Moreover, they pointed proudly to the record of their cordial relations with the Copts, as proof that Sadat's fears were unwarranted. But finally they actually threatened Sadat that unless their demands were met they would be forced to found a clandestine organization.[86] But, whatever past records of intercommunal relations may prove, Coptic fears and outright opposition to the Brethren's demands regarding the application of the Shari'a, and especially the *hudud*, to all Egyptian citizens, have not ceased since they were first put forward. In April 1979, there were reports about anti-Christian activities in the University of Asyut. Muslim student groups were accused of violent attacks on the Copts and of distributing pamphlets against the Coptic Patriarch Shenuda III. While an anti-Sadat paper accused the regime of 'stirring up sectarian dissension in order to suppress political movement and to fragment national opposition',[87] the fact that tension did indeed increase as a result of militant Islamic propaganda cannot be denied.

Until January 1979, Sadat and his government were willing to tolerate the Muslim Brethren's outspoken criticism, even when it was aimed against Sadat's peace initiative. But in January 1979 *al-Da'wa* came out with an open attack on Sadat himself, accusing him of collaborating with the United States secret services and Israel against all Muslim movements including first and foremost the Brethren themselves. *Al-Da'wa* claimed that Sadat had decided to implement a secret report, written ostensibly for the C.I.A. by Dr Richard Mitchell, in which it was proposed to lure the leadership of the popular Muslim movements into the religious establishment, by offering them high sums of money, while those leaders who could not be bought would be exterminated.[88] The government promptly ordered the closure of the magazine and vehemently denied its allegations.[89] In an interview with the London based paper *al-'Arab*, on 30 April 1979, the Egyptian deputy prime minister, Hasan al-Tuhami, stated that the C.I.A. report for 'quelling the Islamic movement in Egypt' was completely false. He claimed that 'anti-Muslim evil scheming hands are behind this and have fabricated this report ... Its aim is to foment sedition, which we hope that God Almighty will spare the Islamic nation'.[90] But Sadat went even further when in his speech to the faculty of Tanta University he accused the Russians of fabricating this report and then using Qadhafi to smuggle it into Egypt.[91]

In the early years of Sadat's presidency the Muslim Brethren were on the whole more outspoken in their criticism of the regime's shortcomings in its internal politics than they were in their declarations on its foreign relations. Their rejection of Nasser's so-called Arabism, blaming it for distorting Muslim history, was probably an extension of their opposition to the regime's secular ideology. They therefore supported Sadat in denegrading pan-Arabism. The Brethren claimed that history text-books taught in Egyptian, Syrian and other Arab schools were in fact a war against Islam. Arabism had replaced Islam in these text books, while the pre-Islamic *jahiliyya* was being extolled because of its Arabism, despite its barbaric and anti-Muslim nature.[92] But, while the Brethren thus supplied Sadat's policies with Islamic-ideological backing, they also denounced the new creed of 'Egypt First', labelling it a pagan pharaonic approach.

But by far the most important challenge to Sadat's foreign policy was waged by the Brethren against his peace initiative with Israel. Their *jihad* against the Jews in Palestine, even before Israel became an independent state, had put the Brethren in the forefront of those fighting against the so-called Zionist threat. Their Secret Army — the *jawwala* (rovers) — had fought against the Jews, especially in the south of Palestine, both before the Arab armies invaded the country on 15 May 1948 and after that.[93] Martyrs Day became an annual commemoration day of the Brethrens' martyrs, many of whom had indeed fallen in the holy war against the Jews. It was therefore no wonder that *al-Da'wa*, since its reappearance in 1976, bitterly and

Islam and Politics in Egypt and the Sudan

continually denounced Israel. It viewed world Jewry as an agent whose services were used by both the United States and the Soviet Union against the Muslim world. Peace with Israel was therefore tantamount to treason while every Muslim was religiously obliged to take part in the *jihad* against the Israeli threat.[94] While these anti-Israel attacks were going on in 1976-77, Sadat had not yet undertaken his peace initiative and hence they reflected to a large degree official Egyptian thinking. But Sadat's trip to Jerusalem in November 1977 and, even worse as far as the Brethren were concerned, his signing of the Camp David accords, were both unacceptable. Israel's true aim was the destruction of Islam and hence peace with it was a betrayal. In a special editorial dealing with the Camp David accords, one of the editors of *al-Da'wa*, 'Umar al-Tilmisani, denounced the agreement as it did not explicitly compel Israel to withdraw from Muslim Jerusalem.[95] Moreover, al-Tilmisani stressed that the Brethren, unlike the Nasserists and the Communists, opposed the peace treaty on religious grounds as, according to Islamic law, it was a sin to leave any Muslim lands in the hands of usurpers.[96] One month later *al-Da'wa* came out with the announcement that peace (*sulh*) with Israel was forbidden according to the Qur'an. In a direct challenge to Sadat, the Brethren declared that Islamic history would pass judgment on those who were willing to sell their dignity and beliefs for questionable material benefits.[97] Thus, in the first half of 1979, Sadat felt compelled to denounce openly his Muslim antagonists, accusing the Muslim Brethren of attempting to create a state within the state not unlike the communists. During his last year in office Sadat was faced with an acute dilemma. Should he ban the Brothers, his erstwhile allies, and thus risk their becoming once again a violent underground movement? Or should he tolerate their vehement criticism of certain of his policies in the hope of maintaining their support for his fight against enemies such as communists, Nasserists, and the more militant Islamic groups? Until September 1981 he tended to follow the second alternative while the Brothers became even more radical in their denouncement of his policy. In September Sadat changed course and arrested the Muslim Brothers' most prominent leaders, as well as other critics of his regime, thereby opting for an open confrontation.

The phenomenon of neo-Mahdist movements in Egypt enjoying the tacit support of certain of the more extremist groups within the Brethren, started in the early 1970s but did not at that time present a real challenge to the regime. After Sadat came to power several such neo-Mahdist groups appeared, especially on university campuses, and openly defied the regime. Their appearance, made possible by Sadat's more liberal policy, enabled such groups to be established and once they had become strong enough they usually committed acts of sabotage or even assassinations under the banner of their Islamic fundamentalist principles. It was then that the government stepped in, arrested as many of the movement's leaders and members as it could lay its hands on, and had those directly responsible imprisoned for long terms or even executed. All of the more notorious Mahdist groups were accused of enjoying the support of some external enemies of Egypt, in most cases Qadhafi's Libya.[98] Of those, one of the better known was the Shabab Muhammad, who in an attempted coup, in April 1974, stormed the military college in Cairo. But the most famous such group and one enjoying wider support was *jama'at al-takfir wa'l-hijra*, whose leaders, headed by Ahmad Shukri Mustafa, a one-time Muslim Brother, were executed following their July 1977 kidnapping and assassination of Shaykh Husayn al-Dhahabi, a former minister of waqf. The reappearance of another *jihad* movement in Egyptian universities, with views similar to those of *jama'at al-takfir wa'l-hijra*, was reported in December 1979 by the Kuweiti *al-Anba'* and indicated that despite government measures the movement had not been crushed. Most of the members of this movement were apparently rounded up and imprisoned in October 1979. However, one of its leaders, 'Ali Mustafa al-Mughrabi, was caught only in January 1980, following a fierce battle, in his hideout in Alexandria. He confessed, before he died of his wounds, that he and his followers had planned to disrupt public order by throwing bombs in places of worship.[99] Of the 3,000-5,000 active members who belonged to *jama'at al-takfir*, the largest concentrations were discovered in Cairo, Alexandria and Asiut, mostly among university students and from rural backgrounds. The leaders and some of the members of these groups had previously belonged to the Muslim Brethren. However, they became impatient with the Brethren's peaceful co-existence within the regime and founded their organizations in order to act in a more resolute and, if necessary, violent, manner to assert their views.

Ideologically there is no great difference between these movements and the Muslim Brethren. They regard the Shari'a as the basic solution for all society's shortcomings. Their fundamental commitment is to the poor and they regard social justice as a major aim. Along with

Islam and Politics in Egypt and the Sudan

the Brethren they demand the implementation of the *hudud* in Egypt, regardless of the individual's religion. While non-Muslims should be tolerated they should have no say in the politics or in the management of public affairs. Violence against Copts is therefore not ruled out, and has in fact erupted on a number of occasions. Their foreign enemies include both the imperialist and the communist blocs with Zionism as an appendage of the former. Hence Sadat's treaty with the United States and Israel was an act of anti-Islamic treason which had to be opposed and, if possible, punished.[100] However, a basic difference between the moderate wing of the Brethren and the militant neo-Mahdists is the former's negation of the Mahdi and their rejection of violence to achieve their aims.

It is hard to assess the present strength of these movements or their actual membership. But what is probably more important is the popularity of their message. It seems that especially since 1973, fundamentalist Islam of the more militant brand has made headway in all sectors of Egyptian society. The major reasons for this revival are to be sought in the decline of other ideologies, such as socialism, marxism or even pan-Arabism, all of which have been largely discredited. Moreover, while it is easy for the regime to denounce the above ideologies as alien to Islam, it is much harder to suppress those who preach fundamentalism. A case in point is that of 'Abd al-Hamid Kishk, the blind *imam* of a Cairo mosque, or that of the *imam* Ahmad al-Mahlawi from Alexandria, whose sermons, bitterly critical of the government, attracted thousands of worshippers, while cassettes of their sermons were sold throughout Egypt to thousands more.[101] Therefore, while these neo-Mahdist movements are, as stated, probably too weak to endanger the regime, their extremism and popularity predominated among the *jama'at Islamiyya* in the universities and may drive the more cautious and better organized Muslim Brethren to follow a more extremist line. This, in turn, may bring to an end the period of peaceful co-existence between the regime and the Brethren whose popular support is believed to be widespread and effective.

ISLAM AND POLITICS UNDER NUMAYRI

In the case of the Sudan, it is rather more difficult to define the exact borderlines separating the Islamic establishment from such popular Islamic movements as the Ansar, the Muslim Brethren, or the Khatmiyya *sufi* order. The reason is that the paramountcy of the popular Islamic movements had, prior to Numayri's coup, been so overwhelming that they had become the most dominant part of the establishment. Thus the Umma party, the political arm of the Ansar, headed the Sudanese government for long periods both before the 1958 military coup and after the popular uprising which overthrew it in October 1964. It seems that on the eve of Numayri's coup the Mahdist leaders were on the verge of seizing complete power. In fact, Muhammad Admad Mahjub, a leader of the Umma and a close associate of the Ansar, related in his memoirs[102] how al-Hadi al-Mahdi and al-Sadiq al-Mahdi, the spiritual and political leaders of the Ansar respectively, had agreed on 23 May 1969, following a long period of bitter strife, to unite forces with the Khatmiyya oriented Democratic Unionist party and realize their ambition to turn the Sudan into a presidential republic with an Islamic constitution. The two Mahdist leaders also declared their intention to compete in the forthcoming elections, the first for the presidency, the second for the post of prime minister. As Mahjub related with some bitterness, 'they thus seemed to consider the rule of the state a booty to be inherited and divided between them, to the exclusion of the other members of the [Umma] party who did not belong to the Mahdi family'.[103] The Numayri coup, a few day later, brought this dream to an end. It would therefore seem that, unlike in Egypt, it was the popular Islamic leadership which supported the *status quo* as long as it enjoyed power. Their fight for an Islamic constitution was probably one of their major concerns in the pre-Numayri period.

I

Why was it so difficult to declare in a Sudanese constitution that Islam was the religion of the state and that the Shari'a was a major source of legislation? One of the main reasons was the precarious unity of the Sudan which depended not only on the Muslim majority but also on the non-Muslim Southern Sudan which accounted for nearly one third of the population. The southern uprising, which started in August 1955 and was only brought to its end in February 1972, after seventeen years of civil war and enormous bloodshed, centred around southern fears of northern Muslim domination. This domination had already, prior to independence, expressed itself in concentrated efforts to enforce Arabic and Islam on the tribal population of the south. It was southern fear of Arab-Muslim domination which brought about proposals for a federal type of government or, as the more extremist southerners demanded: southern independence. In fact, the southern leadership only supported the northern plan for an independent Sudan in December 1955, with the clear understanding that federalism, granting equality to Christianity and English with Islam and Arabic, would be seriously considered by the constitutional sub-committee. However, in December 1957, southern demands for regional autonomy were rejected out of hand by the northern Muslim majority as an expensive façade. It was on these principles that the southerners fought the February 1958 elections. But while the south overwhelmingly supported these demands, the Umma dominated government forced a new constitution on the Constituent Assembly. Fear of Islamization and Arabization were thus the main reason for the southerners' boycott of the Assembly as of June 1958.[104] Under 'Abbud's military dictatorship Islam and Arabic were forced on the south despite courageous and, at times, desperate resistance. English was barred from the schools and Arabic teaching Muslim schools were opened instead.[105] Lastly, on 27 February, 1964, Islamization was further boosted when all Christian missionaries were expelled from the country. However, the basic demands of southern autonomy and of equal status for Christianity and English to Islam and Arabic, continued to stir up strife in the south and were to a large extent instrumental in overthrowing the 'Abbud regime in October of that year. And so in 1965 the new parliamentary government was once again faced with the same dilemma. A draft constitution was finally hammered out, but it was never ratified. Muhammad Ahmad Mahjub who, as prime minister, was directly involved in the constitutional debate, wrote in retrospect:

There should have been no quarrel on whether the constitution should be Islamic or secular. The Sudanese could have had a constitution without calling it Islamic, thereby practising their Islamic faith and using the tolerance embodied in its tenets. This would have allowed us to have a permanent constitution without much trouble.[106]

Such a statesmanlike approach might have helped the Sudan to overcome this deep conflict had Mahjub fought for it in his own Ansar-dominated Umma party, while he was prime minister before Numayri's coup. However, all the major Sudanese parties, with the sole exception of the communists, supported an Islamic constitution. Even the National Unionists, led by Isma'il al-Azhari who prided themselves on their secularism, did not oppose an Islamic constitution, probably for fear of losing support. Oddly enough, in May 1965, while the Round Table Conference, the only serious attempt to hammer out a logical compromise with the south, was in full swing, al-Azhari publicly declared the centrality of the Muslim-Arab heritage for the United Sudan. It is no wonder therefore, that the Muslim Brethren, organized in the Islamic Charter Front, openly advocated an Islamic constitution saying 'We cannot have a God who cares only for religion, but one who cares for all aspects of life'.[107] Thus, the question of whether or not Islam was to be declared the religion of the state was much more determinative in the case of the Sudan than it was in Egypt. For the Sudan, voluntary unity between north and south depended on religious and cultural tolerance. True, 'Abbud's dictatorship and even the sectarian Muslim dominated parliamentary governments succeeded in forcing Arabization and Islamization on the reluctant south. But the price was enormous: continuous bloodshed and destruction as well as a growing alienation and hostility of the southern population, of whom some three million escaped across the borders to Ethiopia, Kenya, Uganda, Zaire and the Central African Republic.

This was the situation when Numayri came to power in May 1969 and a month later announced his plan for granting regional autonomy to the south. Indeed, only a strong military dictatorship could adopt a plan which had been bitterly opposed by all major political parties and was probably unpopular among the conservative Muslims in the rural districts. However, Numayri and his colleagues did not face elections, nor did they fear uncensored opposition in the press. The solution they adopted, which ultimately led to the Addis Ababa peace settlement between north and south in February 1972, was largely based on the programme advocated by the Sudanese Communist Party ever since 1954.[108] However, stable peace in a united Sudan required a new and tolerant approach to the divisive issue of the constitution. In September-October 1972, a People's Assembly was elected for the sole purpose of drafting a permanent constitution, which was approved and promulgated on 8 May 1973. In part one of the constitution the Sudan was declared a 'unitary, democratic, socialist and sovereign republic, ... part of both the Arab and African entities'. Islamic law and custom were declared 'main sources of legislation', while non-Muslims were granted the right to be governed by their own personal laws. But even more significant was the wording of article sixteen where both Islam and Christianity were stated to be 'the religion': the first of 'the majority', the second of 'a large number of citizens', thus attempting to overcome southern fears of Islamic domination.[109]

II

This policy of limiting Islam to the purely religious role of personal beliefs was part of a general drive to end sectarianism and especially to crush the Ansar, a task which was undertaken with great brutality and efficiency in March 1970 when between five and twelve thousand Ansar were killed by bombs and rockets on Aba Island, their spiritual centre.[110] Numayri and his colleagues must have lived under the misapprehension that now that they were free of Ansari political pressure they could move towards a secular society. An example of this illusion was the so-called 'Cultural Revolution' initiated by the R.C.C. in the summer of 1972 with the aim of 'reshaping society in its trends, values, practice and skills', hardly a modest endeavour. In the long debates surrounding this 'revolution', modernization, science and technology were definitely more important than Islam. The late Ja'far 'Ali Bakhit, who had been a central figure in drafting the constitution, expressed extremely critical views of the traditional Muslim value-system of the Sudanese masses. He demanded 'a shake-up in the traditional society that now exists, in such a way that it leads to the creation of vacuums that, in turn, lead to struggles leading themselves to the predominance of values'. There can be little doubt that the values which Bakhit sought to implant were not the traditional Islamic ones. His colleague, Professor 'Abd al-Rahman al-'Aqib, expressed his contempt for the old values even more blatantly when he defined the 'Cultural Revolution' as an expression of 'indignation at all the obsolete legacies' and an invitation to society to change its prevailing views.[111]

However, these expectations were as premature in the Sudan as they had been in Nasser's Egypt. Already in 1972, the three major right-wing traditionalist parties had formed the 'National Front' whose declared aim was to overthrow Numayri and then to initiate the revival of Islam in a modern democratic state. The three parties which founded the Front were the Umma, the Democratic Unionists and the Islamic Charter Front (Muslim Brothers), representing the major sectarian divisions in Sudanese Muslim society.[112] It was therefore quite clear that the Ansar, despite the March 1970 massacre, were again on the march, united, at least temporarily, with their erstwhile rivals of the Khatmiyya and the Muslim Brethren.[113] The two most prominent leaders of the National Front, al-Sadiq al-Mahdi and Husayn Sharif Yusuf al-Hindi, representing the Umma and the Democratic Unionists respectively, were the grandsons of two of the most venerated popular-Islamic leaders of the Anglo-Egyptian Sudan.[114] Following the massacre of the Ansar, in March 1970, al-Mahdi had been exiled to Egypt, where he was for some time under house-arrest. Once he was allowed to leave Egypt he started to organize the anti-Numayri Front. Al-Hindi, who on the eve of the Numayri coup had served as minister of finance in the last civilian coalition government under Muhammad Ahmad Mahjub, had escaped to Aba Island, the Ansars' stronghold, when Numayri assumed power. Once in exile, al-Hindi had joined forces with al-Mahdi and the Ansar, as well as with the Islamic Charter Front. The newly formed National Front soon enlisted the aid of several of the Sudan's unfriendly neighbours, headed by Qadhafi's Libya, but including at times such strange bedfellows as Saudi Arabia and Marxist Ethiopia. The Front, with its new allies, tried unsuccessfully to topple Numayri's regime on at least two occasions: in November 1975 and July 1976.[115]

In order to overcome the mass following enjoyed by the sectarian popular Islamic movements, Numayri tried to create institutionalized popular support for his regime. Following in Nasser's footsteps, he set up the Sudanese Socialist Union (S.S.U.), as the only legitimate political organization in the country. But like the Arab Socialist Union in Egypt, the S.S.U. was supposed to demonstrate its loyalty to the regime without gaining any real stake in the political system. 'A large part of the activity of S.S.U. branches revolved around demonstrations of support for government policy.'[116] Genuine and open debate on government policy leading to changes were few and unimpressive. The S.S.U. became a mass organization, lacking grass-roots or independent leadership with a top-heavy bureaucracy made up largely of presidential appointments. In order to overcome the S.S.U.'s inherent weakness, Numayri, following now in Sadat's footsteps, announced his intention to liberalize the political system, relax censorship and hopefully encourage greater popular involvement in Sudanese politics. However, as long as the leaders of the National Front remained in exile and were doing their utmost to

Islam and Politics in Egypt and the Sudan 229

overthrow Numayri, there could be no real liberalization of the political system. Following the failure of the abortive, Ansar-led coup in July 1976, both the leaders of the opposition National Front and President Numayri decided to reconsider their previous strategy. The July 1976 coup had been the most dangerous challenge to Numayri's regime since the abortive communist inspired coup of July 1971.[117] The coup was led and executed by well-trained and equipped Ansar and by the time the fighting had ended some seven hundred lives had been lost and ninety-eight additional Ansar were later executed. The failure of this coup, despite the fanaticism of the Ansar who fought to the bitter end, was due primarily to the loyalty of the Sudanese army and to the immediate support of the Egyptian army units stationed in the Sudan. The coup's failure convinced the leaders of the National Front that Numayri was too strong to be easily toppled. It convinced Numayri, who at first claimed that the coup had been executed by foreign mercenaries emanating from Libya and Ethiopia,[118] that the National Front and especially the Ansar were too strong to be ignored and hence sought national reconciliation.

For Numayri's regime the return of the leaders of the National Front to the Sudan, as partners within the S.S.U. presented both benefits and dangers. It was clear that neither al-Mahdi nor al-Hindi nor Hasan al-Turabi of the Muslim Brothers, would become docile collaborators with the regime and that their presence could create an active opposition within the S.S.U. However, Numayri probably believed that as long as they were willing to denounce sectarianism, join the S.S.U. and work within the regime, their presence in the Sudan would outweigh the dangers of their continued exile. On 8 July 1977, one year after his abortive coup, Sadiq al-Mahdi was therefore invited to Port Sudan in order to discuss the details of reconciliation with President Numayri. The eight point agreement reached between the two leaders was revealed by al-Mahdi in a number of interviews.[119] According to al-Mahdi, Numayri agreed to important changes in the political system; the release of political prisoners; a revision of the constitution, and neutralism in the Sudan's international relations. In return, the National Front would end its armed opposition, dissolve its training camps and return to the Sudan to take part in the national reconciliation. Indeed al-Mahdi openly declared his belief both in the role of the army in the politics of developing countries and in socialism as an essential model for economic development. The one-party system, exemplified by the S.S.U., was, according to al-Mahdi, essential for the present stage of Sudanese politics and all he asked for in return was the restoration of political and civil liberties and a general amnesty for himself and his colleagues. Curiously, Islam did not seem to loom large in al-Mahdi's interviews. The agreement was ratified by the executive of the National Front on 14 July 1977, and at the end of the month some nine hundred political prisoners belonging to the National Front were released on Numayri's orders. Indeed a law, granting general amnesty for illegal acts committed against the regime, was passed on 7 August. This enabled al-Mahdi accompanied by twelve leading Ansar to return to the Sudan on 27 September 1977 after more than seven years in exile.[120] Reconciliation was prepared in the Sudan not only through amnesty but through major changes in the electoral law to the People's Assembly which were announced on 26 September 1977. Furthermore, a special committee was appointed by Numayri in the same month, whose task it was to facilitate the integration of the political exiles into the political, economic and social fabric of the Sudan. These included also the leadership of the Muslim Brothers, headed by Dr. Hasan al-Turabi.

The elections held in February 1978 may be regarded as one of the major fruits of reconciliation. Out of the 304 seats in the People's Assembly, candidates supported by the two main groups within the National Front, the Ansar and the Democratic Unionist Party won thirty seats each, while the Muslim Brothers won another twenty. If one takes into account that about sixty additional seats were won by so-called independent candidates, especially in rural areas, the fruits of reconciliation seemed impressive. On 21 March 1978, Numayri appointed six new members to the S.S.U. political bureau, a substantial figure in this prestigious twenty-nine member body. The new members included al-Sadiq al-Mahdi, Ahmad 'Ali al-Mirghani and Dr. Hasan al-Turabi, representing the Ansar, the Khatmiyya and the Muslim Brothers.[121] Even more far-reaching were the appointments of fifty-one new members to the Central Committee of the S.S.U. which also included the above three leaders as well as many other former anti-Numayri activists. At the time, Ahmad 'Ali al-Mirghani, in line with Khatmiyya tradition, refused to be drawn into active politics and declined the honour conferred upon him by Numayri.[122] Al-Mahdi declared that he regarded his appointment as premature. Yet, a few months later, on 3 August 1978, he reached an agreement with Numayri which enabled him to join the central bodies of the S.S.U.

However, even at this stage when reconciliation seemed to be progressing smoothly, two questions remained unanswered: first, al-Mahdi's political-executive role in the Sudan; and second, his ability to stand by the agreement, namely to bring the anti-Numayri opposition from Libya and Ethiopia back to the Sudan. Right from the first agreement of July 1977, there were consistent rumours that al-Mahdi would be offered the premiership of the Sudan. Indeed when, in one of his periodic government reshuffles, Numayri became prime minister, it was generally assumed that he did so in order to hand the post to al-Mahdi when the latter was ready.[123] These rumours persisted despite constant denials both by al-Mahdi himself and by Numayri who declared that al-Mahdi was not yet ready to assume executive responsibilities. The second, and from Numayri's point of view the more crucial problem was al-Mahdi's ability to sway the National Front exiles and especially the armed forces of this Front which were concentrated primarily in Libya, to return to the Sudan and be absorbed peacefully in its society. Al-Mahdi undertook several trips in 1977–78 to Libya in order to persuade his followers to return to the Sudan. But despite constant reports regarding the success of this operation, about 6,000 exiles remained in the camps both in Libya and in Ethiopia. Apparently the main reason was their refusal to return to the Sudan as defeated refugees, and it took time to make arrangements in the Sudan to absorb them properly and to welcome them back as honorable citizens. To make matters worse, al-Hindi continued to undermine al-Mahdi's efforts, especially in the armed training camps. Consequently in January 1978 the alliance was broken up and al-Hindi with some of his colleagues were expelled by al-Mahdi from the National Front. The government now worked out a separate reconciliation agreement with al-Hindi which was signed in London on 12 April 1978 and was defined as an 'historic agreement' and 'a new dawn'. In fact it repeated most of the points which had already been agreed upon between Numayri and al-Mahdi in July 1977 and thus it seemed that al-Hindi had given up most of his previous demands.[124] But while it seemed until mid-1978 that national reconciliation was gradually moving forward, it was virtually suspended in the following months. Following Numayri's support for the Camp David accords, al-Mahdi resigned from the political bureau of the S.S.U. and left Sudan on his way to the United States, ostensibly for private reasons. However, while al-Mahdi did not declare that reconciliation had failed, he clearly indicated his dissatisfaction with two aspects of Numayri's policy: first, his subservience to Sadat's foreign policy, and especially his backing of the Camp David accords; and second, the lack of progress with regard to the promised amendment of the Sudan's constitution along Islamic lines.[125] Two months later, in January 1979, al-Hindi went even further when he stated that reconciliation had come to an end and that armed struggle, both in the Sudan and from across the borders, would be resumed.[126]

If proof was needed that the Sudan's internal politics, including reconciliation with the Ansar, depended on external factors, this was supplied in the second half of 1979. In May of that year a rapprochement between the Sudan and Libya brought some 500 Ansar back to the Sudan. A special celebration to welcome their return was held at the Mahdi's tomb in Omdurman. Shortly afterwards Sadiq al-Mahdi himself returned to the Sudan stating that while his views on Egypt's inter-Arab policy still differed from those of Numayri, their relationship was one of dialogue and not of confrontation.[127] In October 1979 there were massive demonstrations in the Sudan against Sadat's peace agreement with Israel.[128] Numayri held a meeting with army and police personnel, aimed at 'the mobilization of national action ... to secure it from sabotage by the enemy of the revolution'. On the same occasion he emphasized the Sudan's Arab identity and reiterated its loyalty to the Arab cause.[129] Even more telling was Numayri's attendance at the Tunis Summit Conference, organized by the Arab League in November 1979. Having refrained from participating in the Baghdad Summit in November 1978, this indicated a definite change in policy.[130] The change became clear when on 25 November 'Abd al-Hamid Salih, chairman of the Sudan's People's Assembly, made a statement on the Middle East peace process. In it he asserted that the Sudan had never fully supported the Camp David accords, and now that Sadat's peace efforts had failed, due to Israel's intransigence, the Sudan fully supported Arab solidarity regarding the Arabism of Jerusalem and the creation of a Palestinian state ruled by the P.L.O.[131] This point of view was reiterated a few days later by the foreign relations committee of the S.S.U.[132]

So it seemed that the combined economic and political pressures were at last bearing fruit. Numayri was constantly accusing Iraq of plotting in the Sudan. But it became quite clear that the 'power blocs' who were accused of being involved in these intrigues within the Sudan were not limited to the communists who had been the most convenient scapegoat ever since their July 1971 coup.[133] In one of the periodical purges of the S.S.U. political bureau and the reorganization of its secretariat, under Numayri himself in 1979, those who were ousted included not only the Muslim leaders, al-Sadiq al-Mahdi and Ahmad 'Ali al-Mirgani, but also several prominent southern leaders such as Joseph Oduho and Bona Malwal. So it seemed that while the Sudan was half-heartedly moving back into the Arab orbit, internal opposition was not limited to the handful of student provokers, as claimed by the regime. Among the southern leaders Bona Malwal stood out as the most serious challenger of Numayri's national reconciliation, which he regarded as a threat to national unity. Malwal resigned from his post as minister of information and editor of the prestigious government weekly *Sudanow*, and openly attacked al-Sadiq al-Mahdi and Hasan al-Turabi for attempting to turn the Sudan into an Islamic theocracy. While he supported reconciliation, as an essential step towards the Sudan's national unity, Malwal opposed a plan which would put the non-Muslim minority at a clear disadvantage.[134]

III

It would, however, be a mistake to assess the role of Islam in Sudanese politics according to the changing political fortunes of the leaders of the Ansar or the Muslim Brothers. Ever since reconciliation started there has been a gradual but consistent move towards the 'Islamic path' within both the People's Assembly and the S.S.U. There are those who claim that Numayri's traumatic experiences during the July 1971 communist coup turned him from secular socialism towards Islam. But even more important, at least politically, was his growing conviction that Islam, especially in its popular *sufi* manifestations, was the only 'language' which was both understood and accepted by the broad masses of Sudanese Muslims. This conviction was clearly expressed by Numayri in his book *Al-Nahj al-Islamic Limadha?*[135] published symbolically in November 1980, the eve of the fifteenth century of the *Hijra*. The unity of the Sudan and the end of the conflict between north and south, which played a predominant role in Numayri's political life, are expressed in equally strong terms in this book. Numayri refutes the claim that the civil war between north and south was one of Arabs against Africans or of Islam against Christianity. He defined the role of the Sudan as a bridge between the two worlds of the Arab-Muslim and the African. Hence the Sudan had to beware of becoming a party to any Arab-African confrontation, since this would be the end of its own united existence. The Islamic path, as advocated by Numayri, was one of liberalism based on broadmindedness and justice, and seemed at the time to be more in line with the Islam propagated by the Sudanese Muslim group of the Republican Brothers than with the *salafi* interpretations of the more orthodox Ansar or Muslim Brothers. Numayri had propagated an enhanced role for Islam since 1973. In his report to the first Congress of the S.S.U., in January 1974, he publicly announced that 'religion was the cornerstone and basis of all social and political institutions in society as a whole; as such, religion should be the basis of solidarity'.[136] Like his Egyptian mentor, Anwar al-Sadat, Numayri adopted public postures to convey his new religious image to the Sudanese public. He surrounded himself with shaykhs of *sufi* orders and visited and subsidized their *zawiyas*. By 1976 many such orders were incorporated into the S.S.U. and they fully endorsed his 'national reconciliation' policy which was started a year later. However, even before reconciliation materialized, Numayri had set up a special committee for the revision of Sudanese laws in conformity with Islamic principles. In his directive to the committee, Numayri stressed the Sudan's social, cultural, and psychological diversity and hence expressed his hope 'that by using the Shari'a as a source of legislation we shall take from Islam its spirit, and from the facts of life in Sudan their reality, so that in the end we have a unity embraced by Islam'.[137]

It was this commitment which enabled the Muslim Brothers to reach a satisfactory arrangement with the regime. Their aim of establishing an Islamic state, based on the Shari'a, while taking the country's cultural diversity into account, broadly coincided with Numayri's new 'Islamic path'. Dr. Hasan al-Turabi thus became the natural choice for the post of attorney general and for chairing the committee for implementing the Shari'a principles in Sudanese law. Turabi and his followers hoped to influence the regime from within and to exploit their massive following among the students and the intelligentsia in order to increase their impact on the decision-making process.[138]

Unlike Sharif al-Hindi, who remained in exile until his death, and Sadiq al-Mahdi, who has fluctuated between cooperation and opposition, the Muslim Brothers under Turabi have opted for pragmatism and have, as a result, benefited politically. This was evident in their success in the 1980 elections to the People's Assembly as well as in their increasing representation in cultural government positions. While this brought about a split in the ranks of the Muslim Brothers' leadership and increased the opposition of the Khatmiyya to what they criticized as Turabi's opportunism, the latter succeeded in enhancing the Brothers' bargaining power to a considerable extent. In 1978 Muhammad 'Uthman al-Mirghani established the Committee for the Revival of Islam, which was founded as a *sufi* front organization and aimed at withstanding the onslaught of the 'Orientalist', 'Westernized' Ansar and Muslim Brothers.

EPILOGUE

The equating of opposition and religious unbelief and of the dominant order and orthodoxy is an old political stratagem. While it persists, both the rulers and their opponents will tax the *turath* with their claims: the rulers with demands for total obedience, for religious vindication of what has been done in this grubby world; their opponents with a vision of a successful order that makes today's necessities and shortcuts look like treason and more compromise. The struggle becomes all the more difficult, for once religious orthodoxy is called upon to sustain political authority there is a natural urge on the part of those pushed out of the world of power to claim that they too wish to recreate God's world and to purify the religious heritage.[139]

Fouad Ajami's statement, though made in a different and broader context, is a very concise description of the present dilemma faced by the ruling élites of Egypt and the Sudan. This study, which has attempted to observe how both 'orthodox' and 'popular' Islam were involved in the political process in Egypt and the Sudan over a relatively short period, has arrived at similar conclusions. For even with these self-imposed limitations a number of characteristics stand out. First, that Islam means different things to different people. The 'language of Islam' as 'spoken' by the fellahin or the urban lower middle class differs as one moves southwards from the Delta along the Nile valley, and is not similar to that of the Azharites or those who wield power in Cairo or Khartoum. Second, that while those in power are opposed to the introduction of religion into politics and derogatorily define the fundamentalists whom they accuse of practising it as sectarians, the rulers themselves mix religion and politics whenever it seems to serve their own purpose. Third, that despite certain similarities between the two sister countries inhabiting the Nile valley there are very significant differences in their attitude to Islam, in their political structure and in the manner in which they attempt to resolve what may be defined as 'Islam in politics'.

Looking first at what we defined as the Islamic establishment, the paramount position of al-Azhar has to be taken into account, since no Islamic institution with similar prestige exists in the Sudan. Hence, the Egyptian authorities, whoever they happened to be, sought to receive the blessings of this revered institution for their diverse political aims. If one turns to the *sufi* leadership, the similarity grows but the differences persist. Here, under both Nasser and Sadat, a concerted effort to harness the *sufi* shaykhs to serve government policies paid considerable dividends, especially in the rural areas. In the Sudan, because of the absence of a strong central Islamic institution, sufism assumed far greater importance. Practically every political leader in the Sudan could claim his adherence to this or that *sufi* order, even if he was not an active member. Among the *sufi* orders the Khatmiyya was of course predominant. Thus, in 1978 the Khatmi shaykh, Muhammad 'Uthman al-Mirghani, founded with his fellow *sufi* leaders the Islamic Revival Committee. The *sufi* shaykhs thereby responded to the growing influence of Turabi's Muslim Brothers or al-Sadiq al-Mahdi's Ansar and hoped to enhance the political importance of their respective orders without being tarnished through active participation in politics.

Turning now to the more militant radical Muslim movements, we see the differences between Egypt and the Sudan become even more evident. Militant Islam has, on the whole, been weaker in Egypt. Under Nasser's authoritarian regime the Muslim Brothers and similar movements were strictly suppressed and their leaders were generally behind bars. Their vitality became evident during the period of their 'collaboration' with Sadat, which ended gradually after 1977–78. But even during their hey-day they have not, so far, ever become a real threat to those in power. True, certain militant neo-Mahdist groups turned to violence, and one such group assassinated Sadat; but they did not possess the power nor command the following necessary to translate a single act of violence into a political victory.

The reverse is probably true in the Sudan. Had the Ansar succeeded in their July 1976 coup, they would have had all the following they required in order to topple the regime. Moreover, since they had been the first to rule the Sudan, in the nineteenth-century Mahdist state and then in the twentieth-century independent Sudan, they never had the same hesitation or reluctance towards assuming power when they had the chance. Therefore, Numayri moved in a direction diametrically opposed to that of Sadat. Numayri started in 1977–78 to move towards 'national reconciliation' and began to integrate the leadership of the Ansar and the Muslim Brothers into the political system, while Sadat, in the same years started to clash with the more militant Muslim groups, including the Brothers, and became convinced that he had to keep them out of the political process, even if it meant the use of force. Now that Sadat himself has been violently removed from the scene, it seems that with the leaders of the most radical neo-Mahdist movements safely behind bars, the Egyptian regime, headed by Mubarak, is attempting to resume the pre-1977 *modus vivendi* in cooperating with the more 'reasonable' leaders of populist Islam both from within the Muslim Brothers and the *jama'at al-Islamiyya*. In the Sudan the dangers of a populist Muslim revolt seem to be greater, despite 'reconciliation'. This is so because the strength of the Ansar is not only greater but has already been tested politically. Furthermore, with Ansari followers concentrated in the western regions of Kordofan and Dar Fur, in close proximity to an unpredictable ruler like Qadhafi, the very precarious unity of this vast Sudanese state could be threatened. But while both the Ansar and the Muslim Brothers seemed to be advocating a gradualist approach to the Islamization of the legal system, the more extremist elements, both within these groups and especially in the universities, advocated the outright application of the Shari'a throughout the Sudan. Numayri's announcement in September 1983 that the *hudud* as prescribed in the Shari'a would be applied to all Sudanese Muslims seems to be another indication of the paramount position of Islam in Sudanese society and politics. Yet with the resumption of civil war in the South, and the economy on the verge of bankruptcy, this may well be an act of desperation.

NOTES

1. See for instance my study 'From Ansar to Umma: Sectarian Politics in the Sudan, 1914–1946', *A.A.S.* 9/3 (1973): 101-153.
2. Nadav Safran, *Egypt in Search of Political Community*, Cambridge Mass., 1961, especially pp. 209-28.
3. See C. D. Smith, 'The Crisis of Orientation: The Shift of Egyptian Intellectuals to Islamic Subjects in the 1930's', *I.J.M.E.S.* 4 (1973) pp. 382-410.
4. The appearance of a *mahdi*, leading the attack on the holiest shrine of Islam in Mecca, on the eve of the 15th Century of the *hijra* is noteworthy.
5. For details see Gabriel Warburg, *Islam, Nationalism and Communism in a Traditional Society: The Case of Sudan*, Frank Cass, London 1978, pp. 21-66.
6. In J. H. Thompson and R. D. Reischauer (eds.), *Modernization of the Arab World*, New York 1966, pp. 26-36.

7. Ibid., pp. 26-7.
8. Ibid., p. 31.
9. H. Sharabi, 'Islam, Democracy and Socialism in the Arab World', in M.C. Hudson (ed.), *The Arab Future: Critical Issues*, Washington D.C. 1979, pp. 95-104.
10. *New York Times*, 7 Oct. 1979.
11. E. Sivan, 'How Fares Islam?', *The Jerusalem Quarterly*, 13 (Fall 1979), p. 33.
12. Safran, pp. 147-8; It is noteworthy that Hasan al-Banna did not regard the *Shura* as binding. His view, as related by his deputy Salih al-'Ashmawi, was that following consultation it was the leader's prerogative to make up his own mind, regardless of the advice given him by the majority of his colleagues. Quoted from *al-Da'wa*, 12 Feb. 1952, by Tariq al-Bishri, *Al-Haraka al-Siyasiyya fi Misr, 1945–1952*, Cairo 1972, p. 373.
13. M. Milson (ed.), *Society and Political Structure in the Arab World*, New York 1973, pp. 3-27.
14. L. Binder, *In a Moment of Enthusiasm*, Chicago 1978, p. 376.
15. A. el-Sadat, *In Search of Identity*, New York 1978.
16. Ibid., p. 3.
17. Ibid., p. 3.
18. See Gabriel Warburg: 'Popular Islam and Tribal Leadership in the Socio-Political Structure of North Sudan', in Milson, pp. 231-41.
19. Ibid., pp. 273-6.
20. J.B. Mayfield, *Rural Politics in Nasser's Egypt*, Austin 1971, pp. 53-4.
21. D. Crecellius, 'Al-Azhar in Revolution', *MEJ*, 20 (1966), p. 34.
22. N. Rejwan, *Nasserist Ideology, its Exponents and Critics*, Jerusalem 1974, pp. 38, 46-67; for details on the al-Azhar reform see Crecellius, pp. 31-49; see also *al-Watan*, 22 January 1980, which reports the decisions of the Islamic Conference held at al-Azhar to denounce the Soviet invasion of Afghanistan. The conference, which included representatives of all Muslim associations in Egypt, including *sufi* orders and student organizations, called upon Sadat to return to al-Azhar all its 'usurped assets' in order to make it independent of government control. It also advocated the election of the Rector of al-Azhar by 'ulama from all over the Islamic world, in order to enable this venerated institution to become, once again, the leader of the Islamic community, quoted in *FBIS-MEA*, v 021 (30 January 1980).
23. P.J. Vatikiotis, 'Islam and Foreign Policy in Egypt', in J. Harris Proctor (ed.), *Islam and International Relations*, London 1965, pp. 138-45.
24. M. Berger, *Islam in Egypt Today*, Cambridge 1970, pp. 43-4.
25. F. de Jong, 'Aspects of the Political Involvement of *Sufi* Orders in twentieth century Egypt (1907–1970), an Exploratory Stocktaking', in G.R. Warburg and U.M. Kupferschmidt (eds.), *Islam, Nationalism and Radicalism in Egypt and Sudan*, New York 1983, pp. 196-200.
26. Berger, pp. 70-1.
27. Rejwan, pp. 35-7.
28. S. Shamir (ed.), *The Decline of Nasserism 1965–1970*, Tel Aviv 1978, pp. 36-7 [in Hebrew].
29. S. Shamir, *Egypt Under Sadat*, Tel Aviv 1978, pp. 58-60 [in Hebrew].
30. G.H. Gardner and S.A. Hanna, 'Islamic Socialism', *The Muslim World*, 56 (1966), p. 75.
31. Baer, p. 16.
32. R.D. McLaurin, M. Mughisuddin, A.R. Wagner, *Foreign Policy Making in the Middle East*, New York 1977, p. 56.
33. On the Copts' compliance with the Regimes' policies see E. Wakin, *A Lonely Minority: The Modern Story of Egypt's Copts*, New York 1963, especially pp. 54-6.

34. For details see J. O. O'Kane, 'Islam in the New Constitution: Some Suggestions in al-Ahram', *M.E.J.*, 26 (Spring 1972), especially p. 37; An English translation of the Constitution was published in *M.E.J.*, 26 (Winter 1972), pp. 55-68; see also R. S. Humphreys, 'Islam and Political Values in Saudi Arabia, Egypt and Syria', *M.E.J.*, 33 (Winter 1979), pp. 1-19.
35. Abd al-Monein Said Aly and Manfred W. Wenner, 'Modern Islamic Reform Movements: The Muslim Brotherhood in Contemporary Egypt', *M.E.J.* 36/3 (Summer 1982): 349-50; see also Israel Altman, 'Islamic Legislation in Egypt in the 1970s', *A.A.S.* 13/3 (1979): 199-219.
36. R. M. Burrell and A. R. Kelidar, *Egypt, The Dilemma of a Nation: 1970–1977*, London 1977, p. 43.
37. R. W. Baker, *Egypt's Uncertain Revolution Under Nasser and Sadat*, Cambridge, Mass., 1978, pp. 165-6.
38. Quoted by *FBIS-MEA*, v. 14 (21 January 1977).
39. *FBIS-MEA*, v. 216 (6 November 1979), quoting *al-Ahram*, 5 November 1979; for details see below.
40. Gamal Abdel Nasser, *The Philosophy of The Revolution*, Buffalo 1959, pp. 62, 77.
41. Vatikiotis (1965), pp. 120-2.
42. Ibid., p. 124.
43. Sadat, p. 136.
44. Berger, p. 47.
45. Ibid., p. 48.
46. M. S. Kramer, 'An Introduction to World Islamic Conferences', Shiloah Center Occasional Papers, Tel Aviv 1978, pp. 20-3.
47. See for instance Mayfield, p. 54.
48. Kramer, pp. 30-1.
49. M. H. Heikal, 'Egyptian Foreign Policy', *Foreign Affairs* (Summer 1978), p. 727.
50. Anouar Abdel Malek, *Egypt: Military Society*, New York 1968, pp. 249-57.
51. Ibid., p. 261, quoted from *'Uruba wa Din*, Cairo n.d., p. 63.
52. *FBIS-MEA*, v. 154 (8 August 1979).
53. *FBIS-MEA*, v. 088 (4 May 1979), quoting MENA, 3 May 1979.
54. *FBIS-MEA*, v. 090 (8 May 1979), quoting MENA, 7 May 1979.
55. *FBIS-MEA*, v. 093 (11 May 1979), quoting Sadat's speech to the people of Kafr al-Shaykh, from R. Cairo, 10 May 1979.
56. *FBIS-MEA*, v. 231 (1 Dec. 1977), quoting R. Cairo, 30 Nov. 1977.
57. I. Altman, 'Recent Radical Trends in the Positions of the Moslem Brothers', Shiloah Center Occasional Papers, Tel Aviv 1979 [in Hebrew], p. 9, quoting from *Ruz al-Yusuf*, 12 Dec. 1977; *al-Ahram*, 28 Sept. 1978.
58. *FBIS-MEA*, v. 98 (18 May 1979), quoting MENA.
59. *FBIS-MEA*, v. 247 (21 December 1979), quoting *October*, Cairo 16 December 1979; (the Zamzam is the holy well in Mecca): see also *FBIS-MEA*, v. 104 (29 May 1979) quoting Radio Cairo.
60. Quoted from *FBIS-MEA*, v. 192 (2 Oct. 1979).
61. Quoted from *October*, 30 December 1979, by *FBIS-MEA*, v. 252 (31 Dec. 1979).
62. *October*, 6 January 1980, *FBIS-MEA*, v. 5 (8 Jan. 1980).
63. *FBIS-MEA*, v. 250 (27 Dec. 1979), quoting R. Cairo, 25 Dec. 1979.
64. *FBIS-MEA*, v. 244 (18 Dec. 1979), quoting R. Cairo, 15 Dec. 1979.
65. R. P. Mitchell, *The Society of Muslim Brothers*, London 1969, pp. 105-25; see also C. P. Harris, *Nationalism and Revolution in Egypt: The Role of the Muslim Brotherhood*, The Hague 1964.
66. See Harris, pp. 195-203; The Brethren's reform proposals were published in *al-Ahram*, 2 Aug. 1952.
67. Ibid., pp. 213-16.

68. 'Abd al-Azim Ramadan, *Al-Ikhwan al-Muslimun wa'l-Tanzim al-Sirri*, Cairo 1982, pp. 133-5.
69. For details see P. J. Vatikiotis, *Nasser and His Generation*, London 1978, pp. 90-91; see also Ramadan, pp. 136-8; on 'Awda's subsequent involvement in the pro-Neguib demonstrations see ibid., pp. 138-9.
70. Sadat, p. 124.
71. Vatikiotis (1978), pp. 144-5.
72. Harris, pp. 222-3, quoting from *al-Jumhuriyya*, 18 Nov. 1954.
73. Shamir, *The Decline of Nasserism*, pp. 36-7.
74. Sayyid Qutb, *Ma'alim fi al-tariq*, Cairo 1964, as quoted by E. Kedourie, 'Anti Marxism in Egypt', in M. Confino and S. Shamir (eds.), *The U.S.S.R. and the Middle East*, Jerusalem 1973, pp. 325-6; see also Sylvia G. Haim, 'Sayyid Qutb', in *A.A.S.* 16/1 (1982), pp. 153-5.
75. J. Waterbury, *Egypt, Burdens of the Past Options for the Future*, Bloomington 1978, p. 241; The figures are quoted from *Akhbar al-Yaym*, 29 March 1975.
76. Sadat, pp. 49-50, 165.
77. For details see S. Shamir, 'The Marxists in Egypt: The "Licensed infiltration" Doctrine in Practice', in M. Confino and S. Shamir, pp. 293-317.
78. Sadat, p. 50.
79. Ibid., pp. 22-3; in his book *Asrar al-Thawra* Sadat related in particular his admiration for the armed and trained 'Secret Apparatus' of the Brethren, which, he hoped would back the Free Officers after their first strike against the regime; quoted by al-Bishri, p. 472.
80. Shiloah Center, Occasional Papers, Tel Aviv 1978.
81. *FBIS-MEA*, v. 250 (27 Dec. 1979) quoted from *al-Anba'*.
82. Said Aly and Wenner, pp. 350-4.
83. Israel Altman, 'Islamic Movements in Egypt', *The Jerusalem Quarterly*, 10 (Winter 1979), pp. 87-94 [hereafter Altman, *JQ*].
84. These and many other criticisms are cited by Sivan, pp. 34-9; see also *FBIS-MEA*, v. 021 (30 Jan. 1980), in which the decisions of the recent Islamic Conference at al-Azhar include the denunciation of the Egyptian mass media for its venomous attacks against Islam, as well as the demand for the application of the *hudud* as specified by the Shari'a (quoted from *al-Watan*, 22 Jan. 1980).
85. Sivan, pp. 41-2; Altman, 'Radical Trends', pp. 4-5.
86. Altman, *JQ*, pp. 92-3.
87. *JPRS-Near East Report*, 1996 (18 July 1979), quoting *al-Hawadith* London, 27 April 1979; while denouncing Egyptian authorities for stirring up dissent, the paper itself 'hinted' that it was odd that only the Coptic grandson and namesake of Butrus Ghali Pasha, the prime minister assassinated for signing the 1899 Condominium Agreement with Britain for The Joint Administration of the Sudan, could be found to sign the new treaty of 'subjugation' with Israel.
88. Altman, 'Radical Trends', p. 10.
89. *FBIS-MEA*, v. 087 (3 May 1979), quoting from QNA.
90. *FBIS-MEA*, v. 085 (1 May 1979).
91. *FBIS-MEA*, v. 095 (15 May 1979), quoting from MENA.
92. Sivan, pp. 39-40.
93. For details see Vatikiotis (1978), pp. 91-4.
94. Altman, *JQ*, pp. 94-95, quoting from *al-Da'wa*, Oct. 1976, Nov. 1976, May 1977, July 1977.
95. *FBIS-MEA*, v. 194 (5 Oct. 1978), according to *al-Da'wa*, Oct. 1978.
96. *FBIS-MEA*, v. 199 (13 Oct. 1978), quoting from *al-Siyasa*, 10 Oct. 1978.
97. Altman, 'Radical Trends', pp. 7-8. This was supported by the al-Azhar Conference in January 1980; see *FBIS-MEA*, v. 021 (30 Jan. 1980), quoting from *al-Watan*,

Islam and Politics in Egypt and the Sudan

22 Jan. 1980; for further details see Saad Eddin Ibrahim 'An Islamic Alternative in Egypt: The Muslim Brotherhood and Sadat', *Arab Studies Quarterly* 4/1-2 (1982), pp. 85-8.
98. Altman, *JQ*, pp. 97-9.
99. *FBIS-MEA*, v. 250 (27 Dec. 1979).
100. Altman, *JQ*, pp. 101-3; see also Saad Eddin Ibrahim, 'Anatomy of Egypt's Militant Islamic Groups: Methodological Note and Preliminary Findings', *I.J.M.E.S.* 12 (1980): pp. 423-53.
101. *New York Times*, 28 Nov. 1979. See also J. G. Jansen, 'The Voice of Sheikh Kishk' in A. Van de Koppel & R. Peters (eds.) *The Challenge of the Middle East*, Amsterdam 1982, pp. 57-66.
102. M. A. Mahgoub, *Democracy on Trial*, London 1974, pp. 224-5.
103. Ibid., p. 224.
104. For details see K. D. D. Henderson, *Sudan Republic*, London 1965, pp. 108-9, 179-80.
105. For details see R. O. Collins, *The Southern Sudan in Historical Perspective*, Tel Aviv 1975, pp. 74-7.
106. Mahgoub, p. 181.
107. P. K. Bechtold, *Politics in the Sudan*, New York 1976, p. 81.
108. See Warburg, *Islam, Nationalism and Communism* ..., pp. 157-8.
109. The Democratic Republic of the Sudan, *The Permanent Constitution of the Sudan*, Khartoum, 8 May 1973; in a rather symbolic act, which took place one month later, R. Omdurman announced that the Islamic college in Omdurman had at last been granted university status and would teach the Islamic and Arabic heritage — a clear indication as to the place of Islam in official thinking; *JPRS-Translations on Near East*, No. 977 (19 June 1973).
110. For details see Mahgoub, p. 237.
111. *Joint Publication Research Service — Translation on Near East*, No. 843 (18 Oct. 1972).
112. The following is in part based on my article 'Islam in Sudanese Politics', *The Jerusalem Quarterly*, 13 (Fall, 1979), pp. 47-61.
113. For details see *M.E.C.S.* Vol. I, 1976-77, pp. 586-8.
114. Al-Hindi's grandfather, al-Sharif Yusuf al-Hindi, headed the Hindiyya *sufi* order, an offshoot of the Samaniyya, in which the nineteenth century Mahdi had been a shaykh. Sadiq's grandfather was 'Abd al-Rahman al-Mahdi, the founder of the Ansar.
115. See *M.E.C.S. 1976-77*, pp. 586-8; see also below.
116. T. Niblock, 'Political System begins to relax', *Financial Times Survey*, 13 July 1978.
117. For details on this coup see H. Shaked, E. Souery and G. Warburg, 'The Communist Part in Sudan, 1946-71', in M. Confino and S. Shamir, pp. 335-74.
118. *Arab Report and Record* [hereafter *ARR*], No. 1 (1977), p. 19.
119. *The Middle East*, London Nov. 1978, pp. 12-13; *ARR*, 14 (1977), p. 608; *Le Monde*, 13 Sept. 1977.
120. *M.E.C.S., 1976-77*, p. 591; *ARR*, 18 (1977), pp. 796-7.
121. *Washington Post*, 11 April 1978; *ARR*, 6 (1978), p. 211; it should be remembered that al-Hindi, the leader of the Democratic Unionists had not returned to the Sudan before his recent death.
122. *Al-Dustur*, 10-16, April 1978.
123. *M.E.C.S., 1976-77*, p. 594.
124. See al-Mahdi's interview in *Sudanow*, Khartoum, Oct. 1978; for Numayri's interview see *The Middle East*, London, Dec. 1978; see also *M.E.C.S., 1977-78*, pp. 698-9, 704-7.

125. *Al-Hawadith*, 29 Dec. 1978.
126. *Al-Watan al-Arabi*, 11 Jan. 1979.
127. For details see *M.E.C.S. 1978–79*, pp. 777-9.
128. Quoted by *FBIS-MEA*, v. 200 (15 Oct. 1979): the report on the coup appeared also in the Lebanese daily *al-Liwa'*, 15 Oct. 1979, which reported that the coup took place on 8 October. The report was denied by the Sudan News Agency (SUNA) on 18 Oct. 1979, see *FBIS-MEA*, v. 203 (18 Oct. 1979).
129. Quoted by *FBIS-MEA*, v. 209 (26 Oct. 1979) from SUNA, 25 Oct. 1979.
130. In an interview with the Sa'udi *'Ukaz* Numayri claimed that his absence from the Iraqi Summit was caused by Iraqi threats. *FBIS-MEA*, v. 085 (1 May 1979).
131. *FBIS-MEA*, v. 229 (27 Nov. 1979), quoting SUNA, 25 Nov. 1979.
132. *FBIS-MEA*, v. 231 (29 Nov. 1979), quoting SUNA, 29 Nov. 1979.
133. In an interview with the Saudi Arabian *al-Riyad*, 20 Nov. 1979, Sudan's vice president and minister of foreign affairs, Rashid al-Tahir, claimed that 'the communists have been reduced to small groups and isolated individuals', quoted in *FBIS-MEA*, v. 232 (30 Nov. 1979).
134. Bona Malwal, 'Reconciliation with the Mahdi', *Sudanow* (Dec. 1978).
135. Ja'far Muhammad al-Numayri, *Al-Nahj al-Islami Limadha?*, Cairo 1980.
136. Quoted by A. S. Cudsi, 'Islam and Politics in the Sudan', p. 10, paper presented at Conference on Islam in the Political Process, The Royal Institute of International Affairs, London 24-26 June 1981.
137. Quoted in ibid., pp. 11-12 from *Sudanow* (Nov. 1979).
138. *M.E.C.S., 1977–78*, pp. 696-8.
139. Fouad Ajami, *The Arab Predicament*, London and New York 1981, p. 190.

Index

Aba Island, 7-8, 192, 227-8
'Abbas Hilmi, II 28-30, 32, 34, 53 58, 71, 94, 98, 107, 134
'Abbud, Ahmad, 40, 148
'Abbud, Ibrahim, 7, 193, 225-6
'Abd al-Latif, 'Ali, 16
'Abd al-Latif, Mahmud, 214
'Abd al-Nasir, Jamal *see* Nasser
'Abd al-Qadir (Imam Wad Habuba), 53
'Abd al-Ra'uf, 'Abd al-Mun'im, 214
'Abdallah b. Muhammad, the Khalifa, 13-14, 19, 42, 192
Abdel Malek, Anwar, 208
'Abduh, Muhammad, 34, 190
Abdulhamid II, 93-4, 190, 192
Abu-Talib, Sufi, 203
Abukir, 162
Acre, 106
Addis Ababa, 226
Adowa, defeat of the Italians at, 14
al-Afghani, Jamal al-Din, 190, 192
Afghanistan, 174, 181, 211
'Afifi, Hafiz, 37
Aflaq, Michel, 208
Africa, African, 2, 5, 11, 12, 26, 38, 59, 117, 120, 140, 162, 166, 171-2, 175-6, 178-9, 182, 185, 204, 209, 226, 233
  East, 161, 169, 182, 207
Ahmad, 'Abd al-Maqsud, 37
al-Ahram, 198
Ajami, Fouad, 173, 235
Alexandria, 69, 150, 214, 222-3
  bombardment of (1882), 27, 129
'Ali, Kamal Hasan, 178

Allenby, E., 2, 30, 35-6, 41, 64-72, 79-82
  ultimatum (1924), 2-3, 17, 79-81
America, American, 99, 168, 171-4, 183
Amery, L., 97
'Amir, 'Abd al-Hakim, 167, 200, 215
'Amr Mosque, 149
Anatolia, 163
al-Anba' (Kuwait), 222
Anglo-Egyptian
  agreements: (1936), 4, 27, 38-9, 42, 99, 104-5, 113-15, 116-20, 124, 126, 130, 137, 164; (1953), 25
  negotiations: Milner-Zaghlul (1920), 68, 116; 'Adli-Curzon (1921), 66, 70; Zaghlul -MacDonald (1924), 69-70; Sidqi-Bevin (1946), 96
Anglo-Egyptian Condominium, 1-3, 17, 24, 42, 49-50, 52, 54, 57, 63-4, 71, 80, 164
Angola(n), 176
Ansar, 2, 3, 8, 13, 15, 17-19, 22, 25-6, 176-7, 192-3, 197, 223-4, 227-30, 232-7
  revolt (July 1976), 172, 176, 229, 236
  see also Neo-Mahdism; Sudan
Aqaba, 90-1, 94-6, 104, 106, 108
  the Gulf of, 3, 90-1, 93, 107-9
  Naqb al-Aqaba, 90
  Port of, 107-8
al-'Aqib, 'Abd al-Rahman, 227
Arab(s), 5, 6, 97, 123, 147-8, 165-84, 193-4, 205-11, 215, 218, 220, 226, 232-3

revolt (1936–39), 165
socialism, 194-6, 199, 201, 205-6, 213, 215, 218
Summit Conferences (1964–65), 168
units in Sudan, 78-9
unity, 5, 148, 167-70, 173, 186
al-'Arab (London), 210
Arab League, 148, 165, 179, 181, 208, 211
Summit in Tunisia (1979), 177, 181, 211, 232
Arab Socialist Union (ASU), 200, 215-16, 228
Arabian peninsula, 15, 163, 169, 179, 207
Arabic, 136, 202, 218, 225
Arabism, 5, 167, 169, 179, 207-8, 211, 220
Nasserist, 179, 182, 198-9, 207-8, 220
see also nationalism, Arab; pan-Arab
Arabization
of the Red Sea, 176, 179
Sudan, 225-6
'Arafat, Y., 174, 183
Archer, G., 20, 80-1
Asad, Hafiz, 174, 183
Ashiqqa', 22
'Ashmawi, Salih, 218
Asia, 11, 12
Aswan, 48, 185
high dam, 167
Asyut, 222
University of, 219
'Atallah, Ibrahim, 139
Attlee, C., 22
Austria, Austrian, 28, 106
Awda, 'Abd al-Qadir, 213
al-'Ayidi, Rajab, 180, 210
al-Azhar, Azharite, 5-7, 120, 131, 139, 149, 180, 189-90, 197-204, 206, 209-10, 214, 218, 235
Majallat al-Azhar, 199, 205
al-Azhari, Isma'il, 22-3, 43, 165, 225-6

'Azuri, Najib, 53
'Azzam, 'Abd al-Rahman, 121-3, 138, 165

Baer, Gabriel, 195-6
Baghdad, 183
Arab summit 1978, 171, 176, 232
pact, 166, 206
al-Bahi, Muhammad, 199
Bahr al-Ghazal, 14, 162
Baily, R., 81
Bakhit, Ja'far 'Ali, 227
Baldwin, S., 79
Balkan
German invasion of (1941), 130
Balta Liman (1838), Treaty of, 11
al-Bana, Hasan, 141, 191, 213, 216
Bandung Conference, 166-7, 168
Bank Misr, 37
Baqqara, 14, 19
al-Baquri, Ahmad Hasan, 180, 199, 208, 210, 212
Barakat, Fathallah, 132
Baring, Evelyn *see* Crommer, Lord
Bateman, C., 126
Ba'th party, Ba'thist, 167-8, 178, 208
Beersheba, 210
Beja, 19
Belgium, Belgian, 14, 28
Belgrade, 167
Ben Gurion, David, 169
Berlin, 14
Bevin, E., 96
von Bieberstein, A.F.M., 94
Binder, L., 196
Bissar, 'Abd al-Rahman, 204
Bonaparte, Napoleon, 161-2
Bowker, J., 98
Boyle, H., 94
Brook, C., 18
Burrell, R.M., 173

Cairo, 1, 5, 23, 25, 28, 33, 41, 49, 50, 52, 54, 56-9, 63, 66, 69,

Index

73-4, 78, 82, 98-9, 108, 112-13, 118, 125, 127, 138, 146-7, 161, 163-4, 174, 177-9, 181-3, 190, 196, 201, 203, 206, 213, 222-3, 235
Caliphate, 201
Camp David accords, 172, 174, 176, 180, 182, 210, 216, 221, 231-2
Campbell, R.J., 151
Cecil, E.H.G., 53
Central African Republic, 226
Chad, 175, 177-9
Chamberlain, A., 77, 80, 82
Childers, H.C.E., 27
China, 204
  Sino-Soviet conflict, 168
Chou En-Lai, 166
Christianity, Christian(s), 15, 56, 210, 218, 225, 227, 233
  in Egypt, 59
  missionary in Sudan, 57, 225
Churchill, W., 40, 69, 142, 145-7
Ciano, Count, 114
Clayton, G., 57, 62, 67
Cold War, 5, 182
Colvin, A., 26-7
Communism, Communist(s), 5, 209, 223
  Egypt, 203, 216-18, 221
  Sudan, 175, 193, 208, 226, 229, 232
the Congo, 14
Constantinople, 109
constitutions:
  1923, 36, 38, 72, 112, 116, 190, 193
  1930, 31
  1971, 202-3
Copt(s), Coptic, 6, 57, 59, 121, 134, 140, 202, 219, 223
Cromer, Lord, 28-9, 32, 34, 37, 48, 50-3, 57-8, 61, 63, 66, 91, 94-5, 98, 104, 107-9, 134, 142, 190
Cuban troops in Libya, 174
Currie, J., 20, 59
Curzon, Lord, 64, 67-9, 72, 76

Cyrenaica, 99
Czechoslovakia, arms deal with Egypt (1955), 166

Daba, 106-7
Daily Express, 67
Daily Herald, 66-7
Daily Telegraph, 66-7
Damascus, 183
Danaqla, 19
Dar Fur, 19, 106, 162, 237
Davies, R., 75
al-Da'wa, 6, 218-21
Deeb, M., 31, 126
Delhi, 167
Delta, 138, 235
Democratic Unionist party, 224, 227-8, 230
al-Dhahabi, Husayn, 222
Dinshiway, 129
Djibuti, 179
Dongola campaign (1896), 48, 185
Drummond-Wolff negotiations (1877), 27

Eden, A., 32, 39-40, 97, 119, 125, 131, 136, 140-2, 145, 147-50, 165
Eilat, 90
Eisenhower doctrine, 167
effendiyya, effendi class, 16, 20, 126, 137
El-Arish, 91, 93-6, 98, 104, 107-8
El-Shatt, 114
English, 225
Equatorial regions, 1, 162
Eritrea, 179, 209
Erlich, H., 217
L'Etendard Egyptien, 58
Ethiopia, Ethiopians, 5, 14, 38, 116, 118, 162, 172, 174-5, 178-9, 208-9, 226, 228-9, 231
Europe, European, 2, 6, 11, 12, 14, 27, 35, 38, 41, 120, 147, 161, 191-2, 195

Fallaci, O., 194
faqih, 194

Farid, Muhammad, 91
Faron, island of, 91
Faruq, King, 4, 24, 26, 28, 32-4, 38-40, 42-3, 116-51, 165-6, 190, 213
Fascism, Fascist, 38, 120, 147, 195
Fashoda, 97
Faysal, King (Saudi Arabia), 173
Fidaiyan-i Islam, 213
Fiki(s), 15
Fischer, W.J., 95-6
France, French, 5, 14, 26, 27, 48, 93, 166-7, 169, 182
Franjieh, S., 173
Free Officers
  Egypt, 4, 5, 24, 26, 34, 40, 165, 188, 191, 193, 195, 197, 199, 205, 212-4
  Sudan, 193
Fu'ad, Ahmad, King, 28, 30-2, 35-6, 38, 42, 71, 81, 116, 118, 134, 139, 190

Gallagher, J., 11, 13-14, 26-7
al-Gaylani, Rashid 'Ali, 132
George V, King, 60, 70
George VI, King, 124
Germany, German, 14, 15, 32, 37, 39, 93-4, 110, 123, 127, 130, 132
  Nazi, 118, 120
Gezira (Sudan), 19, 62, 77
Ghali Pasha, Butrus, 57
Ghali, Butrus, 184-5
Ghazali, Mahmud, 149
Gillan, A., 21
Gladstone, W.E., 26-7, 29
Gordon, Charles, 192
Gordon Memorial College, 20, 54, 59
Gorst, E., 29, 34, 50, 52-5, 61, 63, 66
Graduates' General Congress, 21-2
Granville, Lord W., 27
Grey, E., 62

Habre, Hisseine, 175
Hadi Pasha, 105

Halifax, Viscount C.L.W., 122, 125-6, 135
Halim, 'Abbas, 138
al-Harakan, Muhammad 'Ali, 209
al-Harb, Salah, 122, 138
Harb, Tal'at, 37-8
Hardinge, C., 35
Hartington, S.C., 27
Hasan, King (Morocco), 173
Hasanayn, Ahmad, 33, 125, 132, 136, 143, 147, 150
Hashemite(s), 165-7, 182
Haykal, Muhammad Husayn, 128-9, 132, 135, 138, 191
Heikal, Muhamed Hassanein, 173, 207
Hejaz, 89, 93, 106-9, 162-3
Hejaz railway, 91
Henderson, N., 19, 20, 80, 82, 105
Heyworth-Dunne, J., 123
al-Hilali, Najib, 24
al-Hindi, Husayn Sharif Yusuf, 228-9, 231-2, 234
Hiwat (Ahyawat) tribe, 93
Horn of Africa, 172, 174, 178-9, 208
Howson, C., 98, 104
Hudaybi, Hasan, 213-14
Huddleston, H., 79
Hungarian troops in Libya, 174
Hünkar Iskelesi treaty (1833), 163
Hussein, King (Jordan), 169

Ibrahim Pasha, 163
'Ilwan, Muhammad Mahmud, 200
imam(s), 198, 200-1, 209, 223
India, Indian, 13, 26, 93
Integration Charter (*mithaq al-takamul*), 185-6
International Court of Justice, 99, 115
Iran, 172, 174, 211-12
  Islamic revolution, 179, 188, 194, 217
Iraq, 123, 132, 162, 166-8, 174, 177
Islam, Islamic, Muslim(s), 5-8, 14, 15, 37, 57, 120-1, 123, 126,

Index

134, 140-1, 162-3, 165, 179-81, 184, 188-237
   reformism, 190
al-Islam wa'l-Tasawwuf, 200
Islamic Charter Front, 226-8
   see also Muslim Brothers (Sudan)
Islamic Congress, 206
Isma'il (khedive), 106-7, 113, 162, 182
Ismailiyya, 191
Israel, Israeli, 3, 34, 100, 168-71, 177, 183-5, 191, 206-8, 219-21
   invasion of Lebanon, 184
   Sadat's peace treaty with, 5, 170, 172, 177, 180, 183, 210, 223, 232
   see also Camp David accords
   Sinai disengagement agreements
   Wars (Arab-Israeli)
Istanbul, 161
Italy, Italian, 39, 93, 112, 114, 117-18, 120, 122, 127
   in Ethiopia, 14, 38
al-I'tisam, 6
Izzet, Hasan, 123

Ja'aliyyin, 19
Jama'at al-Islamiyya, 202, 204, 217, 223, 237
jama'at al-takfir wa'l-hijra, 222
Jeddah, 106, 206
Jenings Bramly, W. E., 89-91, 93-4, 96-8, 104, 108, 113
Jerusalem, 209, 221, 232
   governorate of, 89, 93, 109
   Sadat's visit to, 174, 176, 180, 210, 221
Jew(s), Jewish, Jewry, Judaism, 94, 101, 165-6, 210, 220-1
jihad, 15, 192, 206, 220-1
   movements, 184, 222
Johnson, Lyndon, 168
Jordan, 167, 183

Kababish, 19
Kamil, Husayn (Sultan), 53, 110

Kamil, Mustafa, 1, 58, 140, 163, 190
Kantara, 105, 114
Kelidar, A. R., 173
Kelly, D., 28, 122
Kenya, 106, 179, 226
Keown-Boyd, A., 64-5
Khalil, Mustafa, 211
Khalwatiyya, 200
Khartoum, 1, 7, 13, 20, 52-4, 56-61, 66, 77, 79, 81, 174, 178, 185, 192, 235
Khatmiyya, Khatmi, 3, 13, 15, 22-3, 56, 224, 228, 230, 235-6
Khomeini, 194, 199, 211
Killearn, Lord see Lampson, Miles
Kishk, 'Abd al-Hamid, 223
Kitchener, H. H., 14, 15, 34-5, 52-3, 55, 58, 62-3, 65
Kom Ombo, 37
Kordofan, 19, 21, 106, 237
Kufra, 177
Kuttab, 198
Kuwait, 173

Labour party, 33, 40, 67-9, 72, 77
Lado Enclave, 61
Lampson, Miles (Lord Killearn), 4, 20, 21, 28, 31-3, 38-40, 101, 116-51
Lancashire, 62
Lansdowne, Lord, 14
Lausanne Treaty (1923), 95, 97, 100, 104, 111
Lawrence, T. E., 95
League of Nations, 4, 68, 99-100, 115
Lebanon, Lebanese, 122, 167, 173, 208
   in Egypt, 59
   Israel invasion of, 184
Leopold, King, 14, 61
de Lesseps, F., 113
Liberal Constitutionalist Party, 30-1, 36-7, 71, 121, 128, 131, 138, 141, 191
Little, T., 128
al-Liwa, 58

Lloyd, George, 30, 34, 82, 97-8, 100, 105, 112
London, 16, 25, 35, 60, 70, 73-4, 78-80, 90, 118, 122-3, 127, 133, 144, 162, 220, 231
Loraine, P., 31
Lugard, F., 18
Lyttelton, O., 136-7

Ma'an, 91
MacDonald, R., 68-9, 76-8, 112, 118
MacLean, F., 100
MacMichael, H.A., 18
Maffey, J., 18, 20
al-Mahdi, Muhammad Ahmad, 7, 13, 15, 19, 56, 192, 197, 199, 232
Mahdism, Mahdist(s), Mahdist state, Mahdiyya, 1, 6, 7, 13, 15, 19, 22, 42, 48-9, 75, 192-3, 197, 236
 Mahdi's family: 'Abd al-Rahman al-Mahdi, 3, 15-17, 19, 22, 24-5, 75, 192
 al-Hadi al-Mahdi, 7, 224
 al-Sadiq al-Mahdi, 7, 224, 228-34, 236
 neo-Mahdism, neo-Mahdist(s):
  Egypt, 6, 188-9, 197, 216, 221-3, 236-7
  Sudan, 19, 53, 197, 224
  revolt, 13, 50, 162, 189, 197
Mahir, Ahmad, 39-40, 120, 126, 132, 137-8
Mahir, 'Ali, 32-3, 120-3, 124-6, 131, 133, 138, 165
Mahjub, Muhammad Ahmad, 22, 224-5, 228
al-Mahlawi, Ahmad, 223
Mahmud, 'Abd al-Halim, 203-4
Mahmud, Muhammad, 118, 121-2, 126
Makwar dam, 77
Malet, E., 27
Malwal, Bona, 233
al-Manar, 190

Manchester Guardian, 66
Mansur, Anis, 181, 211
al-Maraghi, Mustafa, 120-1, 126, 139, 222
Marlowe, J., 127
Marxist(s), 201
 Egypt, 217
 Ethiopia, 174, 228
Massawa, 106-7, 110, 113
McBride, C., 128
McMahon, H., 35, 61, 63
McMahon-Husayn correspondence, 15
McNamara, R., 171
Mecca, 93-4, 162-3, 204, 209
Medina, 162
Menelik, King, 14
Milner, A., 62, 64-5, 68-9, 76
Milner Mission, 64
al-Mirghani, 'Ali, 16, 56, 230, 233
al-Mirghani, Muhammad 'Uthman, 235-6
Misr Air Company, 37
Misr Cotton Exporting Company, 37
Misr al-Fatat, 121, 126, 131
Misr party, 217
al-Misri, 'Aziz 'Ali, 122-3
Mit Abu al-Kawm, 196, 211
Mitchell, R.P., 212, 220
Morning Post, 67
Morocco, 173-4, 180-1, 183, 204, 210-11
Moscow, 171, 174
Mosul, 167
Moyne, W.E., 146
Mubarak, Husni, 178, 183-5, 237
mufti(s), 201
Muggeridge, M., 13
Muhammad 'Ali, 4, 5, 91, 93, 98, 106, 161-3, 166-8, 182
Muhammad 'Ali, Prince, 133
Muhammad, Mushin, 137, 140
Muhyi al-Din, Khaled, 203
Mukhtar Pasha (Turkish Commissioner in Cairo 1906), 108-9
al-Muqattam, 58

Index

Murray, J., 71-2
Muslim(s) *see* Islam
Muslim Brothers
 Egypt, 4, 6, 8, 39-40, 121, 126-8, 131-2, 141, 165-6, 181, 189, 191, 193-5, 198-200, 202, 204-6, 208, 212-23, 237
 Sudan, 7, 8, 226, 228-30, 233-7
 see also Islamic Charter Front
Muslim Youth Association, 180, 210
Mussolini, Benito, 116
Mustafa, Ahmad Shukri, 222
Mutawalli, Mahmud, 128

al-Nahhas, Mustafa, 4, 24, 33, 38-40, 101, 115, 116-51, 208
Najd, 162
Najib, Muhammad, 24-5, 129, 165, 212-14
Nakhl, 90, 93
Nasser, Nasserism, 5, 6, 27, 129, 166-70, 173, 179-80, 182-5, 191, 194-6, 198-202, 212-16, 218, 220, 227-8, 236
 Nasserist(s), 6, 173, 198, 203, 216-17, 221
 pro-Nasserist, Iraq, 167
National Charter of 1962, 195, 201-2, 205
'National Front', 148, 176-7, 227-31
National Unionist Party, 165, 225
nationalism, nationalist, 11, 12
 Arab, 165, 194
 Egyptian, 1, 5, 16, 26, 35, 37-8, 51, 55, 56-9, 62-3, 65, 69, 73, 80, 82, 117, 127, 140-1, 148, 164, 190-1, 208
 Lebanese, 208
 Palestinian, 208
 Sudanese, 3, 7, 13-14, 16, 21, 64, 69, 73, 192, 197
 Syrian, 208
Nationalist party, 1, 57-8, 75, 131, 163, 190
Navarino, 162
Nazism, nazi, 118, 120, 195

Nazli, Queen, 120
Ndjamena, 175
Nehru, J., 166
Nelson, H. (Admiral), 162
Newbold, D., 21
Nigeria, 18
Nile, 1, 2, 26, 48-9, 52, 55, 61, 65, 68, 162, 185-6, 210
 Blue, 178; Blue Nile dam, 55, 79
 upper, 14, 48, 145, 183
 White, 7, 19, 192
Nile Valley, 1, 3-5, 13, 14, 22, 26, 36, 41-3, 48-9, 66-7, 69-70, 104, 117, 119-20, 147, 161-2, 164-5, 169, 175, 182, 185-6, 188, 192-4, 197, 204, 235
Northbrook, T.B., 27
Nuba mountains, 59
Nubia, 106
 Nubian Lake, 185
al-Numayri, Ja'far Muhammad, 7, 8, 169, 175-8, 183, 185, 188, 193, 208, 233-4, 236-7
al-Nuqrashi, Mahmud Fahmi, 39-40, 120, 122, 126
Nurab, 19
Nyala incident (1921), 17

October, 181, 211
Oduho, Joseph, 233
Ogaden desert, 179, 209
Oliphant, L., 105
Oman, 174, 177, 179
Omar Faruq, Prince, 138
Omdurman, 56, 60, 232
 mutiny of Egyptian Army (1900) 58
'open door' policy, 171, 218-19
Ottoman empire, Ottoman(s), 3, 5, 11, 27, 42, 71, 89, 91, 94-6, 100, 106-7, 109-10, 114, 161-3, 190
 see also Turkey
Owen, R., 26
Owen, R.C.R., 90

Palestine, 26, 95-9, 101, 104-5, 112, 150, 165-6, 220

Arab Revolt (1936-9), 165
London conference (1939), 121, 165
Palestinian(s), 168, 174, 177, 181, 184-5, 208, 211, 232
Palestine Liberation Organization (PLO), 168, 183, 187, 232
Palestine Partition Commission (1938), 112
Palestine Royal Commission (1937), 112
pan-Arab, pan-Arabism, 164-70, 173-4, 196, 211, 220, 223
 see also Arabism
 nationalism, Arab
pan-Islam, pan-Islamic, 54, 56-9, 190
Peel Commission, 101
Persian Gulf, 172, 174, 179
Perth, Earl of, 114
pilgrimage (hajj), Egyptian to Mecca, 93-4, 98, 108, 163
Piraeus, 91, 108
Port Said-Suez railway, 114
Port Sudan, 51, 53, 55, 60, 229
positive neutralism, 167, 182, 185
Prophet, 27, 191, 201, 210, 215
Prussia, 106

Qadhafi, Mu'amar, 169, 174-6, 183, 220, 222, 228, 237
qadi(s), 54
Quraishi, Z.M., 127-8
Qur'an, Qur'anic, 6, 195, 202, 208, 221
Qutb, Sayyid, 6, 215

Rabat, Islamic Conference (1979) 180, 209-10
Rabat Summit conference (1969), 169, 206
Rafah, 3, 91, 93-4, 96, 98, 100, 104-5, 108-9, 113, 163
Ramadan, 'Abd al-'Azim, 120, 213
Ras Muhammad, 91, 109
Red Sea, 13, 48, 55, 114, 163, 176, 178-9
Republican Brothers, 234

revolutions in Egypt:
 1919, 37, 64, 164
 1952, 4, 24, 34, 40, 128, 212
Riad, 179, 183
Rida, Muhammad Rashid, 190-1
Robertson, J., 23, 25
Robinson, R., 11-14, 25-7, 41, 43
Robinson and Gallagher controversy, 11
Rogers plan, 170
Rome, 114
Rommel, E. (Gen.), 32, 123, 132, 138
Rose, E.M., 122
Rushdi, Husayn, 35, 70
Rushdi Pasha (commandant of Aqaba), 90-1
Russia, Russian(s), 27, 57, 93, 106, 110, 130, 163, 220
 see also Soviet Union

Sabah family, 173
Sabri, 'Ali, 215
Sabri, Hasan, 124
al-Sadat, Muhammad Anwar, 4, 6-7, 39-40, 123, 129, 170-85, 191, 195-6, 202-4, 206-12, 214-23, 228, 232, 234, 236-7
 assassination of, 178, 183-4, 188, 236
 Nasserist opposition to, 6, 173, 198
 peace initiative, 170, 183, 185, 207, 220-1
 peace treaty with Israel, 5, 170, 172, 177, 180, 183, 210, 223, 232
 see also 'open door' policy
Sa'dist party (*al-hay'a al-Sa'diyya*), 39-40, 127, 131, 138, 141
Safran, Nadav, 191
salafi, 233
Salih, 'Abd al-Hamid, 232
Salim, Salah, 213
Salisbury, 3rd Marquess of, 14
Santa Catarina Monastery, 210
Sarawak, 18
Saudi Arabia, Saudi, 165, 167-8,

Index

173-4, 176-81, 183, 194, 205-6, 210-11, 215-16, 218, 228
Sayf al-Nasr, Hamdi, 139
al-Sayyid, Ahmad Lutfi, 190, 207-8
Scrivener, P.C., 147, 149
Sennar, 106
Seymour, H., 126
Shabab Muhammad, 222
Shalabi, Mahmud, 201
Shaltut, Mahmud, 199, 201
Sharabi, Hisham, 193-4
Shari'a, 6, 202-5, 217, 222, 224, 234, 237
Shari'a courts, 54, 198
Sharifian revolt, 15
Shayqiyya, 57
Shenuda III (Coptic patriarch), 219
Shone, T., 149-50
Shuqayr, Na'um, 58
shura, 6, 195
Siba'i, Mustafa, 201
Sidqi, Isma'il, 31, 34, 40, 97, 118
Sinai disengagement agreements (1974–1975), 170, 176, 183
Sinai Mining Company, 96
Sinai peninsula, 3-4, 89-101, 104-15, 163, 168, 170-1
Siraj al-Din, Fu'ad, 140, 148
Sirri, Husayn, 32, 122, 125-6, 130-2
von Slatin, Rudolf, 54, 56-7, 60
Smart, W., 129, 139, 141-4, 146
Socialism, socialist, 195, 203
   Arab, 194-6, 199, 201, 205-6, 213, 215, 218
   Sudan, 197, 229
Socialist Republican party, 24-5
Somalia, 177-9
South Africa, 148-50
Soviet Union, Soviet(s), 5, 166-72, 174, 176, 178-80, 182-4, 205, 207-9, 220
   see also Russia, Russian(s)
Stack, L., 16, 17, 49, 64-6, 68, 72-5, 77-9, 81
The Standard (Egypt), 58

Stone, R.G.W. (Gen.), 135-6
Suakin, 106, 110, 113
Sudan Gazette, 60
Sudan protocol (1946), 22
Sudan Times, 58
Sudanese Communist Party, 226
   see also communist(s), Sudan
Sudanese Defence Force (SDF), 17, 78, 80
Sudanese Socialist Union (S.S.U.), 228-30, 232-4
Sudanow, 233
Suez, 91, 94, 96, 98, 100, 104, 108, 112, 115, 163-4
   Gulf of, 93, 113-14
Suez Canal, 4, 27, 48, 67, 69, 91, 93-5, 98-9, 104-5, 108-9, 112-15, 119, 148, 162, 163, 196
   Concession, 113
   Convention (1888), 113-14
   nationalization of, 166
Suez Canal Company, 37, 113
Sufism, *sufi* orders
   Committee for the revival of Islam, 235-6
   Egypt, 189, 200, 204, 236
   Sudan, 3, 13, 15-16, 182, 192, 233-6
Supreme Sufi Council, 200
Symes, S., 18, 20
Syria, Syrian(s), 90, 104, 106, 109, 112, 162-3, 165, 167-8, 173-5, 178, 181-3, 190, 208, 211, 215, 220
   Egypt's conquest of, 5, 162-3, 165-6, 182
   in Sudan, 76

Ta'aisha, Ta'ishi, 14, 42
Taba Incident (1906), 3, 89-96, 104, 108-9
al-Tabi'i, Muhammad, 125, 127
Tahir Pasha, 138
Taj, 'Abd al-Rahman, 198
Taka, 106
al-Tal al-kabir, the battle of, 129
Tal'at, Yusuf, 214
Tanta University, 220

Tarabin, 93
Tawfiq (khedive), 27, 106-7, 192
Tedder, A. (Marshal R.A.F.), 97-8
Tharwat, 'Abd al-Khaliq, 35-6, 70-1
Tignor, R., 29
Tigranne Pasha, 94, 107-9
al-Tilmisani, 'Umar, 218, 221
The Times (Great Britain), 67, 69-70
Tiran, Straits of, 168-9
Tito, J. Broz, 166
Tory, Tories, 68-9, 82
Toynbee, A.J., 95
Transjordan, 95, 99
Triple Alliance, 14
Tripoli (Libya), 169, 175, 178, 183
al-Tuhami, Hasan, 209, 220
Tunisia, Arab League Summit (1979), 177, 181, 211, 232
al-Turabi, Hasan, 229-30, 233-6
Turco-Circassian, 27
Turco-Egyptian, 27, 29, 42, 55, 162, 192
Turkey, Turkish, Turk(s), 15, 90-1, 93-6, 98, 100, 104-5, 107-11, 114
see also Ottoman Empire

'Ubayd, Makram, 39, 139-40, 143, 146, 148, 208
  Black Book, 140-1, 143-4
Uganda, 61, 68, 226
'ulama', 180
  Egypt, 195, 197-9, 201, 204, 209-10
  Sudan, 57, 189, 197
'umda(s), 76
Umm Rashrash, 90, 93
Umma party (Egypt), 34, 36
Umma party (Sudan), 22-5, 43, 193, 224-5, 227-8
United Nations, 26, 115, 168, 201
United States, 5, 25-6, 167-8, 170, 172-3, 178, 183, 207-8, 219-20, 223, 231
'Urabi, Ahmad, 26

Urabist(s), 27, 190
  rebellion (1882), 192
'Uthman, Amin, 39-40, 129-30, 133, 137, 143-4, 146, 149-50

Vansittart, R., 95, 125-6, 135
Vatikiotis, P.J., 205
Vichi, 132
Victoria, Queen, 192

Wad Habuba rebellion (1908), 53, 58
Wadi Halfa, 13, 164, 185
Wafd, Wafdist, 2, 4-5, 30-6, 38-43, 64, 67, 69, 70, 72-5, 77, 79, 82, 116-21, 123-31, 133, 135, 137-51, 166, 190-1, 207-8, 213
Wafdist party (*al-kutla al-Wafdiyya*), 39, 121, 148
Wahhabiyya, Wahhabi, 162, 190, 194
Wajh, 93, 106-7
al-Wajh (El Wedg) incident (1892), 90, 100
al-Wakil, Zaynab, 140
waqf, 55, 189, 198-9
  Egyptian *Waqf* administration, 54-5
  Khayri, 198
  minister, ministry of, 180, 199, 206, 210, 212, 222
Wars (Arab-Israeli)
  1948 War, 34, 166, 191
  Suez War (1956), 43, 116, 167-8
  1967 June War (Six-Day), 5, 6, 166, 168-9, 182, 206
  War of attrition, 170
  1973 October War, 170, 174-5, 183-4, 207
Washington, 171, 183
Wavell, A., 125
West, western, 5, 6, 166-7, 182-4, 194-5, 206, 218
White Flag League, 16, 75
Wilson, H.M. (Field Marshal), 142

Index

Wingate, F.R., 13, 35, 49, 50, 52-66, 73, 75, 82, 89-90
World Bank, 171
World Muslim League, 206, 209
World War I, 4, 15, 34-5, 52, 60, 95-6, 100, 104, 116, 120, 161, 190
World War II, 5, 13, 18, 22, 26, 33, 39, 41, 117, 123, 164-5, 182

Yakan, 'Adi, 35, 67-70
Yathrab, 210
Yemen
  People's Democratic Republic of, 172, 178
  South, 5, 174, 208
  war (1962–1967), 168-9, 206-7, 215
Young Egypt *see* Misr al-Fatat
Young Turks' revolution (1908), 190

Zaghlul, Sa'd, 34-9, 55, 64, 67, 69-70, 73, 75-80, 82, 118, 140, 190, 207
Zaïre, 176, 226
al-Zayyat, Ahmad Hasan, 199, 205
Zionism, Zionist(s), 98, 105, 220, 223
Ziwar, Ahmad, 93